ROUTLEDGE LIBRARY EDITIONS:
VICTORIAN THEATRE

Volume 4

NINETEENTH CENTURY BRITISH THEATRE

NINETEENTH CENTURY BRITISH THEATRE

Edited by
KENNETH RICHARDS AND PETER THOMSON

Routledge
Taylor & Francis Group
LONDON AND NEW YORK

First published in 1971

This edition first published in 2016
by Routledge
2 Park Square, Milton Park, Abingdon, Oxon OX14 4RN

and by Routledge
711 Third Avenue, New York, NY 10017

Routledge is an imprint of the Taylor & Francis Group, an informa business

British Library Cataloguing in Publication Data
A catalogue record for this book is available from the British Library

ISBN: 978-1-138-92272-3 (Set)
ISBN: 978-1-315-68102-3 (Set) (ebk)
ISBN: 978-1-138-92904-3 (Volume 4) (hbk)
ISBN: 978-1-138-93657-7 (Volume 4) (pbk)
ISBN: 978-1-315-68144-3 (Volume 4) (ebk)

Publisher's Note
The publisher has gone to great lengths to ensure the quality of this reprint but points out that some imperfections in the original copies may be apparent.

Essays on

Nineteenth Century British Theatre

Edited by Kenneth Richards
and Peter Thomson

The proceedings of a Symposium sponsored by the Manchester University Department of Drama

Methuen & Co Ltd

11 New Fetter Lane London EC4

First published in 1971
by Methuen & Co Ltd
11 New Fetter Lane, London EC4

Set in Press Roman by
E.W.C. Wilkins, Ltd., London
and printed in Great Britain
by the Redwood Press,
Trowbridge, Wiltshire

SBN 416 07730 7

Distributed in the USA by
Barnes & Noble Inc.

Contents

Introduction

It is still fairly respectable to know nothing about the nineteenth-century theatre, but it seems unlikely that it will be so for long. The modest literary quality of much of its drama has made this period the poor relation of theatre history. But as we become more aware of the need to see plays not only in their literary, but also in their social and theatrical contexts, and as we increasingly perceive that the roots of much modern drama are to be found in the experiments and extravagances of the nineteenth-century stage, it is certain that the disparagement of the period cannot last.

The Symposium, of which these papers are a partial record, met at Holly Royde College from 10 April to 12 April 1970, and was an attempt to contribute to a growing rediscovery. Our intention at the inception of the project was to bring together a small group of scholars interested in this neglected field, and to persuade a publisher to defy the neglect. The extent of our success surprised us, for we were able to assemble at Holly Royde a more distinguished and sizeable group than we had dared to hope for, and we have enjoyed throughout the organization of the Symposium and the preparation of this book the warm support of Anthony Forster of Methuen.

For those of us who organized it, the Symposium was a memorable experience and we owe a debt of gratitude to all who took part. It was, we believe, the first time that representatives from all the British Drama Departments had met together, and that was valuable for reasons unconnected with the subject of the Symposium itself. In addition, it introduced us to a lively and stimulating group of transatlantic academics, and enabled us to renew contact with the dedicated scholars of the Society for Theatre Research whose labours over the years have done so much to focus serious attention on the nineteenth-century theatre. To all who came we give our thanks, and no one who was there will resent that we give particular thanks for the generous contribution and witty companionship of that doyen of theatre scholars, Arthur Colby Sprague. Finally, it is appropriate to remark that only the untimely death of Alan Downer prevented him from being with us and contributing to lecture and discussion.

We have grouped the papers under three main headings, rather than publishing them in the order in which they were read, but we intend no further comment. The material is unashamedly disparate. It emerged clearly enough from the Symposium that nineteenth-century theatre is the property of enthusiasts as well as scholars, and we can expect, with more justice than is normal in academic publications, to have a majority of enthusiasts among our readers.

Members of the Symposium

James Arnott	University of Glasgow
Clive Barker	University of Birmingham
Miss Kathleen Barker	Society for Theatre Research
Michael R. Booth	University of Guelph
Mrs Eileen Cottis	Society for Theatre Research
Joseph W. Donohue, Jr.	University of Princeton
Robin Estill	University of Manchester
Nicholas Hern	University of Hull
John Hopkin	Hatfield Polytechnic
Mrs Andree Hoyles	University of Hull
David Mayer, III	University of Bristol
Mrs Jan McDonald	University of Glasgow
Rev. W.M. Merchant	University of Exeter
John Prudhoe	University of Manchester
Miss Zena Raafat	University of London
Leslie Read	University of Exeter
Jack Reading	Society for Theatre Research
Kenneth Richards	University of Manchester
Miss Sybil Rosenfeld	Society for Theatre Research
George Rowell	University of Bristol
Donald Roy	University of Hull
William Ruddick	University of Manchester
Arthur Colby Sprague	Bryn Mawr College
George Taylor	University of Manchester
Peter Thomson	University of Manchester
Paul Wadleigh	Washington State University
M. Glen Wilson	Macalester College, St Paul
Graham Woodruff	University of Birmingham

Secretaries to the Symposium:

Miss Susan Dunderdale
Miss Kate Marre

Publisher's Representative:

Mr Geoffrey Strachan

PART ONE

The Theatre

1 CLIVE BARKER

A Theatre for the People

The early nineteenth century was a period of radical and often turbulent social change. The period from 1780 to 1880 has been described by one historian as encompassing 'the origins of Modern English Society' [1]. It is therefore appropriate that any contemporary examination of nineteenth-century British theatre should examine some of the social factors that affected the theatre during this period.

Theatre scholarship has often proceeded as though there were two concepts of time, Social time and Theatre time. The theatre has usually been seen as a development in time set apart from the movement of society. The value of such studies is considerable and I intend no disrespect. The undistracted concentration of a scholar upon one aspect of theatrical history has obvious merit in a field where the object of our studies is ephemeral and essentially beyond recall. The critical task of assessing the performance of an actor in a role and the effect of his performance upon an audience demands the painstaking and microscopic examination of secondary and tertiary sources and evidence and poses very fine problems of judgment in assessing the validity and value of this evidence. The task of relating theatrical events directly to the movement and circumstances of the society in which the performance took place is almost certainly at this point in time too much to expect of any single scholar. The library shelves and bibliographies are stuffed with works that have attempted a broad comprehensive coverage of an age in a form and at a length which gives the writer no opportunity critically to examine his material and which traps him into making generalizations and disguised value judgments which either confuse or exasperate the reader or worse still give the impression of authoritative truth. Worse still are the magpie popular theatre historians who trade uncritically in detail. For some reason which should be a source of concern if not shame to us, a very high proportion of the standard works of reference on the theatre seem to have been written by popular theatre historians and not scholars.

There is an imperative need for theatre studies which go beyond the theatre. As theatre studies move away from textual criticism to the study of the play in performance as the only means of understanding any dramatic work and the evaluation of its content and effect, so they must continue to move towards the study of the play in performance in the movement of society in its time, for precisely the same reasons.

If the events from 1780 to 1880 can be described as the origins of modern British society then they can also be called with some justification the origins of the modern British theatre. I am sure that nineteenth-century British theatre history is at the start of a highly productive period because nineteenth-century history studies are already into a highly productive period. The body of social and cultural evidence which is available to the theatre historian grows almost weekly. G. Kitson Clark, in *The Making of Victorian England,* says:

> The tools for any reconstruction of English nineteenth-century history must be forged from the great mass of evidence which is now available for the student – the very large and varied collections of documents, reams of newspapers local and national, ephemeral literature, the results of Government enquiries etc. It is I believe a larger mass than exists for any country in any previous century.... Upon that mass an almost comparably large swarm of research students has settled, and part of the work of anyone trying to deal with nineteenth-century history must be an attempt, probably an unsuccessful attempt, to cover the relevant work which is being done on his subject; he must also gain for himself some direct experience of the varied evidence which is now so profusely available. [2]

The prospect is daunting but some indication of the possible results can be seen in the recently published *Survey of London,* which deals with the Covent Garden and Drury Lane Theatres [3] and which makes use of material not previously used by theatre historians, and in *London Theatres and Music Halls 1850–1950,* edited by Diana Howard [4], which reveals a wealth of material on theatre architecture in the files of the Greater London Council Architect's Department.

The problems of social studies of the theatre are the problems of the comprehensive social histories that they form part of and should contribute to. Harold Perkin, in *The Origins of Modern English Society 1780–1880,* makes a case for social history as a vertebrate discipline built around a central organizing theme, the history of society *qua* society, of social structure in all its manifold and constantly changing ramifications.

> Comprehensive history of this kind, however limited its success, obviously

> cannot be the unaided work of one historian. Ideally, perhaps, it should be a teamwork, with many specialists, and not only historians, contributing their expertise, though the whole at the end best refined in the reverberating furnace of a single mind. [5]

It is clear that the day has gone when one man could sit at his desk and write definitively about nineteenth-century history. The day might come again but the task now is for explorative studies, wide-ranging and hypercritical of previous authorities.

It must be clear from this lengthy exposition and its general tone that I am about to deal with my failure and my inability to blind you with a sequence of startling revelations about popular theatre in the 1830s. We did have our team of researchers, and we did begin to swarm over the material Dr Kitson Clark lists. Eleven students of the Department of Drama and Theatre Arts working under my supervision contributed to the study. There was certainly no shortage of material produced. Perhaps I do not have the reverberating furnace sort of single mind that Professor Perkin thinks is called for to refine the material, but I think we discovered the enormity of the task that faces any student of theatre history who lets his eye wander outside the stage door.

The problems are complicated and numerous, but it is so necessary and so obviously valuable to tackle them that I have thought it worth while to dwell on them and construct this paper round them rather than to take one particular aspect arising out of research. I could quite easily have concentrated on the 1832 House of Commons Select Committee to Enquire into the state of the Law Affecting Dramatic Literature. We discovered a virgin volume of the evidence presented to this committee, and published by the University of Ulster, on the law shelves of the university library [6]. The evidence constitutes a comprehensive first-hand account of the problems facing the London theatres in one particular year seen from the point of view of involved parties, and is probably unique in the annals of theatrical history. The preliminary notes of the student covering it take up almost the length of this paper. But the reason I have not concentrated on it is that most of the evidence is nearly impossible to evaluate except in a much wider context. One of the principle lay witnesses was Francis Place, the middle-class radical, and this immediately leads into an examination of the Reform movement, since 1832 was, of course, the year of the First Reform Bill [7]. To what extent the reform of the theatre coincided, directly or indirectly, with electoral reforms, is the first question that must be asked. Alfred L. Crauford wrote a novel in 1933 called *Sam and Sallie*, subtitled 'a romance of the stage' [8].

Crauford prefaces his book by saying that whereas most novelists disclaim any resemblance in their characters to any real person living or dead, he makes no such apology. In fact if his characters did not resemble real persons there would be no point in writing it. Still, the book is a novel and therefore open to critical mistrust.

Crauford's book is biography in fictional form of the lives of Sam and Sara Lane, proprietors of the Britannia Theatre, Hoxton from 1841 until Sara Lane's death in 1899. Crauford can be given a great deal of credibility as he was the nephew of Sam and Sara Lane and was manager of the theatre for the last quarter of the century. The novel, where it touches on fact, can often be verified from other sources and Crauford shows little desire to fictionalize the story of the two people, and as a novel the book fails totally for this reason. Being a good theatre man he amalgamates minor characters and occasionally telescopes events and he is careless over details, but his intention appears to be to present the love and life story of two theatre people in a very favourable and sympathetic light – which was not difficult since both Sam and Sara Lane were widely respected both in and out of the theatre.

Early in the novel there is a curiously detailed passage which requires either confirmation or explanation, or both. Sam Lane was a Devonshire lad who came up to London in the mid-1830s to seek his fortune. He worked in the Royal Union Saloon in Shoreditch High Street and in 1839 'came into possession' of it. In defiance of the law, Lane maintained a company not only playing burletta but straight drama. One night in 1839 during a performance:

> An inspector with a dozen constables pushed their way through the entrance doors and up on to the stage. He arrested Sam and ordered him to drop the curtain and dismiss the audience despite the money. The audience rose up on Sam's side. The players were not allowed to change their costumes. A huge hostile crowd met the policemen (and the thirteen actors) as they dragged them to Worship Street Police Station and threw them into prison.

The culprits are brought before the bench and found guilty.

> My decision is that all these persons who have aided and abetted you in your illegal performances shall pay a fine of 10s. each....As for you Samuel Lane, you have wantonly broken the law and you did it with your eyes open. The Houses of Parliament in their wisdom have decreed that theatrical performances shall be entirely restricted to the Patent Theatres of London. For years you have been filling your pockets by this illicit trade and I must inflict a penalty commensurate with your offence. I might make the penalty so heavy that it would be to your utter ruin, but if I refrain from this, it is in the hope that you will never again attempt a similar infringement.

Lane is fined £250 and his licence confiscated.

> The Union affair had made a considerable sensation, not only in the neighbourhood, but throughout London. The newspapers had related the matter very fully, giving details of the sensational parade through the streets of the woebegone players, all in their war-paint; and also the subsequent proceedings at the police courts. Public opinion strongly supported the actors and there was comment in the House of Commons. Sam was now approached by some Chartist agitators. The so-called Peoples Charter was drawn up in 1838 and was a protest on behalf of the working man against the hardship of his lot. They were therefore ready to support any discontent that would be likely to enflame the populace and add some backing to their movement. They urged Sam to put himself at the head of an open-air meeting....Accordingly, one day, when Parliament was sitting, a mob of some hundreds of men, with Sam and some Chartist leaders at their head, marched from Shoreditch, through the City and the Strand to Westminster bearing banners with large letters: 'ONE LAW FOR THE RICH, ANOTHER FOR THE POOR.' 'WORKERS WANT THEATRES' 'FREEDOM FOR THE PEOPLES AMUSEMENTS.' [9]

The meeting attracts a large and ugly crowd who hear an impassioned speech from a Chartist. Sam's speech is interrupted by the police, but as a sequel Sam meets Tom Holmes, M.P. for Hackney, who raises the matter in the House of Commons. Holmes introduces a Private Members Bill which is defeated 242–51 and more meetings follow. The novel then asserts that one of the first acts of Peel's Ministry was to introduce a relieving act amending the Law of Theatrical Amusements.

The story moves on to 1841 when Lane takes over the Britannia Saloon in Hoxton, and is soon up to his old games. However, at the time for renewal of the licences, one antagonist of the theatres on the council of Magistrates brings up evidence of certain saloons substituting the elevating educational plays of Shakespeare for the blood and thunder melodramas. He considers the dignity of labour is sufficient reward for the working class and persuades the other magistrates to refuse licences [10].

Sam re-opens as a variety house selling beer tickets and not charging for the entertainment. In parliament an important and valuable advocate of freedom takes the lead in advocating the sweeping away of the monopoly held by the Patent Theatres. This is Bulwer Lytton. Sam attaches himself to Lytton and organises another mammoth march down Whitehall bearing banners such as 'Freedom for the Theatres'. They are joined by the employees of other saloons. The demonstration makes its effect. Opinion has impressed itself, and at a by-election in London the renewal of saloon licences is made an issue and more pressure is brought to bear on the Government. The Theatres

Regulation Act of 1843 is brought in. Ten further theatres and seven saloons are given full licences and the stage is free. 'It was felt to be a political victory won for the people, another shackle cast off and another step on the road to freedom' [11]. The story contains a number of simple errors. Lytton was not in Parliament from 1841–50 (which hasn't stopped other more serious writers calling the 1843 Act Bulwer's Bill). The Britannia licence was refused in 1842 not 1841. The sequence of events is obviously tailored for a clearer narrative, but is it to be disregarded because of this? On a closer examination some major deficiencies appear. We can find no trace whatsoever in 1839 House of Commons of Tom Holmes nor his Bill defeated in such numerical detail 242 to 51. We can find no record of the Chartist marches with Sam Lane down Whitehall, although it may well be that we have either not looked in the right places, or have not the right information to tell us where to look. A.E. Wilson repeats the story about Tom Holmes and the marches in *East End Entertainment,* but his wording clearly suggests that he took it straight from the novel since he also records that the performance for which Lane was fined was an illegal 'Black-eyed Susan', as in the novel, whereas the court accounts give a less class-conscious sounding bill – 'History of Lumpkins Journey' and 'The Three Lovers Plot and Counter-plot'. But should the story be discarded, when it contains one element at least which is not covered anywhere else – that is, Chartist agitation for the reform of the Theatre? It is for this reason that we have thought it worth pursuing.

Various historical events change their significance as they are viewed from the perspective of other times. In our time the issue that has aroused most discussion in the area of theatre reform has been the abolition of the censorship, and most recent writing on the 1843 Act has naturally centred on the Lord Chamberlain's Office. Watson Nicholson, however, writing in the early years of this century in *The Struggle for the Free Stage in London,* in what is far and away the clearest and most detailed coverage of the subject, pays very little attention to the censorship and takes as his main concern the economic struggle to protect financial investments in the Patent Houses. John Hollingshead, who went on fighting the battle for a free stage throughout the nineteenth century, saw the struggle as a fight between Free Traders and Protectionists [12]. Watson Nicholson has little to say on the 'saloon' and smaller theatres except in so far as they are involved in the economic struggle between the Patent and Minor theatres, but he does, however, say: '..for by 1831 the feeling against the monopolies had become part and parcel of the reform movement' and later, of 1843: 'Reformation along many lines filled the air, and a free theatre for the regular drama came in on the crest of the wave of the general movement' [13]. I would not wish to quarrel with this opinion, and I think it is generally agreed that the power of the Patent Houses was broken a long time before the Act was passed, and that the Act simply tied up the loose ends and took some of the ambiguities out of the law. However, if this is the case then there is every reason for us now to take a new look at the run up to the passing of the 1843 Act in the light of some of the recent historical studies made of the period. Meanwhile, also, poor Sam Lane seems to have experienced his darkest night in 1842 immediately before the dawn – which needs some explanation.

The new audiences

A culmination of factors – social, economic and political – precipitated a violent change in British society after 1780. Most of these factors had developed naturally throughout the eighteenth century.

> At the end of a generation, [says Harold Perkin], all that was needed for the final breakthrough was a suitable cyclical trade boom of a not much more than average kind. That boom came in the 1780's, with the end of the American War and the reopening of the oceanic trade, swept to greater heights by the Revolutionary Wars. [14]

The boom was accompanied by an acceleration in population growth which created both the competition to keep down wages and the market for cheap manufactured goods and food.

> The effect was to remove the built-in brake from the economic system and allow its built-in dynamism full play. In other words, after a long period of acceleration, the lift at last overcame the drag, and the machine was airborne. [15]

Among the results which we are concerned with is the rapid expansion of the population which flooded the towns and cities with people. Between 1750 and 1850 the population of England trebled. Production rose, and both home and foreign trade were stimulated by profit inflation which disproportionately benefited merchants, industrialists, farmers and landowners. At the same time:

> .. a philosophy was developed by which the old regime was comprehensively condemned, new classes emerged to challenge the position claimed by those who had enjoyed a monopoly of privilege and power. What happened in politics was connected undeniably with the romantic movement in literature, and that in its turn was connected possibly even more mysteriously with

> a reawakening in religion. Without doubt the connections between all these movements are often tenuous and always obscure; they moved very different people in very different directions and often enough brought them into conflict with each other. But they all tended to one result. The old regime – oligarchic, superficial, self-satisfied, cruel and corrupt – had been weighed in the balance and found wanting, though amongst whom its kingdom was to be divided was not yet revealed. [16]

Watson Nicholson's *The Struggle for the Free Stage in London* gives a very clear picture of the rise of the Minor Theatres and the decline of the Patent Houses in terms of a struggle between the vested established financial interests of the patentees and the entrepreneurial ambitions of men like Elliston and Davidge to capitalize on a growing audience.

'If you want to have anything done as well as it can be done, you must leave it to competition' [17], says Francis Place in his evidence to the Select Committee of 1832. In this respect the struggle between the Patents and the Minors could well be examined in the light of a new rising class striving to take over the cultural institutions of its predecessor and of a clash of economic principles and ideologies. This would involve a more detailed study of the parliamentary careers of such people as Sheridan, Samuel Whitbread and Captain Polhill and their financial interests in the theatre than has been attempted so far. The career of Whitbread, brewer and rising man of the Whigs, who became in 1809 a member of the managing committee of Drury Lane to form the first theatrical joint-stock company, is particularly interesting in this respect [18].

However, it is much less with the struggles of the old regime to keep power and more with the new movements that I should like to concern myself, although obviously the decline of one is inextricably linked to the rise of the other.

The prosperity and population growth in London produced a new audience. This audience was beginning to be appreciated when Palmer opened the Royalty Theatre in Well-close Square in 1787. Palmer found an audience which the Haymarket had failed to find ten years earlier. To what extent were there two audiences in London at this time? Five thousand inhabitants of Middlesex petitioned parliament in 1787 to grant a licence to the Royalty, and M.A. Taylor, pleading the Royalty's case in Committee in the House, insisted that a theatre in Whitechapel could not injure the 'great' houses and that that part of town ought to be indulged as well as the West End [19].

When the Interludes Bill was presented in 1788 there was a rush of places of entertainment to petition for licences to present legitimate drama. This would seem to indicate an audience not satisfied with non-dramatic entertainment. Who were these people demanding plays? The demand for legitimate drama in places of entertainment in 1788 is reflected later in the evidence to the 1832 Committee from the Minor Theatre managers, all of whom have audiences demanding stronger meat than the burlettas provide. The demand is still there in 1839 when Sam Lane is brought up. The audience want plays and, perhaps surprisingly, they want Shakespeare. The decline of the Patent Houses needs to be examined much more closely in the light of this growing demand for legitimate drama, and I don't think this examination can take place without a much wider reference to factors outside the theatre than has previously been brought to bear on the subject.

It is generally agreed that a new middle-class audience came into the theatre after 1780 but who exactly they were I have never seen established [20]. Certainly in Palmer's time they appear to be citizens living either in the City of London or just to the east of it. The success of Astley's (first covered amphitheatre with stage, 1784) in Lambeth would suggest a further body living in Lambeth. Others, to judge from the efforts of Sadler's Wells to obtain a dramatic licence, lived in Islington and Clerkenwell. Perhaps if we understood more precisely who these people were we would be in a better position to evaluate their drama. A search through street directories, and a demographic map of London and its suburbs, would seem necessary.

It is unlikely that people newly come to London would form the patronage of these theatres. Can we look for a time during which an established but rising stratum of society first of all tried to take over the existing institutions and then, perhaps feeling more secure, or being dissatisfied with what it was offered, formed its own institutions? Kitson Clark says,

> In the first quarter of the nineteenth century it was becoming increasingly clear that what was politically, socially, intellectually and spiritually a new society was growing up in England for which neither the institutions, nor the ideas, that had been inherited from the eighteenth century would suffice. New classes were developing in wealth and self-consciousness and were beginning to demand a place in society which its old traditional order based on hereditary privilege would not grant them. Men were learning to require greater humanity, greater justice, greater common sense in the methods of government and the law. Some men were inspired by the revival of religion to accept for themselves a standard of morality and to condemn practices which the earlier eighteenth century and all preceding centuries had accepted without question. And it was inevitable that men, and in due course women, would demand with increasing insistence, as a matter of right, a share in the control of the state under which they lived. [21]

Dr Kitson Clark is referring particularly to the movement for electoral reform, but the theatre is an institution of society as parliament is. To what extent do the Old Price riots coming, as they do, precisely at the time that the middle-class Minor Theatres are being built, reflect this rising self-consciousness? That there was a new audience was clear to the Earl of Carlisle in 1809 in his *Thoughts upon the present condition of the Stage and upon the construction of a New Theatre.*

> A modern audience would be surprised to hear how the public were accommodated 40 years ago [1770]. The side boxes were few in number and very incommodious, especially when the frequenters of those boxes ever appeared in them in full dresses, the women in hoops of various habilments all calculated to deny convenient space to their neighbours. Frocks were admitted into the front boxes, but they were not usually worn by gentlemen in the evening; women of the town quietly took their station in the upper boxes; and men whom it did not suit either to be at the expense of dress or who had not the time to equip themselves, as before described, resorted to the pit. This of course comprehended a large description of persons such as belonged to the Inns of Court, men of liberal pursuits and profession; and who, by an uniform attendance at the playhouse became no incompetent judges of the drama. [22]

Perhaps the Earl gives us some clue to a section of the new audience with his pit full of gentlemen of liberal pursuits and professions. The increased trade and business offered young single men opportunities for advancement in the City and it is perhaps they, foot-loose and fancy free, with ready cash, who are the undisclosed mob of the Old Price riots. Certainly by 1809 the ladies of the town no longer sit quietly in the second row boxes but have become a major and scandalous part of the theatre's finances at five pounds a box for the season. At the same time the Old Price riots should be seen in the context of the petitions for a third Patent Theatre of 1808, 1810 and 1813, where the argument is put forward that London needs a new theatre because of the increasing audience, but that the prices proposed would put that theatre way beyond the pockets of all but a small section of the population who could afford to pay three shillings in the Pit and one shilling in the Upper Gallery. The motives that inspired the third theatre projectors would appear on examination to be very little different from those of the Patent managers – greater gain from larger houses at higher prices. The extension to a third Patent House would seem to have simply strengthened the forces against any movement for freeing the theatre by adding more vested interests, the general agreement being that the Patent Houses declined because of:

> ... the excessive outlay and the high prices of admission, the consequences of the monopoly, inducing them to build houses which cannot be filled,

> which has ruined them. [23]

Some explanation has still to be offered as to why this should actually be the case, the arguments so far being hardly conclusive. The question has to be answered – why did the Patent Houses do so badly when the Minor Theatres did so well? Or rather why did they not show a revival in popularity when larger Minor Theatres were built in which the auditorium size presented similar problems for the actor to those in the Patent Houses? Why in 1821 was the Haymarket able to spend a small fortune on refitting, when the Patent Houses were dropping deeper into debt?

I don't think these questions can be answered simply, or simply in theatrical terms. The association of the Patent Houses with 'Old Corruption' makes them an anathema to a whole class of people who are becoming more and more aware of their strength and their exclusion from political (and social) power. This class consciousness manifests itself through a multi-directional movement for social reform, which after 1815 begins to see electoral and parliamentary reform as the prime necessity for advancing its class interest.

> Between 1780 and 1850 the English ceased to be one of the most aggressive, brutal, rowdy, outspoken, riotous, cruel and bloodthirsty nations in the world and became one of the most inhibited, polite, orderly, tender-minded, prudish, hypocritical. The transformation diminished cruelty to animals, criminals, lunatics and children (in that order); rid the penal code of 200 capital offences, abolished transportation and cleaned up the prisons; turned Sunday into a day of prayer for some and mortification for all; bowdlerised Shakespeare, Gibbon and other obscene classics; and almost gave a death blow to the English stage. [24]

In this last respect I think Professor Perkin totally wrong, because the period saw a tremendous growth in both theatres and audiences and largely from, in the first instance, the class which promoted the processes of reform he outlines; the class which attempted to impose their values on society at large. Why, asks John Williams, in the *Dramatic Censor* for 1811, should the patent monopolists compel the inhabitants of the city and suburbs of London

> to make a weary and expensive pilgrimage of many miles, whenever they may want to suspend the operations of care, by a visit, with their families, to a colloquial theatre; and why are their ears and eyes offended, when they are there, by a pertinacious and insulting display of vulgar and ungrammatical pronunciation of language, and by debasing spectacles in action. [25]

Francis Place, in his evidence before the Select Committee of 1832, says that:

> ... in the case of the Recruiting Officer and the Beaux Strategem, Mr Kemble and Mr Keeley used words which were much softened from the original yet they caused a sensation in the house which prevented their using them any more. I thought the rebukes they received wholesome and sufficient corrections. [26]

A new audience comes into the London theatre between 1780 and 1830. The first evidence of its existence is seen in Palmer's attempts to open the Royalty in 1787. At this time the section of the population which characterizes this audience is politically weak (and disenfranchized) and Palmer's attempts to keep the Royalty open are an indication of the strength of the entrenched privileged establishment. The subsequent battles to break the monopoly between 1787 and 1832 must be studied in the light of the class struggle between the rising middle class and the established aristocracy and landed gentry. The decline of the Patent Houses, the steady growth of the Minor Theatres with middle-class audiences and the increasing tolerance and even favour that these theatres find with the Lord Chamberlain's office, and the increasing difficulty of the patentees to prosecute the Minors must be seen in the light of this class struggle.

> 'The aristocracy', says Davidge in 1832, 'are no longer patrons of the drama. That honour has merged into the more intelligent though perhaps less affluent class, England's staple children, wrongly termed the middle-class.' [He offers no explanation. [27]

This middle-class audience is, it goes without saying, an extremely diverse grouping of people of widely differing backgrounds, incomes, and tastes, who nevertheless have a great deal in common, which, during the period in question, can best be polarized as a sense of exclusion from playing their full part in the political and social life of the community (which the illegality of the Minor performances and the prosecutions against them serves to heighten), and a sense of belonging to a rising stratum of society. They are the new men. A study of their theatre would in the first place be geographical. The theatre in Tottenham Street, later the Queen's, is obviously built to cater for the people in the new houses around Fitzroy Square and Bloomsbury, and the attack on this theatre by the patentees in 1830, which sparked off the campaign for the 1832 House of Commons Select Committee, shows how such an attack aroused at that time the opposition of influential men. The evidence of the 1832 Select Committee shows a wilful misinterpretation of the law by the Bow Street Magistrates.

The established strength of the middle class is also shown by the strategies which led from the prosecution of the Tottenham Street Theatre to the setting up of the Select Committee in 1832 and the subsequent bill attempting to reform the theatre, which although having no immediate results indicates a significant change in tactics from the presentation of petitions to parliament in the 1810s.

The social strength of the middle classes, and some indication of their integration into the establishment, is shown in the evidence presented to the Select Committee by the managers of the Minor Theatres, none of whom pleaded for a 'free' theatre. They were protectionists to a man and asked only that the protection afforded to the Patent Houses be extended to them. Davidge considered a 'free' theatre injurious to the interests of Patent and Minor Theatres.

In their report, the Select Committee rejected the special pleading of Davidge and the other managers and, accepting largely the suggestions of Francis Place, came out strongly in favour of a theatre free of protection. In this respect they placed themselves firmly within the broad stream of social reform which since the turn of the century had been seeking to reform social conditions without upsetting the social order by revolution. This is not surprising since not only was Place, the principal lay witness, a leading agitator for non-revolutionary reform but so also were members of the Committee. Two of them, Bulwer and Duncombe, were playwrights. Throughout, the cause for theatre reform was often carried on by men who were also campaigning for electoral reform, the repeal of the stamp duty on newspapers and other causes.

Karl Marx says:

> For each new class which puts itself in the place of the one ruling before it, is compelled, simply in order to achieve its aims, to represent its interest as the common interest of all members of society i.e. employing an ideal formula, to give its ideas the form of universally valid ones. [28]

In this light it is not surprising to find that the struggles for political and cultural emancipation go hand in hand. The class which produces the political and social reform leaders produces the cultural leaders, the playwrights and increasingly the actors and the managers. What patently needs examining is the extent to which the theatre of this class reflects their struggle for supremacy, and the form and content of their drama needs to be re-examined as a positive reflection of the class struggle. This is particularly pertinent because of the low opinion held of the plays of this period and the critical view of a crude debased theatre. The surprising thing is the far from frivolous regard for the theatre that is held at that time. John Williams, in the *Dramatic Censor* for 1811, argues the case for a third theatre in terms of the theatre as a source of *education.* The projectors, however sincere or insincere they may have been, recognized the importance of forwarding this argument themselves in their petition. Jerrold, in 1832, considers that the Minor Theatres have improved the morals of the times. Davidge, who has a special case to plead, in 1832 opening the City Theatre, says it is

> high time the stage should meet the growing march of improvement and the desire for recreation and instruction now prevalent in all classes. [29]

Fifteen years later, Mayhew, who has no special case to plead, makes a case for cheap theatre to compete with the penny-gaffs:

> My own experience with this neglected class (the costermongers) goes to prove that if we would lift them out of the moral mire in which they are wallowing, the first step must be to provide them with wholesome amusements. [30]

Between these two dates there are references, too numerous to mention, to the same point. Some perhaps are not genuinely held but are nevertheless indicative of a case to be pleaded for the theatre as a source of education and moral improvement. That these views are prevalent over such a long period and are so divergent from our views on the early nineteenth century theatre is ample argument for a complete re-evaluation of the theatre at this time in its social setting. It also raises so many unanswered questions and possible new interpretations that any further study of the Patent Theatres and their decline must take this evidence into account.

Reform and the Working Class

The period between 1780 and 1832 is characterized by a growing awareness of class identity – class-consciousness. No simple analysis of this historical process can be given, and since the general line of my argument so far has been that future theatre studies of this period must take note of historical developments that are complicated and difficult to understand, I must resist the temptation to 'explain' by over-simplifying. However, it is the argument of historians such as E.P. Thompson and Harold Perkin that class-consciousness arose out of the historical events and processes of this period. Certainly in 1780, to quote E.P. Thompson, working-class consciousness was only to be found in fragmentary form.

> To step over the threshold, from 1832–33 is to step into a world in which working-class presence can be felt in every county in England, and in most fields of life. [31]

Just as the growing class consciousness of the middle classes is reflected in their challenge to the established privilege of the Patent Houses and the founding of the Minor Theatres between 1787 and 1821, so the growing working-class consciousness is reflected in the development of 'Saloon' Theatres, penny-gaffs and other illegal theatres from the late 1820s onwards. In the case of the Royal Coburg and the Surrey, class-consciousness is reflected in a changing audience composition. There is evidence of conflict in the theatres between gallery and boxes. Managers of Minor Theatres attack illegal theatres for jeopardising their trade. At this time the Minor Theatres themselves are feeling the pinch as the growing prosperity of middle-class families encourages them to move out of the city and its immediate suburbs, and from 1830 onwards the fabric of social life in the city is destroyed as the better-off families leave for Stockwell, Highgate and Greenwich [32]. The rapid development of public transport during the 1830s accelerates this redistribution of population. The Royal Coburg changes from a fashionable audience in 1818 to a local audience by 1830 (as the Royal Victoria). Later in the 1830s, with the building of Waterloo Station, the area runs down further and so does the social tone of the theatre and its audience. This shift of population may help explain why, in spite of the fact that the population continued to rise, no theatres were built in central London and Westminster between 1840 and 1867.

One of the main reasons for the exodus of families from central London was the rapidly deteriorating standard of life in the city. The fifty years after 1780 flooded the city with people off the land who entered a world singularly unprepared to deal with them. Suitable houses did not exist and the additional numbers were crammed into every nook and cranny from attic to cellar of old decaying property, or into cottages run up hastily in confined spaces with little or no access to light and air — in alleys, in rows placed back to back, in folds and folds within folds, in the backyards of existing houses or what had been their gardens. Water and sanitation were often not provided at all, and where they were provided there was often a judicious mingling of cesspools and wells, with an occasional overstocked graveyard. A description detailing the horrors of the early nineteenth-century city could go on for ever. The preponderance of coal fires in overcrowded areas produced sulphurous fogs, and the healthy fled. I want to advance one further argument for the decline of the Patent Houses. They were obnoxiously sited. Engels in his list of urban horrors singles out the area.

> In the immediate neighbourhood of Drury Lane Theatre, are some of the worst streets in the whole metropolis, Charles, King and Park Streets in which the houses are inhabited from cellar to garret exclusively by poor families. [33]

Standing immediately to the west of the Patent Theatres were the two worst 'rokkeries' in London – St Giles, teeming with starving Irish, and Seven Dials, characterised by Dickens as the worst area of London. Drury Lane itself in the 1830s was hardly any better and the area suffered badly during the cholera epidemics of 1831 and 1832. The concentration of beggars, prostitutes and criminals in the area obviously made theatre-going at these theatres a hazardous and most unpleasant activity. Perhaps Mr Macready was wasting his time. Small wonder the well-to-do patronized the Opera and the Haymarket.

By the end of the 1820s there existed in London a considerable body of working men who were second generation city dwellers.

> Resilient human nature was forming new ways of life and interests amid the sprawling jungles of back-to-backs and crowded tenements. For these people town life had its own fascination, which they betrayed even in their protests against its squalor. Their literature became informed by new outlooks and the new idiom of urban drama, song, newspapers and criminal slang. [34]

The fact that this new urban working class had a literature was largely due to the middle-class reformers of the late eighteenth and early nineteenth centuries who provided the means by which a literate working-class public was formed. I have already discussed the broad nature of the movement for social reform and how it sought to 'civilize' England. Education was a major instrument of this policy. A great deal of this education was through Sunday Schools and directly attached to moral and religious teaching, no matter to what uses the education was eventually put.

> The middle-class radicals defended the right of the working man to cheap news, as they defended his right to cheap books and the right of his children to national schools. They argued that an educated people was a sober and a responsible people; and that as the working class were determined to obtain information somehow, it was essential that they should have access to 'suitable' knowledge. [35]

Working-class radicals recognized that education was the working-class passport to entering the political community, and in the first three decades an alliance between the middle class and the working class against the established interests seemed to the advantage of both. The cultural literacy of the working class was therefore important to those who wished to avoid the excesses of brutish violence and revolution by civilizing, and those who wished to bring about social revolution through the extension of the franchise. This alliance continued until after the 1832 Reform Bill betrayed the cause of a wide franchise and put the finishing touches to the diverse class-structured society which became the new social order.

The decade which followed 1830 is of great interest to anyone concerned with the problems of class and culture, for it opened with the masses seeking, in an unprecedented way, serious political and cultural reading matter; and in the failure of their aspirations we see a blueprint of many cultural problems that face modern society. The situation was largely the product of historical processes. We have seen already some of the forces that were creating a new self-aware working class from the diverse elements the industrial revolution had brought into the towns. The final coalescence came about in 1830. The popular mood was inflamed by industrial distress (largely blamed on the government) and by news of revolutions in France and Belgium. Great hopes were focused on the Whig Government returned to parliament at the beginning of the year and pledged to reform the electoral system. Then the House of Commons threw out the Reform Bill. An excited nation went to the polls, a new parliament was elected and a Reform Bill passed. When this was defeated in the House of Lords angry meetings broke out at Bristol, Nottingham and Derby and only a policy of restraint by radical leaders prevented wider disorders. At the close of 1831 the House of Lords passed the First Reform Bill.

The mood of militancy aroused by the revolutions overseas and the defiance of parliament, and the subsequent disillusionment at the exclusion of the working man from the vote in the electoral reform, led immediately to the policy of General Unionism advocated by Owen – which saw a rapid and vast combination of working men in the large industrial unions – and the National Union of the Working Classes, which after 1835 moved beyond a programme of social justice towards a programme to provide an alternative system, articulating in 1837 the Chartist demands for household sufferage.

> Chartism was from the very beginning chiefly a movement among working men, though not as yet sharply separated from the bourgeoisie. The Radicalism of the workers went hand in hand with the Radicalism of the bourgeoisie; the Charter was the shibboleth of both. They held their National Convention in common seeming to be one party. The lower middle-class was just then in a very bellicose and violent state of mind in consequence of the disappointment over the Reform Bill and the bad business years of 1837–39 and viewed boisterous Chartism with a very favourable eye. [36]

It is this combination of middle-class Radical, working-class Radical and small tradesman that constitutes a turbulent political and social force in the 1830s.

In the autumn of 1830, just three months after the July revolution in France had recharged popular Radicalism in England, illegal, unstamped anti-establishment newspapers appeared on the streets of London, selling for a penny. Six years later their circulation had far surpassed that of the stamped press and, in consequence of the government's inability to enforce the law, the stamp duty was reduced from sixpence to a penny. The 1830s witnessed a fantastic boom in cheap fiction and illegal newspapers. This trade built on the literacy of the 'aristocrats of labour' who were the readers of *The Poor Man's Guardian* and the like, and the dedicated supporters of the National Union of the Working Classes and the Charter.

The centre of this radical movement was the Rotunda in Blackfriars Road, which functioned as a theatre from 1835. The theatre collections have hardly any material at all on the Rotunda. What do the unstamped newspapers show? A brief dip into what is accessible of these papers shows four of them devoted entirely to theatre. There is one illegal newspaper as early as 1826 – *The Harlequin.* Most of the papers seem to have carried theatrical news and criticism. Several of the Chartist leaders were playwrights. The list of the penny fiction shows a considerable number of 'books of the play'. There is also a possible mine of material on the theatre in the reports of Home Office agents detailed to watch the Rotunda. The theatres on the Surrey side obviously reflected the range of the political movement and this is the main sales area for the pauper press [37].

Very few men could afford to buy all the papers they required and the public houses were often compelled to purchase in bulk for the customers to read. The public house being the centre for many of political and social life, it was often the cultural hub also. Many public houses had free and easy singing, and in some of these houses the processes that had called the Minor Theatres into being during the rise of middle-class consciousness gave rise to a demand for working-class theatre. It also gave rise to a further number of Minor Theatres on the fringe of the city which grew out of pleasure gardens. The brewers' archives are ripe for research.

By this time the war with the Minors and the obvious lack of public support (which vitiated their political and legal support) made such enterprises safe from attack from the Patent Houses but still liable to the penalties of the law. The growth of the Chartist movement and the presentation of the Charter to parliament in 1838 created an explosive political situation which had to be watched very carefully and required further police powers. Meeting places were particularly dangerous. Section 46 of the Metropolitan Police Act of 17 August 1839 states:

> That it is lawful for the said Commissioners of Police by order in writing, to authorise the superintendent belonging to the Metropolitan Police, with such Constables as he may think necessary, to enter into any house or room kept or used within the said district for stage-plays or dramatic entertainments into which admission is obtained by payment of money, and which is not a licensed theatre and to take into custody all persons who shall be found therein without lawful excuse. [38]

Which is why, less than a month after the Act was passed, Samuel Lane found himself raided. He was fined not £250 but £20 – the maximum allowed. The newspaper reports tell us something about his house (which far from rising to his support, scarpered by all accounts as fast as their legs could carry them). There were between 800 and 900 of them, which is not disputed. Of the 70 arrested nearly all of them were young men of the appearance of mechanics or labourers. There are other curious facts. Three servants of an ex-church warden were in the house – people of undisputed good character. Some of the members of the Parish Council sat on the Magistrates Bench and they expressed sympathy for the defendants and disassociated themselves from the proceedings. The church-wardens, overseers and 70 Trustees of the Parish signed a testimonial to the orderliness of the house and the parish authorities paid the fines of all the defendants, who left the court to the loud acclamation of a crowd gathered in the street. The local magistrates were vociferous in their condemnation of the police [39].

Obviously if the house was 800–900 people for a straight play (there was evidence offered of a stage and scenery) then we are dealing with a major theatrical house. Nor was the Royal Union Saloon the only one. The 'saloon' theatres have been shamefully neglected, perhaps because the major newspapers saw no reason to cover them. A search of the local and illegal unstamped press could yield much information.

I have said something about the connections between the illegal theatres and Chartism. Worship Street, where Lane was brought up, was the scene of several large Chartist meetings four months previously. But for more striking evidence, we must jump six years. Henry Mayhew, a member of the Bohemian section of the emerging middle classes, writing at the end of the 1840s in *London Labour and the London Poor,* tackles the costermongers. Now by a curious coincidence – or is it? – Hoxton is a heavy area for costermongers, second only to the area around the New Cut, Waterloo and down to the Blackfriars Road, where stand the Royal Victoria, the Surrey and the Rotunda. The swarming population of London in the early nineteenth century saw a boom in the food trade. The costermongers prospered as well as anyone can prosper who makes his living selling on the street.

> The other amusements (apart from the pub and dances) of this class of the community are the theatre and the penny concert, and their visits are almost entirely confined to the galleries of the theatres on the Surrey-side – The Surrey, the Victoria, the Bower Saloon and (but less frequently) Astley's.'.... Three times a week is the average attendance at theatres and dances by the more prosperous costermongers. 'Love and murder, suits us best sir (says an informant) but within these few years I think there's a great deal more liking for deep tragedies among us. They set men a thinking; but then we all consider they go on too long'. [40]

Following a beautiful and staggeringly exciting description of the Victoria Gallery in full cry, Mayhew tackles the politics of the costermongers: 'The notion of the police is so intimately blended with what may be called the politics of the costermonger that I give them together.' The politics of the people are detailed in a few words – they are nearly all Chartists: ' "You might say" remarked one of my informants, "that they all were Chartists, but as it is better you should be under than over the mark, say nearly all." ' After some discussion of the Chartist organisation among the costermongers and the difficulties that moderate Chartist leaders have to restrain them from beating up the police on demonstrations, the piece ends with a dark threat – 'I am assured that in case of a political riot every coster would seize his policeman.' [41]

I have presented the case for a wider series of studies and a continuing examination of our theatre up to the 1843 Theatres Regulation Act. The Act represents simply a moment in time when the forces inhibiting reform became weaker than the pressures for reform. To detail the shift of this balance would take up even more space than I have used up here. It deals not only with shifts of theatrical balance but more importantly with fine shifts of social and political balance, and in this movement we should expect to find anachronisms, survivals and anticipations which blur the line of cause and effect. I hope I have made a case for a much more detailed examination of the popular theatre of the 1830s beyond the tiny footnote it is usually accorded. I have not of course mentioned anything about the penny theatres and 'dukeries', which are one stratum of popular theatre below the saloons. This area can be neglected very little longer. Mayhew definitely states that they play drama in four of them at least. John Hollingshead remembers actors from Mrs Harwood's penny gaff being marched through the streets of Shoreditch, in the costumes of *Othello,* with eighty members of the audience to Worship Street Police Station [42].

I suppose the next question would be what good did it do? Did it free the theatre? Here the material is more readily available, though almost equally neglected. Lane went on to build the Britannia Theatre, Hoxton, a theatre later described as the most valuable piece of theatre real-estate in England. In the years 1841–1906 it showed a loss on only three years. It had seating capacity of well over 3,000 and when full held over four. It pioneered popular Shakespeare. Anderson played there early in the 1850s and Aldridge not only gave his *Othello* but had Titus Andronicus mounted specially so that his Aaron could be seen. The first Shakespeare commemoration festival took place there in 1864, and in comparison with Stratford's miserable fiasco was an enormous success, running several months. The theatre was still playing the Harlequinade with full transformations of character, costume and scenery at the beginning of the twentieth century, thereby preserving in an almost pure form the popular theatre that came out of the eighteenth century into the age of the silent films.

Surely only a combination of idleness and snobbery allows us to ignore the popular theatre and concentrate on the sterile relics of a dead tradition before 1843? Enough has been written about Drury Lane and Covent Garden. What about the Theatre for the People?

Notes

[1] Harold Perkin, *The Origins of Modern English Society, 1780–1880* (London, 1969).

[2] G. Kitson Clark, *The Making of Victorian England* (London, 1962).

[3] *Survey of London,* Vol. XXXV, 1970.

[4] D. Howard, *London Theatres and Music Halls, 1850–1950* (London, 1970).

[5] Perkin, *op. cit.,* x.

[6] *Report of the Select Committee appointed to inquire into the laws affecting Dramatic Literature – 1832* (Dublin, 1968).

[7] The Bill was passed in 1831, but received the Royal Assent in 1832.

[8] A.L. Crauford, *Sam and Sallie* (London, 1933).

[9] Crauford, *op. cit.,* 143–9 and 152–5.

[10] *Ibid.,* 227–30.

[11] *Ibid.,* 227–30.

[12] Compare J. Hollingshead, *My Lifetime* (London, 1895).

[13] Watson Nicholson, *The Struggle for a Free Stage in London* (London, 1906) 357 and 410.

[14] Perkin, *op. cit.,* 105.

[15] *Ibid.,* 105–6.

[16] Kitson Clark, *op. cit.*, 33–4.
[17] *Report of the Select Committee*, Minute 3739.
[18] *Survey of London*, Vol. XXXV, 21.
[19] Quoted in Nicholson, *op. cit.*, 132.
[20] See also G. Rowell, *The Victorian Theatre* (London, 1956) and A. Nicoll, *A History of Early Nineteenth Century Drama, 1800–1850* (Cambridge, 1955).
[21] Kitson Clark, *op. cit.*, 39.
[22] Quoted in Nicholson, *op. cit.*, 182.
[23] *Report of the Select Committee*, Minutes 3692–6.
[24] Perkin, *op. cit.*, 280.
[25] Quoted in Nicholson, *op. cit.*, 228.
[26] *Report of the Select Committee*, Minute 3736.
[27] Publicity poster in the Enthoven Collection.
[28] Karl Marx, *German Ideology* (1845–6), quoted in Perkin, *op. cit.*, 271.
[29] Publicity poster in the Enthoven Collection.
[30] H. Mayhew, *London Labour and the London Poor*, Vol. 1 (Edition of 1861) 40.
[31] E.P. Thompson, *The Making of the English Working Class*, (London, 1963) 807.
[32] Compare Sir Walter Besant, *London in the Nineteenth Century*, (London, 1909).
[33] F. Engels, *The Condition of the Working Class in England – 1844* (Edition of 1892) 28.
[34] L. James, *Fiction for the Working Man* (London, 1963) 146.
[35] P. Hollis, *The Pauper Press* (Oxford, 1970) 295.
[36] F. Engels, *op. cit.*, 229.
[37] Compare Hollis, *op. cit.*
[38] 2 and 3 Victoria, Cap. XLVII, Clause XLVI.
[39] *Weekly Dispatch*, 15 and 22 September, 1839; *Bell's Weekly Messenger*, 15 September 1839.
[40] Mayhew, *op. cit.*, Vol. 1, 15.
[41] *Ibid.*, Vol. 1, 20.
[42] Hollingshead, *op. cit.*, 23.

2 DONALD ROY

Theatre Royal, Hull; or, The Vanishing Circuit

One of the most distinctive conditions of existence in Hull is the city's comparatively mild but very persistent disaffection from the twentieth century. Human nature and the theatre being what they are, this usually presents itself as a disadvantage, but it can sometimes, and unexpectedly, prove a hidden asset. For instance, I cannot think that in any other part of the country we should have been fortunate enough to unearth so recently and in such quantity rich caches of eighteenth- and nineteenth-century playbills and posters which in Hull had somehow managed to escape the predatory grasp of dealers, antique-pushers and other captains of the nostalgia industry. Admittedly, most of these came up for auction at local sales but others arrived from a variety of unlikely sources, including a bird-seed shop and the backs of several picture-frames. As a result, with the help of the university library, the Department of Drama has, over the last five years, been able to amass a collection of more than 2,500 bills which range from the 1780s to the 1920s and which, taken in conjunction with similar collections at the Hull Central Library and at the Municipal Museum in Wilberforce House, provide an astonishingly complete record of theatrical activity in the city for upwards of a hundred and fifty years. Clearly there is ample material here for research and this brief paper represents no more than a nibble at a very large cake. In fact, none of us in the department has yet had an opportunity to tuck in systematically and do justice to the entire spread, but, for the purposes of this symposium, I felt it might be at least amusing and possibly appetizing if I tasted a few crumbs at random. I therefore chose three years fairly arbitrarily – one at the height of the 'Major–Minor' struggle and the earlier days of melodrama, one in the middle of the century and subsequent to the

Regulation Act, and lastly one towards the end, in the time of Actor Managers and of so-called 'genteelization'. At intervals of a generation these resolved themselves as 1820, 1850 and 1880. I decided to confine my attention to the one Patent House in the city, the Theatre Royal, since the largest proportion of extant bills relate to it, and then to compare the evidence afforded by the playbills of these three years. Not surprisingly, after so modest an effort, I cannot claim to have stumbled on anything startlingly new – though I have managed to attribute a few plays whose authors were hitherto unknown, even to Allardyce Nicoll [1] – but the real value of the exercise for me is that it has helped to define and flesh out, if only in miniature, the overall pattern of nineteenth-century theatrical development which, as an arrant non-specialist in the period, I had accepted too readily in skeletal terms.

In 1820, of course, the Theatre Royal was an important house on the York Theatrical Circuit, then probably the most reputable and highly evolved of the provincial circuits. Tate Wilkinson, who obtained a patent to establish theatres in York and Hull in 1769 and ran the circuit successfully for over thirty years, had died and the management had passed to his son, John, who built a handsome new theatre in Humber Street in 1810, described in a contemporary guide-book as 'one of the best buildings of the kind out of London' and capable of accommodating 'a very numerous auditory' [2]. John Wilkinson relinquished management in 1814 to be followed by a succession of lessees and sub-lessees but he was still referred to in 1820 as 'the Late Manager', still had an interest in the circuit's theatres and was still apparently entitled to a benefit every season, at least in Hull.

The Hull season was a long one, spanning the four winter months from November to March. The inference is fairly clear, I think: the beginning of the season was arranged to coincide, whenever possible, with the well-patronized annual Hull Fair, while its closure was certainly determined by the company's departure to York for the Spring Assizes. The latter weeks of the season, from the turn of the year onwards, became increasingly dominated by benefit performances, largely in favour of the principal actors, who appear in a suitably affecting role for the occasion and often provide a *bonne-bouche* in the form of a song or a recitation, and who are allowed to sell tickets for the performance at their lodgings, presumably pocketing the proceeds. There are, however, other beneficiaries: performances are earmarked for Mr Wilkinson, the late manager, Mr Hope, the Box-Keeper, Mr Vause, the Wardrobe-Keeper and Dress-Maker, Mr Jerom, the 'Play-Bill Deliverer, &c. &c.', the resident 'band' and, of course, any specially engaged artists. One effective device for attracting additional custom at benefits seems to have been the inclusion in the cast of a local amateur performer, whose appearance receives due prominence in the handbill. Further evidence of good public relations work is provided by the frequency of performances given 'under the patronage' of local notabilities, usually, though not always, in connection with a benefit: the military, merchant captains and prosperous tradesmen are represented as patrons and even the local branch of the 'Ancient and Honourable Society of Free and Accepted Masons', on the occasion of the benefit of Brother Clarke, a prominent actor in the company, who took the lead in Addison's *Cato* that evening and obligingly contributed a 'Masonic Eulogium on Free Masonry (explaining also why Ladies cannot be admitted)'.

At this time the stock company appears to have numbered over thirty acting members, including about a dozen actresses, and to have enjoyed a fair degree of stability, for the turnover of players from season to season is not great. The average programme offered to the public implies a considerable versatility of talent, though it is evident from the cast-lists that possession of parts is the norm and that some members of the company are specifically employed as singers, dancers, or singer-dancers as well as actors. The typical 'entertainments' of an evening would comprise, first, the main play (usually, though not invariably, a tragedy or melodrama), followed, after the start of 'second-price', by a 'ballet-dance' or a succession of comic songs and dances and, finally, a farce or 'petite comedy' or pantomime or extravaganza of some kind. The company still have a strong sense of their patented status and consistently proclaim themselves 'His Majesty's' or 'Their Majesties' Servants' in the bills, yet in their repertoire they are at pains to include not only the tragedies, sentimental dramas and farces that Tate Wilkinson played but also the spectacular melodramas and burlettas mounted at London houses like the Surrey and the Lyceum. The year 1820, of course, witnessed the heyday of Scots romanticism in the theatre and it is not surprising to find the company producing, in a single season, *Macbeth,* John Home's *Douglas,* Dibdin's *The Heart of Midlothian* and *The Lady of the Lake,* Barrymore's *Wallace, the Hero of Scotland,* a 'Ballet-Dance, called *the Scotch Ghost',* the 'Grand Pantomime of *Oscar and Malvina; Or, The Hall of Fingal',* an 'Interlude, taken from Allen Ramsay's Scots Pastoral Comedy of the Gentle Shepherd, called *Patie and Roger',* the 'celebrated Historical Piece, called *Robert the Bruce',* and Planché's *The Vampire; or The Bride of the Isles.*

The Vampire was, in fact, seen in Hull only four months after its first performance in London, a measure no doubt both of the York Circuit's enterprise and the play's success. That it was intended as a special production for Christmas is clear from the fact that it was given four consecutive performances and was publicized well in advance, an exceptional departure from custom: for five whole weeks the bills exalted the virtues of the forthcoming production's 'new scenery, dresses and decorations'. It was of course common for day-bills to emphasize these aspects of a production: alive to the increasing threat from the Minor Houses the stock company was quick to draw attention to those incidents in a play, such as storms, explosions, battles, tournaments, trials, dances and processions of all kinds, that were likely to appeal to the public's growing taste for visual spectacle, and particularly to vaunt any special effects they would display in the course of performance. In the 1820–1 season, for instance, they descended on clouds, entered by traps, were drawn on stage by a 'docile lion', struck walls with lightning and felled trees, but the effects of which they seem to have been especially proud were the 'new invented red fire', for conflagrations, and the moonlight: on 25 January 1820 for Dibdin's burletta, *The Sceptre on Horseback,* we hear that 'there will also be exhibited a New Moon, which is expected to be full about Half-price'. In the same spirit, productions of Shakespeare are prodigally sub-titled in the day-bills to stress their spectacular or thrilling qualities; thus, *Richard III*; *or The Battle of Bosworth Field* and *King Henry VIII*; *or The Fall of Cardinal Wolsey*. But clearly this was not enough: with a circus opening that year a matter of yards away in the same street, the Theatre Royal had no alternative but to hire trained performers in this line, like the dogs Carlo and Bruin, whose anthropomorphic derring-do thrilled audiences in a week of canine melodrama in November, while their handler Mr Holland contributed farmyard imitations for good measure, and the renowned Madames [*sic*] Ferzi, who for a week in December performed their 'Grand, Serious, Operatical Feats on the Tight Rope', accompanied by an enigmatic figure known as the Young American, who trod the rope 'from the back of the Stage to the Shilling Gallery, Sixty Feet high from the Pit, and embracing the whole extent of the Theatre' and on his return to the stage was 'surrounded in a brilliant display of Bengal Light'.

By 1850 the competition confronting the Theatre Royal had become more intense and more firmly entrenched. Encouraged perhaps by the Regulation Act, speculators had built a brand new theatre in Paragon Street in the developing business quarter of the town near the North Eastern Railway station. Opened in 1846 for equestrian shows as the New Amphitheatre and later the Royal Amphitheatre, it was re-named the Queen's Theatre in the following year and, with an auditorium seating about 3,000 and a stage ninety feet deep, it was reputed to be the largest theatre outside London. Faced with this challenge, the York Circuit stock company, still occupying their old building in Humber Street, respond in a number of ways. Having already lowered their Box prices some years earlier, in the 1830s, they now reduce the charge for the Pit and First Gallery from 1s. 6d. to 1s. and for the Second Gallery from 1s. to 6d. They continue to observe the traditional season from October or November to March but introduce a further three-week season in September, largely devoted to opera. They lease the house to the Manchester Theatre Royal Company under Henry Beverley, who play two limited summer seasons there, in May–June and again in July–August. Whereas in 1820 performances were given only infrequently on Wednesday and never on Saturday (which Tate Wilkinson even in the previous century had described as a bad night in Hull), it is now the custom to play every night of the week and often to announce for Saturday the second-price performance of a play hitherto given first on the programme, as a means of attracting an audience for that evening. The net result of these innovations is that the theatre is closed far less often in the course of the year, a necessary first step to wooing a clientèle and propping up a weakened economy.

A variety of other features in the 1850 bills strike one as indications of a determined effort to outshine the theatre's rivals. To add lustre to the September opera season five well-known singers are brought up from London to join the company for a week, the accompanying publicity making it clear that 'notwithstanding the very great expense attending this engagement, there will be no advance in the prices'. Advertising his plans for the 1850–1 season, Mr Caple, who has just been appointed manager of the York Circuit in succession to J.L. Pritchard and has inherited a company of about thirty actors little changed from the previous season, achieves a remarkable feat of double-think sales talk when he announces 'New Company! Old Favourites! and New Attractions!!' These new attractions include 'the most Talented Ballet Company in England, from the Theatre Royal, Drury Lane', engaged for two weeks in December to provide a nightly ballet, and two 'grand scientific entertainments' known respectively as the Polytechnic Magnificodioptrica and Dissolvent Diorama, 'displaying, by a powerful Oxyhydrogen Gas Apparatus, an innumerable variety of Dissolving Views', and the Chromatrope, in which 'the Colours of the Rainbow are seen in Rotary Motion, performing the most graceful, yet fantastic evolutions, glittering in all the brilliancy of Noonday Sun'. After a great deal of resourceful advance publicity extolling its 'splendid Appliances' and the London 'Pantomimic Artistes' who will be taking part, the year ends with 'an entirely New, Original, Historically, Historical [*sic*], Local, Imaginary, Operatic, Romantic, Melo-Dramatic, Tyrannic, Pathetic, Allegoric, Eccentric, Heroic, Magical, Legendary, and provokingly Comic Xmas. Pantomime, introducing some startling and unrevealed Passages in Ancient History, abounding with brilliant and expensive Scenery, extraordinary Machinery, beautiful Dresses, gorgeous Properties, indescribable Tricks, Transformations, Hits, Skits, Cracks, Slaps, Thumps, Bumps, Pokes, and Jokes, and first appearance of the Troop of Infant Dancers, with other Novel Introductions, entitled *Harlequin, Jack the Giant Killer; or, the Elfin Fairies of St. Michael's Mount and the Naiades of the Silver Stream*'. Sensing that there is a market amongst children for all this as well as amongst adults the company announces for the first Friday of the new year 'a Grand Juvenile Night, upon which the New Comic Pantomime will commence the Performances of the Evening'.

The 'Infant Dancers' seen in the pantomime were in fact children from Hull, recruited by advertisement in the playbills and trained for the occasion. This is but one instance of the more determined and inventive exploitation of local association which the company is now prepared or obliged to make. Other examples abound: the staging of performances not only for Hull Fair but for the regatta in July, with a specially tailored farce called *The Hull Water Witches*; the inclusion of local scenes or references in the synopses of plays, which are only to be expected of the Christmas pantomime but which assume a more factitious, not to say implausible, air in connection with Blanchard's *Faith, Hope and Charity* or Courtney's *Tricks and Trials! The Modern Tom and Jerry*; *Or, Life as We Find it in 1850*; again, the dedication of a ballet to Lady Clifford Constable, wife of a local gentleman renowned for his support of theatrical activities; and, as might be anticipated, a substantial increase in the number of performances given 'under the patronage' of local worthies, such as the mayor, the sheriff, the landed gentry, aldermen and prominent tradesmen, army officers and stewards of the regatta.

In many other respects, one is struck by a continuity of tradition from 1820 to 1850. The format of the evening's programme is virtually identical, even if the closing piece is perhaps less often a farce. Burlettas, divertissements, extravaganzas, as well as individual songs and dances, are common and even the grand Christmas pantomime always comes last on a generous bill of several items, except on

Juvenile Night when it opens the programme and the evening's entertainment finishes early. Performances still begin normally at 7 o'clock (occasionally at 7.30) with second-price at about 9 o'clock. The benefit system for leading or specially engaged players continues. Handbills, issued daily and delivered by hand, are still the accepted form of publicity, though the announcement on these bills of performances a day or two in advance is met with more often, implying perhaps a greater degree of programme planning. The bills are still prone to make as much capital as possible out of the visually spectacular features of a play, like the procession of '140 auxiliaries' which throng the stage for *The Jewess*, the '80 Fairy Children' used in the pantomime and the 'New Scenery' regularly announced for revivals of old tragedies; but here too one can detect the signs of a shift of emphasis in audience expectations. Antiquarianism dictates that physical appurtenances are best when they can boast a pedigree and the company's publicity has already begun to stress that the armour for *The Jewess* is not only real but manufactured in Paris 'at a cost of £2,000' and, at every possible opportunity, that the costumes are 'taken from Authorities of the Period'. There is even what may be read as an attempt to establish a tenuous connection with Charles Kean's productions in the announcement that the company will stage 'Shakespeare's Play of *King Henry IV*, as Commanded by and Performed before Her Most Gracious Majesty the Queen, Prince Albert and the Royal Family, at Windsor Castle, three weeks since'. By the same token scenic artists are dignified by a mention in the playbill more frequently than dramatists and occasionally separate credits are accorded to those responsible for properties, decorations, dresses, machinery and 'tricks'. The name of the stage manager is now always given on the bill and on the occasion of particularly spectacular productions he is allowed the status of a producer *avant la lettre* in phrases like 'the whole arranged and produced by Mr. W.D. Broadfoot'. The latter is even described as 'Stage Manager and Spectacle Director' in one bill; indeed, before the pantomime, produced 'under his exclusive direction', the theatre is closed for two days to allow him to make final preparations.

Changes in the pattern of theatre-going and consequent changes in organization are implicit in the fact that runs of several consecutive performances are now fairly common: that the Christmas pantomime should be given fifteen performances, twelve of them consecutive, is not perhaps remarkable, but *The Jewess* can claim six and runs of two or three nights are frequent. Moreover, in the extensive advance publicity lavished on the appearances of Miss Goddard, who seems to have achieved a position of eminence in the stock company, we can even see adumbrated the importance attached to stars and star billing that will characterize the Theatre Royal's policy in the later years of the century.

Turning to 1880 one has a strong initial impression of *dėja vu,* for the year opens, curiously enough, with the same pantomime, now calling itself *Jack and the Beanstalk; Or, Harlequin the Wicked Giant, and the Good Fairies of the Moon* and keeping roughly to the same plan, with a dozen scenes devoted to the fairy story culminating in a 'Grand Transformation' for scene 12, followed by a brief 'Harlequinade'. But there the similarity with the practices of 1850 virtually ends. The fact that the pantomime boys are now played by girls and the dames are in 'drag' might almost be seen as an index to the profound changes which have overtaken the whole conduct of the Theatre Royal. For one thing, it is no longer in the same place. The old building in Humber Street had burnt down in 1859 and its splendid successor, erected on the same site six years later by a new group of entrepreneurs (who had bought out the Wilkinson family) and seating a large audience of well over 2,000, had churlishly succumbed to a similar fate during the Christmas pantomime of 1869. Meanwhile its chief rival, the Queen's, plagued by dwindling receipts as tastes changed, had fallen on evil days and, after doing service as a music-hall for a time, had been sold to speculators for a hotel and shop development – with the exception of its vast stage, which ironically provided the site for the new Theatre Royal, opened in 1871. The York Theatrical Circuit, as such, has ceased to exist but, of the cities formerly served by it, two – Hull and Leeds – continue to have theatres under the same management, that of Wilson Barrett, who, as an absentee landlord with larger theatrical fish to fry in London, leaves a resident manager in charge in each city.

The Hull manager in 1880, Mr Alfred Cuthbert, has two main strings to his bow. There is, first, what is to all intents and purposes a permanent company occupying the theatre for an elongated autumn and winter season: they play from what the bills call the 'Commencement of the Dramatic Season' in August until a week after the closure of the pantomime in February, then spend the early spring commuting between Leeds and Hull and touring with the provincial production of Wilson Barrett's latest London success, before returning to Hull for a few weeks at the end of the season, which finally closes in May. For the remainder of the year and for the weeks during which his permanent company is absent, Mr Cuthbert books 'travelling companies'. In all, the Theatre Royal is hired out in this fashion for exactly twenty weeks in the year, and to all manner of companies: to several opera companies, including the D'Oyly Carte twice, to visiting American entertainers and ageing English stars 'supported' by their own companies, to Wilson Barrett's Royal Court company from London, to companies 'specially selected', often by the author himself, to tour a West End success in the provinces. In this case they usually claim the exclusive right of performance: thus, the bill for June 28 announces that Mr F.M. Paget will appear 'by arrangement with Mr. and Mrs. Bancroft (Haymarket Theatre, London) in the celebrated Prince of Wales' Theatre Play, in Four Acts, *Duty*, the Provincial right of which is vested in Mr. F.M. Paget'. Other bills testify to the longevity of these provincial tours: when Mr William Duck, who has the provincial monopoly of several of H.J. Byron's plays, brings his '*Our Boys* Company' to Hull in April he proudly lets it be known that it will be the '1,342nd Night of *Our Boys* in the Provinces'. Conversely, the visiting stars not only select their own vehicles but have plays written or tailored especially for them, like *Otto, a German* played by Mr and Mrs George Knight, *Conrad and Lizette* played by the American comedians Baker and Faron, and a revamping of Sheridan Knowles's version of *The Maid's Tragedy* entitled *The Bridal* 'now compressed into three Acts, and re-arranged with considerable new matter introduced, by W.C. Day, Esq., expressly for representation by Mr Charles Dillon'. In this category, too, one should perhaps put Miss Marriott's appearance as Hamlet on April 3.

Already in 1880 these touring companies are apparently well organized: they bring with them their own acting manager, stage manager or stage director, frequently a business manager as well, are always represented by an 'agent in advance' and arrive with copious 'press opinions' collected from all parts of the kingdom, which are then sprinkled liberally over the local playbills.

As for the permanent company, they clearly cannot afford to overlook the appeal and pulling-power of the star system and throughout their season Mr Cuthbert engages a whole string of established stars to lead the company, either for the première of a new play or for the performance of a play already associated with a particular artist – or even for a spell of Shakespeare and the classics (including, almost inevitably, *The Merchant of Venice*, 'Shakespeare's Play in 4 Acts... Terminating with the Trial Scene').

The entertainment offered to the townspeople of Hull has altered almost out of all recognition since 1850. To begin with, a week's run is now the norm and forthcoming attractions are always announced at least seven days in advance. The permanent company can permit themselves a certain amount of flexibility in this respect and perform a play 'until further notice', thus allowing them to terminate a run in the event of a failure and to extend it in the event of exceptional success or when they wish to make room for the preparation of a new play. Two-week runs are not uncommon and the Christmas pantomime is now so firmly established that it has become a law unto itself and can afford to run for seven and a half weeks. For most of this time the pantomime now stands alone on the bill; only in the last two weeks is it in need of a transfusion of piquancy in the shape of an extra 'comic drama'. Similarly, well established and, at times, new plays are played unaccompanied. For benefit performances, however, tradition still demands a variety of items on the bill, and this tends to be the case in the closing weeks of the permanent company's season as well, when there is also a fairly rapid turnover of plays from night to night. The very last night of the season, for instance, rather like the last night of the Proms, has an 'old favourites' ring about it – a blockbuster double-bill composed of *The Colleen Bawn* and *The Corsican Brothers*. The 'special attractions' booked for the Horse Show week and the August Bank holiday seem equally dictated by this kind of thinking. However, on the whole, one is struck by the remarkable newness of the repertoire in the 1880 season: with the exception of Shakespeare and a handful of sure-fire melodramas there are very few plays more than fifteen years old and the incidence of recently written plays or even premières is surprisingly high.

Other indications of the changing climate in theatrical taste abound in this year's bills. New plays calling themselves 'realistic' have begun to appear, boasting 'realistic' scenery and properties and 'characteristic' costumes. For *Drink*, Charles Reade's adaptation of Zola's *L'Assommoir*, both the costumes and the properties are 'supplied direct from Paris' and for Paget's touring production of *Duty*, as one might expect in a play originating at the Prince of Wales's, the poster is careful to announce that the 'Grand Staircase, Elaborate Properties, Draperies, Carpets and Appointments' used on stage are all guaranteed to come from 'the famous establishment of Messrs. Copeland and Lye'. In other places there is ample evidence that the new 'realism' is of a questionable nature and has not yet usurped the place of spectacle in the theatre. One finds the two modes jostling side by side, even in the same play: the playbill synopsis for Thomas W. Charles's provincial tour of Byron's *Sardanapalus*, for instance, alternates the archaeologically pretentious with the downright sensational descriptions of scenes, while *Drink*, for all its claims to depict 'the Interior of a Public Wash-House' and a 'Home Beggared by Drink' can still find room for 'a Quadrille by the Company'. At least Paul Meritt, Henry Pettitt and Augustus Harris have the disarming, if strategic, honesty to advertise their new work, entitled *The World*, as a 'Sensational *and* Realistic Drama'.

As might be expected, another phenomenon is beginning to make its presence felt in the publicity – that of the producer as distinct from the stage manager. This is certainly true of the companies touring West End successes, which are regularly announced as 'produced under the direction of' or 'under the stage direction of', but it also applies to productions mounted by the resident company: the poster for *Drink* says clearly 'the whole produced under the direction of Mr Alfred Cuthbert' and the two world premières staged at the theatre early in the 1880–1 season are both billed as 'under the personal direction of the Authors'. It would appear that the example of Tom Robertson had not only taken root in the travelling companies but was already influencing the provincial theatre at large.

The terms of the Copyright Acts of 1833 and 1842 (or the repercussions of subsequent litigation) appear at last to have borne some fruit, for the 1880 bills suggest a measure of improvement in the status of the playwright. Certainly, it is now, if not *de rigueur*, at least customary for the author's name to appear and recent adaptations from the French quote the original source as well.

Finally, when one comes to examine the internal management of the Hull theatre, the picture is one of almost complete transformation in thirty years. The enterprise is now securely and profitably established on a commercial footing, with a degree of organization far exceeding anything practised in 1850. The theatre is open all the year round, except for one week in July, given over to a holiday for the entire staff, and a four-day rehearsal break immediately before the Christmas pantomime. Prices of admission are very revealing: there has been no overall increase in scale but greater differentials have been introduced, in keeping, no doubt, with the hierarchical divisions enshrined in the architecture of the new building. The charge for private boxes has been raised substantially to a guinea and 1½ guineas; the First Gallery has been significantly re-christened the Dress Circle and elevated in price accordingly to three shillings, while the parts of the theatre occupied by the lower orders remain unaffected. Clearly, the theatre can now afford to project a markedly different image of itself; the likely corollary is that it has already begun to retrieve the custom of the prosperous middle classes and their social superiors. In step with dining habits there is a noticeable tendency to start the performance later in the evening: the 7 o'clock curtain which has been usual since the beginning of the century is now withheld until 7.30 for the greater part of the year and reverts to the earlier hour only in the winter months. The matinée performance has made its début, in connection with the pantomime: on New Year's Day 1881, a Saturday, there is 'a Grand Illuminated Morning Performance. Doors open at 1.30, Commence at 2', to which children are presumably admitted for half-price, as was certainly the practice at the Grand, Leeds.

The pantomime, in fact, illustrates admirably the administrative gulf which separates the mentality of 1850 from the business acumen and solid commercial achievements of the 1880 provincial manager. There are now late boats from Hull pier and special trains; cheap-day excursions to the Theatre Royal panto are organized to cover a wide catchment area, from Grimsby in the south to York in the north and Leeds and Doncaster in the west, while 'Juvenile Nights' are regular and account for a substantial part of the run. Within the auditorium the manager's first concern has now become his public's comfort and safety. To counter the prevalent early Victorian habit of taking babes in arms to the theatre a regulation has been introduced banning children under the age of three, and smoking is prohibited, the bills telling us in no uncertain terms that 'the Police have imperative orders from the Magistrates to remove anyone so offending'. With the advent of longer runs and forward booking the weekly poster has become the normal medium of publicity in preference to handbills, though the day-bill is still used for weeks of opera in repertoire. There is a free list which is only rarely suspended (for outstanding touring attractions), whereas second-price (and all that goes with it), though still operative, is patently no longer encouraged. It is now available for nowhere in the house but the highly priced Dress Circle and the poster for the D'Oyly Carte tour opening on June 7, which announces that 'during this engagement there will be NO SECOND PRICE', sounds the knell of this long-established custom. Benefits of course continue, usually on a Friday evening, for leading actors in the permanent company, for the resident manager, for the treasurer and for most visiting stars, but one other link with past practice, the energetic cultivation of local affiliations, has virtually disappeared. On only one occasion, in connection with a benefit, is the performance given 'under distinguished patronage' and there is only one reference in the bills to the deployment of local amateurs among the ranks of their professional betters – and that is of a rather special nature, when seamen from H.M.S. *Audacious* in Hull docks add an authentic nautical flavour to a production of *Black Eyed Susan.* Arguably the Theatre Royal is, by this time, so firmly accepted and so respectable an institution that it no longer needs to demonstrate its solidarity with the pace-setters of local society.

I hope that through the dust raised by this hasty scamper over the century some discernible pattern of development has emerged. It seems to me to be one of profound revolution in the conduct of theatrical affairs. Some survivals from the past persist – benefits, the truncated second-price, the fairly frequent after-piece or curtain-raiser and, amongst the imponderables, a lingering affection for visual spectacle and sensation. But in most respects there has arisen already by 1880 an ethos of management and theatre-going which is still recognisably with us in the second half of the twentieth century. I think it likely that the experience of one Theatre Royal is not untypical and that a closer and less superficial scrutiny of the Hull collection of bills than I have been able to undertake for the purpose of this paper would throw a great deal more light on the evolution of the theatre in the English provinces.

Notes

[1] e.g. William Barrymore, *Manfred; or, The Mysterious Hermit,* (1841); John Courtney, *Tricks and Trials. The Modern Tom and Jerry; or, Life as we find it in 1850* (1850); Frank Harvey, *A Wife's Victory* (1879).

[2] *The Tourist's Companion from Leeds through Selby to Hull* (1835) 238.

3 M. GLEN WILSON

The Career of Charles Kean: A Financial Report

Seldom have actors left financial records of significant completeness. Even more rare is the preservation of such records. It is of particular interest, then, when one finds extensive manuscript financial data on an actor, for such information may be revealing of both the individual actor's success and the theatre in which he figured.

Charles Kean was an actor for almost forty years, his career spanning the middle of the nineteenth century rather neatly. He never played anything but starring roles, and his position as leading tragedian for almost thirty years makes him a central figure for study of theatre at mid-century.

Beginning in 1835, and perhaps earlier, Kean kept daily records of his acting engagements, and it is likely he kept detailed accounts throughout his career. He was rather meticulous in such matters, and obviously his antiquarian eye was, later, on future scholarship. The abundant materials Kean left are widely scattered, however, and much has been lost; only a few of his account books are available, though there may be others lodged in unknown libraries or private collections.

In Folger Library there are Kean's account books for the two seasons from July 1835 to July 1837; from September 1848 to September 1850; and for the Windsor Castle Royal Theatricals which Kean directed for nine years beginning in 1848. In the Harvard Theatre Collection there are Kean's account books for the seasons of 1837 to 1839, 1840 to 1842, and for most of the final American tour from 1864 to 1866. Thus, precise accounts exist for more than nine years of Kean's career, and various other manuscript materials permit reliable estimates on sixteen additional years. By projection from this evidence and with knowledge of terms, success and degree of activity, seven other years may be estimated with some confidence. Except for the first eight years of his career, where evidence is scattered and incomplete, it is possible to account for Kean's gross income with a reasonable degree of accuracy. While the accounting here by no means approaches the exactitude or methodology of an auditor, it is conservative and accurate in terms of known data. It will, I hope, suffice for purposes of theatre research.

Proceeding chronologically, Kean's first engagement began at Drury Lane on 1 October 1827, at £10 weekly. His salary was to increase by a pound per week for each of the two following years [1]. Although he seldom played, he drew his salary for about six months of that first season, going to the provinces in April of 1828. From all accounts he fared poorly there. He returned to Drury Lane in December for another four months of very infrequent appearances. On return to the provinces, he was apparently more successful as a result of some well publicized appearances with his father, but he was still earning only enough to support himself as a touring star. In October 1830 he played the last week of the Haymarket season for £20, but for some reason he did not fulfil the third year of his Drury Lane contract. After an abortive tour to Holland, at an unreceived salary of £20 weekly, he went to America where he did rather well for some thirty months as a visiting attraction, but he apparently made no fortune. In 1833 he began an engagement in late February for £30 weekly at Covent Garden, remaining with the company until July, the last weeks being played at the Olympic following a salary dispute with the new Covent Garden manager. When Dunn, the Drury Lane treasurer, suggested to young Kean that a place might be available for him at Drury Lane, Kean voiced his well-known vow never again to act on a London stage for less than £50 a night. He turned to the provinces where he was soon on the road to financial independence. His American savings, whatever they may have been, had apparently gone toward his father's illness, funeral and, perhaps, debts. Edmund Kean's effects were put under the hammer in June 1834 to satisfy creditors, apparently to Charles' helpless distress.

The 'Charles Kean Account Book, 1835–1837' [2] opens with the statement, 'Began this year with £350 at Coutts', and lists sums sent to his mother the previous year, totalling £203. In his accounts, Kean listed all engagements for the respective season, citing dates, plays performed, daily gross receipts, terms of agreement, his share received, and various brief notes concerning weather, health and unusual circumstances, especially those influencing receipts. For example, the first engagement was at Exeter for five nights on terms of one third of the gross receipts and one half on Kean's benefit night. On Monday, July 27 Kean played Sir Giles Overreach in *A New Way to Pay Old Debts* with gross receipts of £17.15s.6d. On Tuesday, *Othello* brought £18.8s.0d., and on Wednesday receipts for *Merchant of Venice* were £30.3s.0d. *Hamlet* on Thursday drew £30.9s.6d., and *Richard III* for the benefit on Friday, July 31 grossed £38.3s.0d. Re-engaged Saturday night, the gross was only £7.10s.0d., and Kean accentuated it with three large exclamation points and noted, 'The heat was *extreme* during the week.' His total share for the engagement was £53.16s.10d.

In larger centres, such as Brighton three weeks later, terms were half the receipts after £10 and half on the benefit. There his engagement was extended from ten to seventeen nights, for which he received £206.10s.9d. In major cities terms were less favourable. At Liverpool, on unspecified terms, he received £131.8s.9d. from a gross of £1095.8s.6d. for fifteen performances. And so on through the season. Kean summarized it: 'From July 20, 1835, to July 20, 1836, I performed 193 nights and received £2573.13.4.' Expenditures had been £1462.11s.1d. for a profit of over £1100. He had sent £215 to his mother, paid £266 in debts and given £25 to a publisher 'for my father's correspondence'.

The following season his terms were higher. He played at most theatres for £10 nightly, but Brighton, Bath and Edinburgh, for example, were much more remunerative. At Edinburgh, he played for half after £30 and a half benefit; for the engagement, extended from eighteen to twenty-seven nights, he received £1026.16s.0d. from gross receipts of £2809.10s.2d. At the end of the account book, Kean wrote, 'From July 20th 1836 to July 20th 1837, I performed 183 nights and received £3455.1s.11d.' Profit for the year was £1790. 19s.2d. [3].

The following season, after a provincial tour, he opened at Drury Lane in January at £50 per night. He played forty-four nights for £2100, giving two gratuitous performances for benefits. Four weeks in Edinburgh and Glasgow brought him £1075, but interruption of the Drury Lane run was unfortunate. He returned there with diminished success, writing on May 14 in the account book, 'In consequence of the houses not being well attended and the actor's salaries not likely to be paid, I resigned my money for these three nights [the first of the engagement] and reduced the remaining ones to £25 per night instead of £50'. His account book summary for the year was, 'From July 20, 1837, to July 20, 1838, I performed 140 nights and received £4567.8.0.' [4].

London success brought increased attraction in the provinces. Half nightly became the standard terms except in Liverpool, Dublin and Edinburgh, where half after £30 and a half benefit were the terms, and in Manchester where he played an engagement of ten performances at £10 nightly. The season ended with a Haymarket engagement of twenty-two performances at £50 per night and a half benefit. Kean's accounts for the season ended with 'From August 1st 1838, to August 1st 1839, I performed 225 nights and received £7242.7.5.' [5] He was no longer listing expenses in his accounts.

There are no extant records for the American tour, obviously unproductive, that came next. Illness plagued Kean, and the National Theatre in New York burned during his engagement, destroying some of his costumes and rendering the manager unable to pay. In 1845 he was still hoping to collect $5,000 owed him in New York [6]. Cutting the tour short, he returned to the Haymarket on 1 June 1840 for twenty nights at £50 per night, but the engagement was twice extended due to his great success in *Macbeth.* The only precisely known income for the 1839–40 season is the £1345 realized in this engagement [7].

The provincial tour that followed was a productive one. Terms were half nightly except for the large cities, and at Liverpool and Manchester Kean played for £20 nightly plus a half benefit. In May 1841 he returned to the Haymarket for twenty nights at his usual London terms, but giving two nights free. During this season he gave a total of seventeen free nights to managers or to actor benefits. At the Haymarket, Ellen Tree was also engaged, at £25 nightly, and Kean noted in his account that he gave Webster six clear nights 'In consideration of extra expenditure to engage Ellen Tree for Romeo.' Kean wrote at the end of the season, 'From August 17th, 1840 to August 17th 1841, I performed 220 nights and received £6474.11.0.' [8] In November following he wrote to Edward Moran of the *Globe,* 'I can boast of receiving more money in one year than ever was received by a British actor or actress, not excepting my father or Miss O'Neill.' [9]

The 1841–2 season was a particularly auspicious one. Provincial tours in the fall and winter were with Ellen Tree, an on 29 January 1842, for Miss Tree's benefit at Dublin, Kean played Beverley in *The Gamester* and Duke Aranza in *The Honeymoon.* In his account book [10] he wrote 'The day I married' and then entered 'Rec'd £480.' It is clear, however, that subsequent engagements this season were made independently, even when the newlyweds played together, until their Haymarket engagement. Of that agreement, Kean noted in his account book,

> My engagement at the Haymarket was £50 per night for 20 nights – ½ a benefit, giving two free nights to the manager – My wife was £25 per night, and without the benefit. In consequence of this I rec'd £1500 and the ½ benefit produced £110. After which I reduced my terms to £100 a week and my wife's to £50, but with an anxiety for the success of the new play, and to aid the manager who had suffered from a bad season, we acted *seventeen nights for nothing*, so in all we received £2000 and £60.

His summary of the season: 'From 1st Sept. 1841 to 1st Sept. 1842 I performed 184 nights and rec'd £6061.6.6.'

Thus, from 1835–42 Kean received, at minimum, £31,679.8s.2d., an annual average of £4525. His accumulated savings must have been something under £18,000, for in a letter of 5 February 1842, Kean wrote, ' ...we start with nearly £30,000 between us.' [11] Confirming various newspaper reports of her fortune before marriage, Ellen Kean wrote after Kean's death of 'the £12,000 I brought him.' [12] From this point the two careers become one, and no separation can be made for purposes of this paper.

The next season was marked by Ellen Kean's difficult pregnancies [13]. She was often unable to act, and Kean was so perturbed that his professional life apparently was somewhat neglected. He played only twelve nights at the Haymarket in 1843, but in 1844 played 21 nights at Drury Lane at his usual terms of £50 nightly. Both Keans were performing regularly in 1844 in the provinces. Their combined talents and high popularity must have exceeded Kean's individual attraction. It would seem that an income of about £5,000 annually is conservatively assumable for these years.

In August 1845 the Keans embarked on a two year American tour for which no accounts are available. Correspondence reveals the usual terms were half nightly, although no letters relating precisely to terms of the New York engagements have been found. The Keans opened at the Park Theatre in New York for a two week engagement that was highly successful, and they were subsequently re-engaged four times at the Park during the next fifteen months. On 30 November 1845, Kean wrote to a friend that he had sent £3000 to Coutts in the first three months in America and that he expected to send £10,000 home during the two years [14]. A letter from Ellen to Kean's mother corroborates Kean's figures [15]. The *Theatrical Times,* 27 June 1846 reported that, to that date, the Keans had played seventy-two nights at the Park in New York with receipts averaging 'upwards of $690 a night'. Figures cited for the last engagement played averaged $740. At this rate, their New York engagements, totalling 120 nights, would have returned them about £16,500 at terms of half the gross receipts.

Good houses continued until the unsuccessful 'getting up' of *King John* in which Kean invested $8,000. Kean regarded $865 for the opening night as poor, and a subsequent night of $600 he emphasized in a letter with exclamation points of incredulity [16]. A forty night engagement with Ludlow and Smith, managers of the New Orleans, Mobile and St Louis circuit, grossed $24,204.50, bringing Kean half that sum, according to Smith's diary [17]. Projecting from these indications and assuming terms of half on all engagements, one can conservatively estimate this American tour grossed about $125,000 (£25,000) for the Keans.

No accounts exist for the 1847–8 season, which, from the evidence, was busy and prosperous. A Kean account book at Folger covers from 25 September 1848 to 25 September 1850, during which period the Keans curtailed provincial touring in favour of 'in residence' starring at the Haymarket, where the terms were £20 per night for three nights weekly and the same for any extra nights. In the provinces, the usual terms of half nightly, or half above £30 and a half benefit in the major cities, were maintained. Kean made no summary for this account book. There is illegibility in one instance, and no terms or receipts for two engagements, but it would appear that receipts were about £10,000. In this period, the Keans performed 387 nights, 234 of them at the Haymarket [18].

In October 1850 Kean began his nine year tenure as manager at the Princess's Theatre. No account books are available. I have been unable to trace the one listed in the sale of Henry Irving's effects for the first season at the Princess's in which Kean and Robert Keeley were partners. At Folger, however, there is a summary financial statement, in Kean's hand, of the first seven seasons [19]. The first season showed a profit of £6969.3s.11d., half of which went to Keeley. In round figures, the second season lost some £600, the third season profited £500, the fourth lost £1550, the fifth lost £550, the sixth lost £1670, and the seventh profited £3000. For the seven seasons, Kean expended £243,859 (about two million pounds in the money of 1970) for a profit of £2627.6s.10d. John W. Cole, Kean's assistant manager, secretary and biographer, wrote that the loss for the eighth season exceeded £4000 [20]. The final season must have been fairly successful, but it was also probably the most expensive one. As a farewell season, it was mainly devoted to reviving the great productions of the previous eight years, and the new *Henry V* was so successful that no Easter piece was produced: it played eighty-four nights and Cole wrote that 'The aggregate receipts went far beyond those of its most successful Shakespearean predecessors [21]'. It is doubtful, however, that the deficit from the preceding year was more than erased.

It would appear that Kean's nine years of management may have profited about £2500, but most likely it was less than this figure. However, it must be recognized that the Keans apparently took no salaries, thus foregoing the income available to them as actors. Calculated at the rate of £5000, their apparent annual income from acting the two years prior to entering management, the income loss at the Princess's would have been £45,000. The evidence seems clear that the Keans were liberal regarding charities, gifts and gratuities, very liberal with their employees, and liberal with themselves in the style of living they enjoyed, and the only source to defray such expenditures was their savings.

In his curtain speech at the final night of his Princess's management, Kean declared,

> To carry out this system, the cost has been enormous; – far too great for the limited arena in which it was incurred. As a single proof, I may state that in this little theatre, where £200 is considered a large receipt, and £250 an extraordinary one [He was speaking to a house that grossed £309.], I expended, in one season alone, a sum little short of £50,000. During the run of some of the great revivals,... I have given employment... to nearly 550 persons.... In improvements and enlargements to this building, I have expended about £3,000. This amount may, I think, be reckoned at or above £10,000 when I include the additions made to the general stock, all of which by terms of my lease (with the exception of our own personal wardrobe), I am bound unçonditionally to leave behind me.... [22]

As a matter of passing interest, Kean was paying £3550 annual rent for the Princess's in 1859 [23].

As director of the Royal Theatricals at Windsor Castle, Kean laboured valiantly but without compensation except when he acted. Standard compensation for all stars was £10 for a performance at Windsor, and Kean acted seventeen times and his wife sixteen times, receiving £330 [24]. However, in 1857 Kean calculated, somewhat vaguely, his 'Loss by Windsor Theatricals' at £1687, which included unrecompensed expenses and losses due to closing the Princess's or due to the Keans' acting at Windsor rather than at their own theatre [25].

It would seem clear that Kean's accumulated savings, which, from calculation of the £30,000 savings at his marriage in 1842 plus one third of subsequent income, may be conservatively estimated at £45,000 in 1850, had been severely eroded by personal and professional expenditures for which no accounts are available (or likely were kept). On leaving the Princess's the Keans promptly set out, with zealous purposiveness, to secure enough for an affluent retirement.

With three supporting players, evidently drawing their salaries from Kean, a series of provincial engagements occupied the next three years, punctuated with appearances at Drury Lane and the Princess's. In a letter of 1863 Kean made clear the financial basis of these provincial engagements:

> ....after closing the Princess's I made a nine months tour through the Provinces acting 160 nights in large and small theatres and my share of the proceeds amounted to £10,000 my terms being a clear half of the gross receipts everywhere with the exception of six weeks between Liverpool and Manchester in the heat of summer where I received a certain sum of £2,000 for 36 nights. The usual prices were always increased and no half-prices ever taken.
>
> Each season has given me over £8,000 – my Drury Lane terms being £60 pr. night. [26]

Evidence of specific engagements would indicate this was no exaggeration; for example, Dublin and Cork in 1860 paid the Keans £2500 for twenty-five nights [27].

On 22 March 1862, at a testimonial dinner at St James's Hall, Kean was presented with silver plate valued at two thousand guineas.

On 6 July 1863, with three supporting players, the Keans left for an Australian tour. The account books of George Coppin, their Australian agent, reveal that terms for the tour were 'clear half of the receipts. £10.0.0. Bonus nightly and a salary of £17 per week for Mr. Cathcart.' and that the agent took twenty per cent of what Kean received. Kean's receipts for 131 nights totalled £10,918.18s.9d. Expenses were quite high, and he was able to send only £3950 to England for investment [28].

From Australia the Keans proceeded to San Francisco, playing there during October and November 1864. Opening night brought $1585 in receipts – $795 for Kean and a profit of $482.50 for the manager [29]. The engagement was a successful one. In Portland, Oregon, and in Vancouver in December, receipts for three nights were $795, $1050 and $800, indicating the outcome of their engagements there [30]. From these figures, the Coppin data [31] and the account book figures for the second San Francisco engagement in January, it can be safely estimated that Kean's gross receipts for the last three months of 1864 were about $20,000 (£4,000).

Beginning on 5 January 1865, Patty Chapman, a niece who accompanied them as a supporting actress, kept a record of receipts for Kean that is now in the Harvard Theatre Collection [32]. Three minor engagements are not recorded with clarity, but in round figures Kean grossed $90,000 (£18,000) for 229 performances from

5 January 1865 to 16 April 1866, when his farewell benefit at the Broadway Theatre in New York paid him $969.50. Throughout the tour, terms had been either half the gross receipts or a flat $500 nightly.

In 1865, Kean wrote to his daughter from St Louis that he was aiming for a retirement goal of £2000 yearly income.

> I now have a yearly income of somewhere about $1500.... My reckoning places my *invested* property at this time £100 less than £30,000 with an annual interest of £1512.... [33]

The Keans docked in Liverpool on 29 April 1866, opening at the theatre there on May 2, and on May 17 they opened at the Princess's again. A two year schedule had been booked from America. Throughout the provinces, they were warmly received as old favourites, international stars and the last representatives of the 'palmy days' of English acting. There is no reason to presume that this last thirteen months was less remunerative than the years following the Princess's management. On 28 May 1867, in Liverpool, Kean's career was ended by a heart attack. He died the following January.

In summary, reliable documentary evidence exists for conservatively determining Kean's approximate income for twenty-five of his forty years on the stage at £110,000, and one could safely hazard that it was nearer £125,000. For seven other years, conservative projection from analogous years adds £35,000, leaving only the first eight lean years as relatively unestimatable. Thus, from 1835, including the nine years at the Princess's, Kean averaged more than £4000 annually as gross income. For the eight and a half years covered by his account books, Kean (or perhaps we should say, the Keans) averaged just over £35 per performance in an age when five shillings was the price for a stall seat in the major London theatres.

But expenses were great, the Keans did not live parsimoniously, and the years at the Princess's apparently cut more heavily into Kean's fortune than has been thought; or possibly some unfortunate investments were made for which no records have been found. An unidentified clipping in the Harvard Theatre Collection reports that Charles Kean 'whose personality has been sworn under £35,000' left by will dated 30 June 1866, a life interest 'in sum of £25,000'. The principal went to his daughter after his wife's death, but all presentation plate, jewelry, etc., went to her at his death. She was also to receive £100 annually while Ellen lived. To Patty Chapman went £1500 and an annuity of £150 [34]. On 29 June 1868, a statement of Kean's estate by his executors showed £22,001.5 in stocks, mostly railroad, plus the freehold house at 47 Queensborough

Terrace, London, valued at £3,000 [35].

Ellen Kean died in 1880. On 29 February 1884, a statement of securities held at Coutts Bank for the executors of Kean's estate totalled £22,082, producing an annual income of £1070.4s.0d. [36]. This evidently passed to the daughter, Mrs Cosmos Logie, who died in 1898 without living issue.

Digressions into various items of interest or indulgence in broader interpretative analysis have not been possible here. It may be noted, however, that exorbitant as Kean's terms may seem, there were only occasional grumbles, and he was usually considerate and generous to any manager in distress. Managers were eager to have the Keans, engagements were frequently extended, and there are several instances, notably Dublin and Edinburgh, where managers often looked to the annual visit of the Keans to turn a season to profit. There were few if any stars to equal the provincial attraction of Charles Kean after 1835, and after his marriage to Ellen Tree there was no equal attraction on the English stage.

If money does 'talk', it would seem that Kean was a more important actor than generally recognized. His work as a manager is also given dimension by understanding of his financial status. Clearly, Kean was astute in business matters, and so was his wife. We must therefore presume that his financial policy at the Princess's Theatre was calculated.

Apparently, Kean was dedicated to a concept and programme of dramatic art without regard to commercial success. This was in the spirit that was to animate the independent theatre movement at the end of the century. Its rationale was surprisingly like that which motivates national subsidies today.

Notes

[1] John William Cole, *The Life and Theatrical Times of Charles Kean, F.S.A.*, 1859. Chapters IX, XII and XIII of Volume I provide details of Kean's early career cited here.

[2] In Folger Library.

[3] *Ibid.*

[4] Charles Kean, 'Journal of Receipts and Expenses, 1837–1839', Harvard Theatre Collection.

[5] *Ibid.*

[6] 'Journal of Edward Shaw Simpson' in Folger Library, a xerox copy of a manuscript owned by Mrs J.S. Brockman.

[7] 'Charles Kean Receipt Book, 1840–41', Harvard Theatre Collection.

[8] *Ibid.*

[9] Charles Kean to Edward Moran, 23 November 1841. Harvard Theatre Collection.

[10] 'Charles Kean Account Book, 1841–1842', Harvard Theatre Collection.

[11] Charles Kean to David Buchanan, 5 February 1842. Missouri Historical Society, St Louis.

[12] Ellen Kean to Cosmos Logie, n.d. Folger Library.

[13] In a Folger document listing of his Haymarket engagements, Kean wrote, 'I cannot find 1843 [evidently referring to the account book] but I acted 20 nights without my wife who was then near her confinement.' In September 1842 she suffered a miscarriage at Brighton, and a daughter was born on 6 September 1843.

[14] Charles Kean to David Buchanan, 30 November 1845. Folger Library.

[15] Ellen Kean to Mary Kean, 30 November 1845. Folger Library.

[16] Charles Kean to Sol Smith, 18 November 1846. Sol Smith Collection, Missouri Historical Society, St Louis.

[17] The diary is in Missouri Historical Society, St Louis.

[18] 'Charles Kean Receipt Book, 1848', Folger Library. It begins 25 September 1848, and ends 25 September 1850.

[19] In a collection of Charles Kean's letters and sundry documents at Folger Library.

[20] Cole, *op. cit.*, II, 313.

[21] *Ibid.*, 353.

[22] *Ibid.*, 383.

[23] Receipt, J.M. Maddox to Charles Kean, for quarterly rent, 3 February 1859. Enthoven Collection, Victoria and Albert Museum.

[24] 'Expenses, Royal Dramatic Performances, Windsor Castle, Charles Kean, Director'. Folger Library. This ledger was kept by George Ellis, Kean's stage manager.

[25] *Ibid.*, at the end of an attached paper and in Kean's hand.

[26] Charles Kean to George Coppin, 25 February 1863. Printed in J.M.D. Hardwicke, *Emigrant in Motley* (London, 1954) 54–6.

[27] Letter, Ellen Kean to Sol Smith, 29 December 1859. Missouri Historical Society, St Louis.

[28] Alec Bagot, *Coppin the Great* (Melbourne, 1965) 267. This book, utilizing data from Coppin papers in Australian libraries, is an excellent source on Kean's Australian and subsequent American tour.

[29] Letter, Ellen Kean to Mary Kean, 9 October 1864. A James Cathcart letter to Kean on 10 November 1864, reveals the manager's expense charge for a benefit was $300. Both letters are in the Sol Smith Collection of the Missouri Historical Society, St Louis, and are printed in William G.B. Carson, *Letters of Mr and Mrs Charles Kean Relating to Their American Tours* (St Louis, 1946) 97–100.

[30] Letter, Ellen Kean to Mary Kean, 6–9 December 1864, and Charles Kean to Mary Kean, 14 December 1864. In Hardwicke, *op. cit.*, 200–6.
[31] Bagot, *op. cit.*, 290–5. Coppin accompanied the Keans to America as their agent.
[32] Charles Kean, 'Journal of Receipts, 1865–66', Harvard Theatre Collection.
[33] Charles Kean to Mary Kean, 16 June 1865. Folger Library.
[34] In Folger Library. (Compare footnote 19.)
[35] *Ibid.*
[36] *Ibid.*

4 PAUL WADLEIGH

Staging Mid-Victorian Drama: Four Seasons at Pullman's Summer Palace

If my attitude toward my topic – four seasons of producing nineteenth-century drama – vacillates from the solemn to the jocular (if not downright frivolous, occasionally) you must bear with me, for I have never really decided how I ought to appear to think about it. The trouble is that doing these revivals is so enjoyable it seems positively sinful. You are probably aware that in most Americans there lurks a trace of our Puritan heritage, part of which says, in effect, that if something is any fun at all it is very likely bad for one, an attitude which frequently manifests itself in intellectual circles in grim and humourless pursuit of scholarly and cultural goals. So, when I read of summer seasons at other American universities, schedules fraught with significance, reminding audiences that 'Life is real; Life is earnest', or when I meet some old acquaintance or other at a conference who tells me he has just finished a season including, say, *The Investigation* and *Rosmersholm*, with a late Shaw for comic relief, and I can only counter with *Lady Audley's Secret* or *Under the Gaslight*, I feel like a grasshopper in a community of ants. The Puritan in me stirs uneasily.

Such twinges are momentary, however, and quickly suppressed, and I have no tendency to vacillate now when I say that our four years of reviving the old plays have been fascinating, challenging and rewarding, intellectually and artistically, for both participants and audiences and that I look forward to the next four with great anticipation.

I am not going to presume to tell you how to stage mid-Victorian plays, if only because I am aware that ours is neither the first nor the only theatre organization to give serious attention to the matter. I can, however, tell you what we have done and how we have gone about doing it. To those of you who have done revivals I offer my remarks in the spirit of comparing notes. If, as yet, you are still only contemplating such productions, I hope this account will encourage you to give it a try and serve at the same time as a guideline. Each summer at Washington State University, in Pullman, the University Theatre, known for the two months of the season as Pullman's Summer Palace Repertory Company, presents four nineteenth-century plays. Since 1966 we have staged fifteen dramas: *East Lynne, Ten Nights in a Bar-room, My Partner, Our American Cousin, The Count of Monte Cristo, The Octoroon, Davy Crockett, Hazel Kirke, Richard III* (Cibber version), *Rip Van Winkle, Lady Audley's Secret, The Drunkard, Bertha the Sewing Machine Girl, Under the Gaslight* and *The Banker's Daughter.* Our 1970 bill will be: *The Shaughraun, The Old Homestead, Two Orphans* and *Horizon.*

The company is composed of around twenty-five students, undergraduate and graduate, most of whom are between twenty and thirty years of age and a majority of whom are either students of theatre arts and drama or teachers of those subjects seeking advanced degrees. The company, then, is non-professional with levels of proficiency ranging, I would judge, from adequate-for-amateurs to the lower reaches of professional competence. As might be expected, performances are uneven from night to night and, at times, a little slap-dash; our basic training is sound, though, and the ensemble effect will give the judicious little cause for grief. We play a seven week season, five nights a week, with a nightly change of bills. The stage is small – proscenium opening is eighteen feet by nine; the audience capacity is 250.

What is it, exactly, we are doing? First of all, we are providing entertainment for audiences – first order of business for any theatre, amateur or professional. More than this, however, we provide entertainment of a special kind as we present the plays as if for audiences of the 1870s. We have worked out a mode of presentation which approximates that of a hundred years ago. We play without parody and with practically no concessions to modern audiences' attitudes and expectations. We state, through the manner of presentation, 'This is the way it was.' Thus, the Palace functions as a kind of theatre museum in which are on display theatrical practices of a century ago as well as the thousands of customs, ideas, ideals, mores, etc. reflected in the plays. The playgoer may come to the shows just to enjoy the old-fashioned stories; he may, however, transport himself back in time, should he choose to exercise his imagination, and gain a notion of what it might have felt like to live in another era as he is seated in the midst of a vanished audience, experiencing the same impressions and stimuli that once moved the hearts and minds of that earlier generation. Finally, for the theatre scholar the Palace can be seen to serve as a laboratory, wherein one is an enthusiast or a dubious critic of the period, and until the plays have been brought to life in a manner something like the author intended all opinions must remain tentative.

From this tripartite conception of the function of the Palace – as theatre, as museum and as laboratory – derives our primary criterion, authenticity, and all of our procedures have evolved as a result. Since I will be using this word, 'authenticity', or referring to it, frequently, I had better establish now that we are not so fatuous as to think we actually are authentic – literally – in our productions. To recreate the theatre of an era is to recreate a way of life – a job clearly impossible; we can be true to the times, though, and we console ourselves with the thought that authenticity, like nirvana, is a state to be approached but never quite attained by mere mortals.

When I set about preparing this report I expected to be concerned mainly with production details. It would consist, I thought, of a relatively straightforward account of our research and its application to mounting the plays. When I got down to reviewing the problems that have confronted us, however, I realized that, although the processes of research, conjecture, decision and translation into practical stagecraft have indeed occupied the greatest part of time and effort expended, the specific details of these processes are pretty much what anyone familiar with the period and with standard theatre practice would expect, given the controlling principle of authenticity. What is not so predictable is one particular difficulty we encountered from the outset which is recurrent and, unless solved, can negate the effect of all our efforts. This is the matter of getting our actors to believe in what they are doing. I don't mean eliminating insincerity, for we have found that merely to be sincere is not enough – the problem is more complex than that – but the solution, when we hit upon it, was simple. It consists of a single rule: *Don't play the role – play the actor playing the role.*

During our first season we concentrated on reconstruction, through research and training, of what we deemed to be an appropriate acting style under the erroneous impression that once we had a degree of mastery of it – voice, gesture, carriage, etc. – all we would have to do would be to learn the lines, arrange the blocking and then simply turn the crank, and Victorian drama would emerge like a Strauss waltz from a restored phonograph. What we got, however, were empty, meaningless charades – mockeries. The plays did not come to life because the actors did not mean them. Consequently they had no appeal for audiences except that of novelty, which wore off after half an hour or so. It is important to understand that the actors were, in fact, acting, that a great amount of energy was expended on stage; no one was slacking. The plays did not live because the performers were not really performing the plays as the authors had intended; they couldn't, for the plays were written to be performed by nineteenth-century actors. The trouble was that our directors and actors either would not or could not eliminate their twentieth-century reservations, usually manifested in one of two ways: those with no faith at all that the old plays could ever work for modern audiences, turned to a kind of parody, quite subtle and often well executed but clearly inviting the audience to titter; those who were genuinely fond of the period earnestly tried to overlook those elements they privately thought to be hopelessly absurd and persisted in thinking of the plays as quaint but still viable modern, *i.e.* realistic, works; this group tried to 'help' the plays by playing their roles in the subdued realistic manner. For all its good intentions this approach was, if anything, worse than parody, for the strange mixture of modern acting and antique dramaturgy made all parties seem to be blithering idiots. There was, or rather, is, for this problem comes up with every season, a third group, much smaller, who instinctively grasp our concepts and have no difficulty at all in convincing themselves and their audiences that they are, indeed, part of the original play. Even these people find our single rule useful, however, in helping them to keep on the right track.

'Don't play the role – play the actor playing the role.' Instead of attacking the role in the nineteenth-century play directly, as one normally would in a contemporary production, the actor is asked to play what amounts to two roles simultaneously: the first is that of a Victorian actor, *the performer of* the play; and the second is the *character in* the play. The first he approaches in the customary (twentieth-century) manner, which is to say that through study, research, insight or whatever, he examines the character (in this case the nineteenth-century actor) and his environment, his culture, his attitudes, etc., and, through a deliberate effort of imagination wills himself to become that actor, to think the way he might, to feel the way he might, to react the way he might react. Now, imbued with the attitudes and values of a nineteenth-century actor (it is to be hoped) our Palace actor approaches his second role, the character in the play, as his earlier counterpart might have. With his twentieth-century misgivings compartmentalized (not eliminated – and this is, I think, most important – we do not expect our people to believe in the old plays so much as to pretend to believe in them) and thus subdued, the actor, be he cynic or enthusiast, finds the plays 'normal', because they are addressed to him now as a Victorian, in his language, about his world and concerning events, values and customs he and the author and their audience share common knowledge about. Now the old plays can come to life, for the outer manner, the nineteenth-century acting style, is illuminated from within by sympathetic understanding – and the old plays glow with a light much brighter than any of us might expect.

This system is simple, merely a mental trick, self-hypnosis if you will, and like all 'simple' rules it doesn't work out as neatly as it appears in the stating. It is all very well, for instance, to urge the actor to step back into the past and see things as a Victorian actor might have. What, precisely, is he to see once we get him back there? What are those attitudes and values? How are they to be assimilated? How can we possibly expect to recreate the thousands of impressions accumulated in a lifetime that make up a man in his totality? Well, obviously, we can't and we don't expect to. It isn't necessary. I have found it desirable that our actors become familiar with as many aspects of everyday life as they can. At the beginning of each season I tell them to do some exploring on their own in the library. They should read some of the fiction of the period, Dickens, of course, perhaps Poe, and certainly Mark Twain to remind themselves that Victorians were by no means solemn and stuffy folk. Dipping into old newspapers is a valuable experience, especially when they can follow a paper through a week or two of successive issues to learn what people thought was important enough to write about. For a visual image of the period, and for an idea of how Victorians saw themselves, I urge them to study collections of genre paintings. They can leaf through books of lithographs, of photographs, read history and ponder the impact on thought of the writings of Darwin, of the railroad's effect on trade, of the telegraph and trans-Atlantic cable on international relations. In short, they should literally steep themselves in the period until it becomes as natural and familiar as their own. Actors are actors, though, and students are students. I like to think that for all of five minutes after my exhortations they are filled with resolve to get started on a self-improvement programme that very day. And they do actually poke around a little, but most of them just don't have the time to do much. Consequently, I find it more realistic just to steep myself in the period and pass along that which seems relevant. The two-role concept makes it likely that our student-actors will keep their modern selves detached from their roles, which is what we are after. At the very least, this approach makes them aware that other meanings for language and other cultural attitudes existed, even if they aren't quite sure what they were.

For a variety of reasons we have chosen to focus on a limited segment of the nineteenth century, the 1870s, and a particular kind of theatre – that which toured the small towns and cities of the United States. This focus eases research problems, of course, which is one reason; staging practices were relatively uniform throughout the country and a good deal of information about details of those practices is still accessible to the researcher. This particular period, furthermore, is transitional both as to dramaturgy and philosophy of representation, falling, as it does, between the Romantic and the Realistic eras (or Early-Victorian and Late-Victorian eras; for practical purposes we regard the twenty-five year span between, say, 1855 and 1880, as homogeneous). Not only would we have technical difficulties in trying to reproduce staging of the earlier period, but I believe that plays of this time would come across to audiences more as bizarre curiosities, difficult to identify with. The theatre of the later period, the beginning of the Realistic era, was not different enough from that with which today's playgoers are familiar and would appear to them merely as dated 'modern' plays.

The restriction to dramas that were popular in small-town America also enhances our striving for authenticity in several ways. First of all, the small theatres in these communities (often known as the 'opera house') were frequently the size of our own Palace. Touring companies that appeared on these limited stages could not present the elaborate scenic spectacles they would have in the metropolitan theatres; they carried less scenery, relied more on stock pieces to be found locally; yet they made an effort to give the audiences an idea of those thrilling visual effects so characteristic of the plays of the period. Thus a company might tour with wing and drop settings even though box sets and levels might have been used 'at home' in the big theatres, yet they would manage a simplified version of the mechanical effects – the train that comes across the stage in *Under the Gaslight,* for instance. For economic reasons our own theatre, The Palace, does not have elaborate staging facilities and does, in fact, duplicate in every dimension many stages to be found in small towns of the 1870s. Working within the limitations of our budget and facilities, then, we can honestly claim a degree of faithfulness to one aspect of the physical theatre of the time – not all nineteenth-century theatre, but that of the 'provinces'.

In this same vein, we find it desirable to establish a fictional context within which the entire company works: we consider ourselves as a second or third rate stock company, permanently based in San Francisco, perhaps, or Denver, or Chicago, on our annual tour. Such companies did, indeed, operate from a large, well-equipped theatre most of the year, going out once or twice with a repertory of several popular plays and appearing in small houses in towns as small as 10,000 to 20,000 population. Such a company would have had three or four experienced and reliable leading actors, a dozen or so younger actors on their way up and would have depended upon local people for supernumeraries. We do not literally impersonate such a company, with everyone sticking to one line of business in every show and so on (although the idea is intriguing and we might try it some day just to see what happens). The concept is useful mainly to the directors and to me in that it sets a standard of achievement; provides a distinct image to strive for. The make-up of our own company resembles this combination remarkably, not in age, of course, but in spread of experience and talent; so, while we could not convincingly (authentically) impersonate first rate troupes like Booth's or Daly's, we felt we could certainly come up with performances analogous to those of a mixed bag of journeymen and apprentices and pick-up supers of the 1870s, even down to the occasional mishaps with which the annals of the nineteenth-century theatre are graced.

As a matter of fact, we do not need to create mishaps for the sake of verisimilitude; with student actors they just happen. Take the last act of *Richard III*, for example. We happened to have two excellent villains that year, both mature and experienced performers, so we double-cast Richard, each to do five performances. On the second Richard's first night he stood on stage, surrounded by his followers, Catesby, Norfolk and the rest; at the back a seedy little army of three pikemen and a standard bearer stood in their baggy tights and silver painted burlap chain mail, fairly quivering with determination to do or die in the best tradition of the super, as Richard howled defiance in that great crescendo ending, 'St George inspire me with the rage of lions – Upon 'em! Charge! – Follow me – !' Whereupon he started off left. The other Richard, however, had always gone off right and unfortunately the rank and file responded to habit. It was only a couple of steps, but by the time both parties had got themselves organized and off right (Richard realized at once that he could not go left, for that was where Richmond and *his* three man army – the rest of the supers – were waiting) the climactic moment had somehow lost its effect for the audience. Sometimes, you will see, we are more authentic than we need be; also, it must be understood that incidents such as these are rare, unintentional (enjoyable though they may be in retrospect) and that we avoid any kind of parody at all times.

In setting up a training programme for our students in 1966, I now blush to confess I was naive enough to think that all I had to do was spend a month or so in the library with pencil and note cards to unearth a 'typical' training programme an actor of the period might have undergone, the idea being that our student actors would go through a similar programme. A period of fruitless digging was required before I remembered the obvious: nineteenth-century actors learned as apprentices, working at the sides of older actors, acquiring skills and stage lore by observation and as occasion arose, not in accordance with any particular plan. And no one, I soon discovered, had anticipated our need for a training course for twentieth-century actors to enable them to learn in five weeks what their predecessors learned during a lifetime. Now we had the apprentices, all we lacked were the old actors for them to observe and learn from. With the shortage of Victorian actors, the job fell to me and I had to work out a period acting style, not all at once but by keeping one page ahead, so to speak, and passing along the results in bits and pieces as required during rehearsals. What follows is a brief outline of our findings and practices, all of which have undergone constant modification and correction as trial-and-error experience has dictated.

And reconstruction of an acting style suitable to the plays has been nothing else if not a trial-and-error process. Everyone connected with the profession seems to have written about it in diaries, journals, articles, observations, critical reviews and reminiscences. They share with their readers their dreams and their fears, their successes and their agonies, details of their childhood, funny stories about colleagues, sad stories about their colleagues, views about women, God, the theatre, life, towns visited, favourite managers and carpenters – and especially their theories of acting, either those they employ themselves or those they think others should use. It seems impossible not to be able to obtain from the vast literature of the nineteenth century a visual image of acting style useful to our purposes; but I have found very little concrete information as to what the actors actually did on stage. When one must fill up two hours of stage business one needs to to know more than the fact that Mr A's tendency to rant was distressing to his listeners or that Mrs B's voice thrilled to the marrow of one's bones. The clues are there, of course, but since it never occurred to the writers that word pictures would ever be useful to someone a century later the clues must be sought between the lines. I recommend Michael Booth's article, 'Melodramatic Acting', to anyone embarking on this search, for he has brought together a most valuable collection of specific descriptions of actors in action [1].

Pictorial sources are not as immediately helpful as might be expected. There are few photographs which depict actual stage posture. Poster illustrations are useful when allowances are made for artists' tendencies to exaggerate for commercial purposes. Numerous books are available to us on elocution with photographs of the Delsartian poses; these, we have reasoned, must have derived from stage posture, however formalized and stilted they had become.

Even with a reasonably large collection of specific materials, verbal and pictorial, we found we still had a long way to go in developing a convincing acting style. What we had was essentially a number of 'stills', mere glimpses of actors frozen in motion. We still had to fill in the gaps. How much eye contact with the audience was customary? What was the range of gesture? Did villains really leer across the footlights at the audience, or is that concept just one of our modern parodies? And, for that matter, how did they handle those asides, where did they look, what did others on stage do?

Besides a liberal application of common sense to answer these questions, we have found early motion pictures and phonograph recordings extremely valuable. I have not had access to any films or recordings made earlier than around 1910, some thirty years after 'our' period, but since the performers in early motion pictures often came from the stage and either would have learned their craft as early as the 1870s or would have been influenced by their older colleagues who had, it seemed reasonable to conclude that what we saw on film would not be too much different from earlier stage practice. The earliest film we own is of Sarah Bernhardt's company in their stage production of *Queen Elizabeth,* filmed with their actual sets. When we obtained it and were about to view it for the first time we were in anticipation of startling revelations from the past – we felt as if we were present at the opening of King Tut's tomb. At first it struck us as disappointingly modern – unexpectedly good cinematography, rather 'normal' manner of movement and grouping of characters. We found the most striking difference occurred at moments of emotional stress; only then did the actors use what is now regarded as excessive gesture, sweeping movements. So convincing was this emotional acting, though, that it did not jump out at us on first viewing and we had to watch for it and analyze it to discover what, exactly, was being done. It was through careful study of this film and others that our people learned that bigger than life acting need not be mere posturing, that it can be motivated and, thus, convincing in the context of overall style.

In working on voice we found (and find) that our student-actors usually want to head for one of two extremes when confronted by the flowery, rhetorical dialogue – mechanical sonority or naturalistic murmuring. Either they failed to think at all of what they were saying and simply declaimed it, or they tried to read their lines as if Terence Rattigan had written them. From this difficulty came another simple dictum that has been useful: *Approach and deliver your lines as you would Shakespearean dialogue.* It works, even for prosaic westerns such as *My Partner,* certainly for high-powered scenery-chewers like *East Lynne* and *Lady Audley's Secret.* The reason is, I am convinced, that just as Shaw was the Culture Hero for the realistic dramatist so was Shakespeare for the Victorian. After having lived with fifteen of the plays (well, fourteen, since it hardly seems logical to include *Richard III* as an example), I believe that authors and performers alike, whatever the particular subject, felt the rhythms, conceived the characterizations and heard the thunder of the Bard in their inner beings. I am not prepared to cite chapter and verse from internal evidence in support of my statement, but the theory works in practice. We are fortunate in having for study a small collection of phonograph recordings by such American actors as Edwin Booth (very brief passage from *Othello*), Otis Skinner, Julia Marlowe and E.H. Sothern, all of whom flourished in their profession as Shakespeareans during the latter half of the nineteenth century.

Staging the low comedy scenes is sometimes more difficult than one might expect, for most of it must have been visual (except for absolutely hopeless puns) since the scripts present us with inexplicable bits of dialogue accompanied by directions such as 'business with hat'. Our students have had to learn to handle these as vaudeville comedians, inventing their own business and changing the lines which obviously referred to contemporary events of which modern audiences would be unaware.

What has evolved in movement and gesture as our acting style has turned out to be not so very 'different' after all. It resembles a cross between traditional grand opera and traditional Shakespearean acting. Pantomimic gesture is more literal than today's; we spell it out more. Gestures are of greater sweep and precision. We are more stately in movement and tend to strike attitudes a little more frequently than contemporary practice allows. And we finally concluded that asides and soliloquies should be handled just as they are in modern playing of the classics, as thoughts spoken aloud, and not as messages delivered to the audience. In short, we have concluded that the differences between today's acting styles and those of a century ago are more of degree than of kind, more of outer details than inner attitude; that actors crossed, sat, rose, shook hands, embraced, fought, kissed about the same way they do these actions today.

One important aspect of our training programme hardly requires elaboration here, since it is a common problem in modern theatre training, too (at least in America). This is the difficulty in getting student actors to understand the difference between the theatrical, or presentational, mode and the realistic. For some reason, our people want to *be* the characters rather than impersonate them and they tend to resist the precisely structured stage mannerism we ask them to adopt. 'It doesn't feel natural', they say. 'Of course it doesn't feel natural', we tell them. 'It isn't supposed to be natural. Victorian audiences went to the theatre to see a *show.* If they wanted naturalism all they had to do was stay at home and watch the family next door.'

Working out a rationale for what we think to be authentic blocking has not been especially troublesome. Fine points of making stage movement and picturization an integral part of the artistic whole had not reached lesser companies in our era; the underlying assumption is that important points in the action were usually played at or near centre stage and generally close to the curtain line or on the apron. When working below the curtain line, out on the apron, which is four feet out into the house, we block as we would for any thrust or platform stage. This basic assumption is supported by the few photographs of actors actually on stage we have found, by the more numerous paintings and drawings of stage groupings, by poster illustrations and by Garret Leverton's useful analysis of prompt books of the period [2]. Stage directions in the scripts give clues, of course, but these are often as baffling as they are informative. On the whole, then, we have established a conventional system of movement patterns and groupings; big scenes are played in the prominent locations and lesser characters and supers have standing instructions to fall back and form rough ranks unless told otherwise.

Whatever else The Palace contributes, it provides good training for student actors, demanding, as it does, more technique than much of our contemporary drama programme. The students are soon disabused of any notion they might have entertained that Victorian drama is easy to act. They become better actors for any kind of drama as a result of their Palace work (although in some cases they need a short period of readjustment to effect the transition back to the twentieth century, during which some of them have a tendency to stride to centre stage and declaim their lines and to want to exit via L.2 instead of through the door).

As a teacher, I find especially rewarding the fact that our people develop a tolerant respect for the niceties of scholarship as a result of their work in the Palace; and, for a few, this tolerant regard develops into passion for history.

As far as mounting the plays is concerned, we have discovered that just as inner conviction seems to supply the missing element needed to bring the plays to life so does a two-dimensional painted setting complete the visual background, revealing it to be more important than we had previously thought. Detailed scene paintings are difficult to execute well and painters are hard to come by in this age of Appia and the plastic setting, but every effort should be exerted to obtain as realistic effects as possible. When the old plays are seen in front of the drops everything falls into place and they are suddenly complete. In all of our staging we try to be faithful to the period. Lighting is general illumination, without dramatic spotlight effects. (Does anyone living today know what a stage looked like under gaslight or calcium?) All music and sound effects are live. When we have no idea of how a sound effect was originally created we figure it out as we assume our predecessors would have. For the climactic scene in *Under the Gaslight,* when the train roars across stage, we had an 'orchestra' of seven off-stage pounding, scraping and rattling an exotic collection of noise-makers; we received several compliments on the quality of the recording. Fire effects come from a modern smoke machine and a red spotlight instead of the time-honoured pan of red fire (a compromise, of course; actually, I suppose, since we are so taken with the idea of authenticity we ought to burn the place down every four or five years).

The only major liberties we take with the scripts are in cutting. We shorten them to a maximum playing time of one hour and forty-five minutes. With intermissions and the short variety show afterwards this makes a long enough evening for modern playgoers accustomed to one hour television programmes and two hour motion pictures.

In one respect alone do we change the scripts because of modern attitudes. Nineteenth-century America was pretty much the domain of the white Anglo-Saxon Protestant. Its drama, as drama will, reflects this in its sometimes crude and offensive depiction of ethnic minorities. I see no compelling artistic need to offend American Negroes by displaying the obsequious comic 'darkie' on our stage. I have written several such characters out of our shows and have softened the cruelly stereotyped portraits of Jews and Chinese that appear now and then. We have long wanted to do *Uncle Tom's Cabin,* a good melodrama, not at all the play most people think it is, which would not be found offensive by most Negroes when seen in its historical context, as we would play it. The problem lies in our requirement of authenticity, for most stage Negroes were played by whites in blackface and woolly wigs and to do this today would be looked on as a gratuitous insult to racial pride – yet to use Negroes in the roles would be false to history and would give an entirely misleading effect, an impact of realism not then sought after. Someday we will do *Uncle Tom's Cabin,* and the stage Negro will take his place on the Palace stage alongside the stage Irishman, the Jew, the silly-ass Englishman, the boasting American westerner, etc., without causing pain to a sensitive people. In the meantime, to gloss over racial stereotypes of the period is one compromise with authenticity I make without hesitation.

A pseudo-problem has arisen occasionally in regard to audience reaction to our productions that I would like to dispose of in concluding. It stems from the fact that the public persists in regarding the Palace not as a proving ground or a museum but as a theatre for entertainment. It soon becomes apparent that they cannot take the plays seriously, as plays. They are respectful, they get properly sentimental at times, they watch and listen intently, enjoying the plays as stories – but they laugh now and then at the 'wrong' places. It is a friendly laughter, of course, not raucous, even sympathetic, but it can be disconcerting to performers and directors who, as they must, believe in the dramas during performance. We have come to see such reaction as inevitable and have learned to live with it. Some of our directors, though, anxious and over-protective, want to subdue those elements causing the laughter – the florid diction, the bigger-than-life acting, the naively realistic scenery, etc. I am convinced that this not only does not help the plays but does them an injustice, for to modernize them would be to wrench them out of their cultural context and set them, mutilated and muted, against an alien background. To do so is in its way, as patronizing of the culture that produced them as is parody. If one finds value in the plays one should present them on their own terms, and let the laughter come as it may.

It would, in fact, be surprising if audiences did not find the old plays amusing, for human nature persists in regarding Now as normal and Then as funny – a phenomenon to be found as close as home, when the children discover the wedding pictures. Laughter need not be punitive. It can and does come as often from wellsprings of delight and affection and understanding. Audiences find the plays amusing in exactly the same way they find an antique automobile, chugging along a road, amusing, or one of those marvelous merry-go-round band organs with its trumpets and drums and cymbals going full blast. I am most definitely not thinking of parody when I suggest that when a nineteenth-century play is underway in full and lively restoration – chugging, as it were, down the road with exhaust popping, smoke billowing, fenders flapping and goggled occupants hanging on for dear life – anyone who can look on without a chuckle or two must indeed be sober-minded.

Notes

[1] Michael R. Booth, *English Melodrama,* (London, 1965) 190–210. This style of acting, according to Professor Booth, emerged as a distinct variation with recognizable characteristics by the mid-nineteenth century; there is no reason, however, to suppose that these variations were anything but intensification of the tragic style in general use. We use this chapter as a guide – not as a book of rules.

[2] Garrett H. Leverton., *The Production of Later 19th Century American Drama* (New York, 1936). This book, out of print now, presents a complete treatment of the feasibility of producing the old plays, with especial attention to blocking.

PART TWO

The Drama

5 PETER THOMSON

The Early Career of George Colman the Younger

In his aptly titled autobiography, *Random Records,* George Colman the Younger recalls with admiration his father's friend, Bonnell Thornton:

> When Thornton was on his death bed, his relations surrounding it, he told them that he should expire before he had counted twenty; and covering his head with the bed clothes, he began to count: – 'One, two ... eighteen, nineteen, twenty.' He then thrust out his head, exclaiming, 'By 'od! it's very strange! but why aren't you all crying?' [1]

Colman's contemporary reputation as a wit was high, rivalling, and in some quarters outshining, Sheridan's. I was first startled into contemplation of this fact by one of Byron's sudden jottings, made the morning after the night before perhaps:

> If I had to choose, and could not have both at a time, I should say, 'Let me begin the evening with Sheridan, and finish it with Colman.' Sheridan for dinner, and Colman for supper; Sheridan for claret or port, but Colman for every thing, from the madeira and champagne at dinner, the claret with a *layer* of *port* between the glasses, up to the punch of the night, and down to the grog, or gin and water, of daybreak; – all these I have threaded with both the same. Sheridan was a grenadier company of life-guards, but Colman a whole regiment – of *light infantry,* to be sure, but still a regiment. [2]

A mighty pleasant epitaph. It is a pity, perhaps, that so little of Colman's table-talk is preserved. He cherished his name as a wit more than his name as a playwright. At the height of his dramatic career, he wrote to the journalist William Woodfall, 'Being a stage hack, I have no style, and every style: a Jack-of-all-trades, but master of none.' [3]

But he was never so careless of his social prowess. Byron's comment rounds out a picture of Colman as a Regency *bon viveur,* easy to like, witty without malice, and socially energetic. The picture can be easily reversed, of course, as it was by such enemies as John Wilson Croker, and Colman will emerge as a timeserver, undeserving of literary reputation or noble patronage, weak-willed and self-indulgent. A full study of the life and works would, I think, lend support to both accounts.

Colman was a dramatist for forty years, a theatre-manager for thirty and the Examiner of Plays for twelve. He had his first play performed in 1782, when he was less than twenty, and his last in 1823, when he was sixty-one. Until 1806 he produced at the rate of about a play a year, after that a play every two years. He abandoned writing only when, on 19 January 1824, he was appointed into 'the place and quality of Examiner of all Plays, Tragedies, Comedies, Operas, Farces, Interludes, or any other entertainments of the stage of what denomination soever, in the room of John Larpent, Esq., deceased'. [4] I don't intend to say anything of Colman's career as Examiner. It has left him with the posthumous title of arch-hypocrite, a licentious ex-dramatist turned office-bearing prude. At the time, the appointment must have had its supporters. For several years Colman had been recognized as the ambitious playwright's surest guide to theatrical success. Not only had no play of his ever finally failed, but he had been responsible for others' successes. His contribution to the popularity of Henry Heartwell's *The Castle of Sorrento* [5] was openly acknowledged. The famous case of Drury Lane's *The Forty Thieves* (1806) is less clear, but it seems almost certain that Colman's advice was sought. The editors of *Biographia Dramatica* record the contemporary guesses at the authorship of this spectacular and highly successful operatic romance:

> The programme of this piece, we have been told, was sketched by Mr. Sheridan; the dialogue written by his brother-in-law, Mr. Ward; and some finishing touches are said to have been given by the pen of Mr. Colman. [6]

Jeremy Bagster-Collins's list of plays on which Colman's advice was sought [7] includes *The Cataract of the Ganges,* whose sensational staging at Drury Lane preceded Colman's appointment as Examiner by less than three months. Not only as playwright, but also as theatre-manager, Colman could be expected to understand the problems of the contemporary stage. He was, in effect, sole manager of the Little Theatre in the Haymarket from the summer of 1789, when his father's mental degeneration required that he be put in the care of 'a person at Paddington', until 1805 when, regrettably as it turned out, he went into partnership with two businessmen. He continued to participate in the management of the theatre between 1807 and 1810, when he was detained in the King's Bench Prison, and resigned his share only in

1819. According to George Raymond [8], at some time between 1817 and 1819 he declined an offer to become manager of Drury Lane, a decision which Sheridan might have envied from the other side of the grave.

It is as an eighteenth-century dramatist, pointing confusedly towards the confusion of the nineteenth-century theatre, that I wish to survey Colman. But his career and the story of the Little Theatre in the Haymarket are not separable. His fondness for the small summer theatre was genuine, and his work contains a number of shrewd hits at 'those covered Salisbury Plains which now characterize the two grand winter houses'. [9] As his place among the leading dramatists of the age became assured, he was increasingly courted by Drury Lane and Covent Garden. It was probably financial reward rather than any change of theatrical loyalties that governed his partial surrender to them after 1798. R.B. Peake records the following details:

> Colman received very considerable sums for his plays. For 'The Poor Gentleman' and 'Who Wants a Guinea?' he was paid £550 each, then the customary price for a five-act comedy; that is to say, £300 on the first nine nights, £100 on the twentieth night, and £150 for the copyright. For 'John Bull' (the most attractive comedy ever produced, having averaged £470 per night for forty-seven nights), Mr Harris paid £1,000, and Colman afterwards received twice an additional £100, making £1,200. [10]

Once he had joined the opposition, Colman made fewer attempts to beat it; but before 1798 his voice was not the least considerable in the chorus of protests against the size and customs of the Patent Houses. He had, after all, few rivals at the head of his profession: Sheridan certainly, but that was in another decade, and besides the urge was dead; Richard Cumberland, who was sixty-eight in 1800; O'Keeffe, always a favourite among actors; Thomas Morton, whose best play, *Speed the Plough,* is clearly indebted to Colman; Holcroft, who had done himself no good by exaggerating Godwin's political notions; Dibdin, Reynolds, 'Monk' Lewis. The list could be extended, but not by much. With the decline of Sheridan, the search for the great dramatist that was to occupy so many people for so long was on. Meanwhile, George Colman was a leader of the competent. If his talent is underrated now, it has to be admitted that it was overrated then. In 'English Bards and Scotch Reviewers', Byron appeals to him in the tone of Wordsworth's apostrophe to Milton. After listing some of the catchpenny dramatists of the time, he writes:

> Who but must mourn, while these are all the rage,
> The degradation of our vaunted stage!
> Heavens! Is all sense of shame and talent gone?
> Have we no living bard of merit? – none!

> Awake, George Colman! Cumberland, awake!
> Ring the alarum bell! let folly quake!

The verse is as uncertain as the judgment, but Byron is rare among critics in looking for the stage's salvation at the hands of men who have proved their knowledge of stage conditions. The continuing popularity of the English theatre through the nineteenth century cannot be accounted for in literary terms. In the rift between men of letters and men of the theatre, Colman is decisively on the theatrical side. By tracing his early career, I hope to illustrate some of the tricks and traditions he bequeathed to the nineteenth century.

Colman was nineteen and an indifferent student at King's College, Aberdeen, when his first play, a farce in two acts called *The Female Dramatist,* was given a benefit performance at the Haymarket. It was, Colman admits in *Random Records,* 'much TOO BROAD to have escaped the erasing hand of the Examiner of Plays, in the present day', [11] and since he was by then the Examiner, the remark has some authority. Beyond this, *The Female Dramatist* merits no comment. Colman considered *Two to One,* produced two years later at the Haymarket, his first play. The reviews were enthusiastic, and *Two to One* was performed nineteen times during the summer of 1784, a flattering success. The plot sounds familiar. Charlotte loves Beaufort, but her father insists that she marry Townly. Beaufort and Townly meet on their way to the house and agree that Beaufort shall impersonate Townly and Townly his own servant, so that, while Townly flirts with Tippet the maid, Beaufort sets about marrying Charlotte. It goes back to *The Beaux' Stratagem,* to *She Stoops to Conquer,* and to countless 'plays from the French', just as the effectively contrasted Dupely brothers owe their creation to Charles and Joseph Surface. This playing of slight variations on stock dramatic situations seems to have been read as piety rather than plagiarism. Successful playwrights in the years between 1750 and 1850 needed, or at least exploited, a greater knowledge of other men's plays than at any time before or since.

In a revealing passage of *Random Records,* Colman describes how he wrote *Two to One*:

> I had no materials for a plot, further than the common-place foundation of a marriage projected by parents, contrary to the secret views and wishes of the parties to be united; and which, of course, is to be obviated by the usual series of stratagems, accidents and equivoques. Alas! what those stratagems, &c., were to be or how the second scene was to be conducted, I had not any idea, while I was writing the first: – but, having finish'd the first, I hurried on into the second, with as little forecast about the third; – and so on, from scene to scene, spinning out stage *business* (as it is term'd)

> as I went along, and scribbling at hap-hazard, 'as humours and conceits might govern,' till I came to the conclusion of *Act One*....
> In this improvident way I have written all my dramas, which are not founded on some historical incident, or on some story or anecdote, which I have met with in print; and, of those thus founded, I never made out a scheme of progressive action before I began upon the dialogue. [12]

Since Colman valued his reputation for facility in composition, we should read this with caution, but we need not dismiss it. There is much in the plays of Colman and his contemporaries to support the description, not least their reliance on 'the usual series of stratagems, accidents, and equivoques'.

In terms of Colman's subsequent career, two significant things emerge from the production of *Two to One.* Firstly, that a young dramatist should set about writing his second play so complacently suggests that experience, flattered by success, was unlikely to increase his sense of awe. Colman's unwillingness to exert himself was, in the view of Leigh Hunt [13], one of the causes of the decline of English comedy. Secondly, this was the first of Colman's plays to provide a part for John Bannister Junior. Their collaboration is one of the best examples of the actor/author link in which the period is rich. Colman recalls it in his autobiography:

> Up to the year 1796, inclusive, I scribbled many dramas for the Hay-market and one for Drury Lane; in almost all of which the younger Bannister (being engaged at both theatres) perform'd a prominent character: – so that ... he was of the greatest importance to my theatrical prosperity, in my double capacity of Author and Manager; while I was of some service to him, by supplying him with new characters. [14]

Bannister was a versatile actor, who had considerable success with the one-man shows he performed under the title of 'Bannister's Budget', but he was at his best in sentimental comedy. His long-winded biographer talks of 'a sort of midway character, uniting the pathos of tragedy with the hilarity of comedy, in which he was peculiarly great'. [15] The Haymarket had its mug-cutter in John Edwin, and Colman provided parts for him too, full of the outrageous puns that he could never resist, but it was in suiting Bannister that he came closest to guaranteeing the success of his plays. The writing of parts for popular comedians was common practice, and has been too often overlooked in histories of the drama. Mrs Mathews goes so far as to claim that many writers, among them Theodore Hook, gave her husband only the outline of the character, allowing him to write in all the dialogue except the cue-lines [16]. Whilst this is probably an overstatement, we need to admit our ignorance of the relationship between the printed texts and the plays as performed. There is abundant evidence of radical textual changes in rehearsal, in which the actor's voice was louder than the author's. The details of the Bannister/Colman relationship are lost; but it is clear that Bannister propped up Colman's plays where they are weakest – in their appeal to the sentiment.

Two to One was followed by an equally undistinguished musical comedy, *Turk and No Turk*. In retrospect, Colman was aware of its defects:

> I doubled all the faults of my first composition in my second. Instead of splashing carelessly with a light brush, I now deliberately laid it on with a trowel. [17]

'Musical comedy' is a misleading description of this and countless pieces of the period. They are broken-backed compilations in which the songs make no contribution to the action and scarcely a nod in the direction of the mood. The underlying motive is simple, now as then. If an audience can be assumed to like plays and songs, it will like a play with songs twice as much as one without them. Such pieces were recognized as legal fare at the minor theatres. Colman was contributing to the dilution of English comedy by offering them to a theatre with a licence to perform the legitimate drama.

His father's fame was so far an incalculable asset to Colman, but on 4 August 1787, his first notably original work opened at the Haymarket. *Inkle and Yarico* is based on Arietta's story in the eleventh number of Steele's *Spectator* (13 March 1711), though Colman's first knowledge of it probably came, through Bannister, from the reference in Arthur Murphy's popular afterpiece, *The Citizen* [18]. The play's peculiar interest lies in its placing of familiar eighteenth-century stage types in unfamiliar surroundings. Colman had a taste for dramatic globe-trotting. As well as *Inkle and Yarico,* there are *Blue Beard,* according to Michael Booth the first Eastern melodrama [19], *The Africans, The Gnome-King* and *The Law of Java.* The characters remain outstandingly unaffected by their new geography. It is not great literature of course, but too many surveys of the drama of this period suggest that we would find the popularity of its popular plays mysterious. There is nothing in the popularity of *Inkle and Yarico* that need surprise a country hospitable to the tirelessly touring D'Oyly Carte company.

Steele's story is one of simple greed. Thomas Inkle, a young man trained by an eminent father to a love of gain, sets sail for the West Indies. When the boat is forced to seek shelter in an American creek, crew and passengers go ashore. Inkle is one of the few survivors of a Red Indian attack. He is found and protected by a naked Indian maid, and for several months they live as lovers. They make their escape together on a boat bound for the Barbados:

> To be short Mr. Thomas INKLE, now coming into *English* Territories, began seriously to reflect upon his loss of Time, and to weigh with himself how many Days Interest of his Mony he had lost during his Stay with YARICO. This Thought made the Young Man very pensive, and careful what Account he should be able to give his Friends of his Voyage. Upon which considerations the prudent and frugal Young Man sold YARICO to a *Barbadian* Merchant; notwithstanding that the poor Girl, to incline him to commiserate her Condition, told him that she was with Child by him: But he only made use of that Information, to rise in his demands upon the Purchaser.

Despite his considerable verbal ingenuity, Colman could never match the restraint of this, nor the exquisiteness of Steele's earlier description of the romance. Steele's imagination keeps him constantly alert to linguistic challenges; Colman's imagination is, by contrast, sluggish. This is a major loss. But it is fascinating to see how a thousand-word tale is transformed into a three-act comic opera shrewdly suited to public taste.

First of all, of course, there is the change of heart. Repentance, in the final act of eighteenth-century comedies, rarely owes much to character development. Even so obtuse a critic as Walwyn is alert to the inadequacy:

> A writer of taste, ingenuity, and feeling, will always prefer the change of circumstance from passion, to the change of passion from circumstance. [20]

And Colman would have agreed. In *Random Records* he cites with amusement the case of a miser, who was required in a fifth-act stage direction to 'lean against the wall, and grow generous'. But what was he to do? *Biographia Dramatica* records the existence of an unacted tragedy on the Inkle and Yarico theme. Colman's version was for the stage, Bannister was playing Inkle [21] and public taste is public taste. The result is a final heart-heaving submerged imperative:

> Ill-founded precept too long has steeled my breast – but still 'tis vulnerable – this trial was too much – Nature, 'gainst habit combating within me, has penetrated to my heart; a heart, I own, long callous to the feelings of sensibility; but now it bleeds – and bleeds for my poor Yarico. Oh, let me clasp her to it, while 'tis glowing, and mingle tears of love and penitence.

Inkle has very few of the play's good lines. I doubt whether Colman's sentimental writing is ever free of flippancy. The real strength of the piece lies in a second major innovation. Inkle is given a manservant, and Yarico a maid. Trudge is a low comedy part with strong sentimental overtones, written for and created by John Edwin. The implausibly named Wowski strikes the same note on the comic scale. Her English is much less perfect than Yarico's and her skin much darker. The really significant thing about these two is that they are, in every theatrical sense, more important to the play than Inkle and Yarico. There is nothing more perplexing in late eighteenth- and early nineteenth-century comedy than the relationship between major and minor characters. In such a play as *Speed the Plough* the adjectives become almost reversible. The main plot concerns Sir Philip Blandford's guilty conscience, his implausible brother Morrington, and the marriage of the uninteresting Miss Blandford to the unbearably virtuous Henry. Fortunately, these characters are allowed less stage-time than the 'minor' comic figures of Farmer Ashfield, Sir Abel Handy and his endearingly feckless son, Bob. Trudge and Wowski do the same kind of salvage work for *Inkle and Yarico.* It is as if Touchstone and Audrey had made a bid to take over the real business of pleasing the audience. I cannot resist the conclusion that contemporary audiences shared with modern readers a preference for sub-plot fun over main-plot sentiment.

The third of Colman's major additions to Steele's story is a theme of thwarted young love which admits a common hypocrisy of sentimental dramatists. Narcissa's real dilemma is nothing to do with the choice between two lovers, but with how to implement a decision already made. Lip service is paid to the drama of choice, but all that is enacted is the comedy of intrigue with its predictable scenes of mistaken identity.

And finally, there are the songs. At his best, Colman handled light verse gracefully. Here is Wowski, singing to Trudge:

White man, never go away –
    Tell me, why need you?
Stay with your Wowski, stay:
    Wowski will feed you.
Cold moons are now coming in;
    Ah, don't go grieve me!
I'll wrap you in leopard's skin:
    White man, don't leave me.

And when all sky is blue,
    Sun makes warm weather,
I'll catch you a cockatoo,
    Dress you in feather.
When cold comes, or when 'tis hot,
    Ah, don't go grieve me!

Poor Wowski will be forgot –
    White man, don't leave me!

And here, cleverly exploiting the growing craze for nonsense jingles, is Trudge to Wowski:

Your London girls, with roguish trip,
    Wheedle, wheedle, wheedle,
May boast their pouting under-lip,
    Fiddle, faddle, feedle.
My Wows would beat a hundred such,
    Diddle, daddle, deedle,
Whose upper-lip pouts twice as much,
    O, pretty double wheedle!

Rings I'll buy to deck her toes;
    Jemmy linkum feedle;
A feather fine shall grace her nose,
    Waving siddle seedle.
With jealousy I ne'er shall burst;
    Who'd steal my bone of bone-a?
A white Othello, I can trust
    A dingy Desdemona.

Inkle and Yarico leaves many regrets. The story is a favourite one in the literature of the noble savage [22] but Colman shirks most of the implications. In his defence, it should be said that anti-slave-trade agitation was in its infancy in 1787, but the play's abolitionist tendencies are sentimental rather than egalitarian. There is a good deal of honest John Bullery in Colman's portrait of the planters as unprincipled scoundrels, but his voice was never publicly raised in support of Wilberforce. If *Inkle and Yarico* added any strength to the movement, it was by accident. The eighteenth-century man of feeling was bound to be abolitionist when his subject was the noble savage. No doubt much of Wilberforce's support was as flimsily based. Where there is satire in *Inkle and Yarico* it is in the form of laugh-lines.

Colman's next play, *Ways and Means,* is his closest approach to the comedy of manners. By this time the battle for supremacy between sentimental comedy and comedy of manners had passed its peak, though it might be expected still to have presented an apprentice dramatist with a difficult choice. Certainly it was a problem that taxed Thomas Holcroft during this decade [23]. It is probably inadequate and certainly unhelpful to assume that manners comedy implies the author's belief in the fundamental corruption of man's nature, and sentimental comedy a rival belief in its fundamental goodness. It is a question not of philosophy but of technique. The mistaken assumption of too much sentimental comedy is that the exhibition of virtue and the recital of morality are competent incitements to virtue and morality. The 'fun' of sentimental comedy, generally confined to the sub-plot, escapes towards farce through caricature. The historical succession appears retrospectively inevitable. The main plots of sentimental comedies found a home at the turn of the century in melodrama; the sub-plots separated off into farce and burletta. Comedy as a recognizably unique genre virtually ceased to exist.

Ways and Means met some opposition, which Colman countered in a sulky preface to the first edition; but he took the easy way out by leaving manners comedy alone for the rest of his career. This is regrettable, for *Ways and Means* contains some excellent writing. Before leaving it, we may illustrate by its fate a typical procedure of the time. Having written it originally in five acts [24], Colman cut it to three before the opening night. Later it was cut again to two acts, and was a popular afterpiece until well into the nineteenth century. Colman's ability to cut his own plays turned *The Iron Chest* from failure to success. It would save a deal of rehearsal time if dramatists like Hochhuth would follow his lead.

The Battle of Hexham, first staged at the Haymarket in 1789, might have been a landmark in the history of the British theatre. It defies categorization. The plot is derived from history, but relies rather on legend in its treatment of Henry VI's queen. It is, at one level, a drama of heroism and loyalty, a history play, built largely on the Shakespearean plan; but Colman's eye for the theatrically expedient led him to introduce music into a piece that has no obvious room for it. There are ten songs in the three acts of *The Battle of Hexham,* ranging from the comic, provided for Edwin's Gregory Gubbins, to the patriotic and the pathetic. This inextricably mixed form was almost certainly Colman's invention, and, considering its success, it had a surprisingly small progeny. Two years later Colman followed it up with *The Surrender of Calais,* but that was his last attempt at musical history. Jorh Arden's play of Nelson, *The Hero Rises Up,* reminds me of the form, and the tone, though not always the songs, can be heard sometimes in Scribe, Dumas and Shaw (I am thinking of *The Man of Destiny* and *Caesar and Cleopatra*). Historical figures play a minor role in Colman's two plays. The hero of *The Battle of Hexham* is the unhistorical robber leader, Gondibert, and of *The Surrender of Calais* the unhistorical Ribaumont, who shares the honours with his devoted servant, La Gloire. It is a clever way of finding a home in high places for the bourgeois hero of serious drama. George Barnwell began to look much happier when the theatre found him his proper place, in melodrama. *The Battle of Hexham* clearly helped him on his way.

Colman owed the firmness of his reputation above all to *The Surrender of Calais* and *The Battle of Hexham.* They merit some consideration for having created the taste by which they were enjoyed, but they are defective in obvious ways. Firstly, they are emotionally irresponsible. The sudden switches of mood are conditioned by nothing more than immediate effectiveness. These are not the revelatory shock tactics of *Oh What a Lovely War*! Colman's emotional immaturity scars the whole of his literary output, and made severe inroads on his life as well. Secondly, the plays are dishonest, for they interpret history sentimentally. There is, admittedly, no attempt to interpret history, but even exploitation is a kind of interpretation. Thirdly, they are, for all their innovations, reactionary. The avowed imitation of Shakespeare was anachronistic. A play with the main plot in blank verse and the comic sub-plots in pseudo-Elizabethan prose has nothing to do with the progress of English drama into the nineteenth century. *The Mountaineers* applies the style of *The Battle of Hexham* to a sombre, neurotic fiction, and Colman was still ready to exploit it in 1822, when he wrote *The Law of Java.* It was soon identified with the Haymarket Theatre. James Boaden describes Morton's melodramatic *Zorinski,* first performed in 1795, as 'diversified by scenes of comedy and music, and composed in three acts, upon the declared summer model.' [25] Boaden himself was indebted to the mixed form popularized by Colman for his only dramatic successes, a debt which is curiously and definitively enshrined in his *Memoirs of John Philip Kemble*:

> The masterly presentment of Ambrosio in the Monk, by Mr Lewis, though not original, struck me forcibly in the perusal, and I worked, as I thought, rather successfully upon the subject, in a sort of Colman drama of three acts. I showed it to Mr Kemble, and he at once decided that he would act the monk. "But," he said, "why *three* acts? Why innovate upon established usage? – a play should be in five acts, for this sound reason among others, that it affords *four* pauses; and consequently the *relief* which is necessary to the attention. In a full piece you *must* occupy the usual three hours, and you create a heaviness by compelling the audience to listen to an uninterrupted business, or act, one hour long.
>
> (Vol. II, 227–8)

Boaden was persuaded, and *Aurelio and Miranda* opened at Drury Lane on 29 December 1798. Despite the presence in the cast of Kemble and Mrs Siddons, it lasted only seven nights. There were two problems. The immorality of the subject offended part of the audience, and 'it was weak in its structure; the two last acts were entirely an *hors d'oeuvre*'. He should have had more faith in the efficacy of 'Colman drama'.

Colman's next three pieces can be briefly treated. *Poor Old Haymarket* (1792) was an occasional prelude, opening the summer season with several shrewd digs at the Patent Houses. *The Mountaineers* (1793) was widely considered Colman's finest work to date. It gave Kemble a moody part as a deranged misanthrope, in which he continued to delight audiences for the rest of his career. I find the play extremely silly. *New Hay at the Old Market* (1795) has an interesting stage history. It is composed of two entirely separate scenes. In the first an out-of-work actor and an unacted playwright meet and talk as they wait to see the theatre-manager. In the second, we are moved for some further hits at the Patent Houses to the actual stage of the Haymarket, where an apparently impromptu conversation takes place. The first scene was soon separated off, and became extremely popular under the name of the out-of-work actor, *Sylvester Daggerwood.* It offered attractive scope for virtuoso performance. When J.L. Toole played it, he managed to get in 'something like five-and-twenty imitations of popular actors'. [26]

I turn, finally, to *The Iron Chest,* which had its ill-fated opening at Drury Lane in 1796. Michael Booth calls it 'a high-quality melodrama'. [27] Colman called it a tragedy. It begins with a glee, sung by a starving family, and ends with a tenor solo. It contains low comedy, high drama, pathos and danger. At the same time as it exposes Colman's literary shortcomings, it reveals his sense of the theatrical. The part of the guilt-ridden Sir Edward Mortimer was written for Kemble, who failed in it, re-created at the Haymarket by Elliston ('It is thought by many a bold attempt, but by none more so than myself' [28]), and found its finest exponent in Edmund Kean. It became one of the classic 'secret guilt' roles, and was bound to catch the eye of the master of secret guilt, Irving, who staged it at the Lyceum in 1879. The play is, indeed, melodrama *avant la lettre.* There is just sufficient complexity in the main characters to attract actors without confusing audiences. There is just enough adventurousness in the telling of the tale to distinguish it from its Gothic competitors without overstretching scenic resources. And it is, for Colman, unusually well made. But there is a snag. Let Colman introduce it:

> The difficulty ... of transplanting a Novel, chapter after chapter, from the Library to the Theatre, is very obvious. This difficulty I experienced in my play of *The Iron Chest,* taken from the very interesting Novel call'd 'Caleb Williams'; and after much cudgelling of my brains, I abandon'd the task, in great measure, as hopeless. – I follow'd some of the most prominent points, and mingled them with scenes of my own, whereby poor Caleb was greatly 'curtail'd of his fair proportions'; but I was over-loaded with Mr Godwin's good things, and driven to relinquish a large portion of them,

as sailors are sometime obliged to lighten the ship, by throwing their valuables overboard. [29]

You will not think highly of *The Iron Chest* if you come to it, as I did, from *Caleb Williams.* Colman discards the whole of volume one of the novel, Godwin's best writing, and rejects the book's political tendency, 'which is thought, by many, to inculcate levelling principles, and disrespect for the Laws of our Country'. The story is inevitably trivialized, and reduced, finally, to a concentration on the contents of the iron chest, whose centrality is the play's most glaring device and its most intractable flaw. I have to admit at this stage a sympathy with Leigh Hunt, Colman's most persistent critic, who found the son less interesting than the father, 'for he had not a particle of gravity'. [30]

The story of Kemble's failure in *The Iron Chest* is well told elsewhere. He was ill, and perhaps drunk, on the opening night, and Dodd, who played Adam Winterton, was dying. Colman and Kemble had a bitter public quarrel. Colman cut and altered the play for its Haymarket performance in the summer of 1796. Its success there was the sweetest Colman ever smelt.

Before 1800, Colman had added to his list of popular plays *The Heir at Law* (1797), his first five-act comedy, *Blue Beard* (1798), a spectacular melodrama, and *Feudal Times* (1799), another spectacular melodrama which lacks the excitement of *Blue Beard.* Ahead of him were two further five-act comedies, *The Poor Gentleman* (1801) and *John Bull* (1803), his best play, as well as a number of shorter pieces whose common characteristic is an eye and part of an ear for the theatrically expedient. Colman outlived his own reputation, indeed his activities as Examiner of Plays did much to destroy it, but he was not forgotten in the nineteenth century. I have done no study of his plays' stage-history, but cite as an example of a continuing interest the staging by the younger Mathews of *John Bull* at the Gaiety in the 1872–3 season, and the run of *The Heir at Law* at the Strand in 1870. Apart from the Bagster-Collins volume, there has been only one serious attempt to restore Colman's literary eminence. Professor G. Wilson Knight's argument that Colman wrote 'Don Leon' relies, in the end, on 'a kind of submerged tradition', and the attempt to strengthen the case by reference to plays and poems known to be by Colman seems to me far-fetched [31]. 'Don Leon' is an epistolary poem in heroic couplets, offering an explanation of the failure of Byron's marriage. It is witty and obscene. If Colman wrote it, and Knight dates it about a year before Colman's death, it was the best thing he ever did. But it needs to be remembered that the ascription of such an obscene poem to the Examiner of Plays would have been an amusing way of starting a rumour. One of the many scurrilous books on Madam Vestris was ascribed to Arthur Griffinhoofe, Colman's pseudonym during the production of his earliest plays. According to a more recent biographer of Madam Vestris, Colman had been dead for three years when it was published [32]. I can only say that Knight's method of arguing back from a work of admitted quality and uncertain authorship towards a re-appraisal of works known to be Colman's seems to me dangerous, and his judgments extravagant. He discovers in Colman's plays a 'Shakespearean emphasis on emotional integrity'. I do not. He rises from a discussion of the poem, 'Two Parsons', to an assertion that 'as a master of comic narrative, Colman reminds us of Chaucer; and as a denouncer of cant, of Byron'. I find this comparison surprising. Colman made few extravagant claims for himself. Bagster-Collins finds him lacking in ambition. To those who said there was a dearth of legitimate dramatists, he answered:

> ... it may be so, – it has been averr'd to be the case in all ages; – but few regular shoemakers are inclined to take the trouble of making shoes, when they find so much encouragement given to them for cobbling [33].

The self-portrait is just, and the image striking. Colman was a cobbler who now and then showed signs of an ability to make shoes. In deciding to include songs in 'serious' drama, he accelerated the triumph of melodrama. It is, perhaps, his most notable achievement. If the reasons were aesthetically unsound, subsequent events proved them historically sound.

The ultimate failing of the popular dramatists – one that broadly persists until the emergence of Tom Robertson at the Prince of Wales's – was their refusal to write plays from their response to life. Their plays are about the kind of people who appear in plays. The intention to keep the stage separate from life was generally a conscious one, though not openly admitted. That was how the public liked it. There is a contemporary play that throws an interesting light on this characteristic. Vapid, who has the title role in Frederick Reynolds's *The Dramatist* (1789), is in Bath on the look-out for dramatizable situations. There is a good deal of inventive comedy, but Reynolds clearly anticipates that his audience will find the initial situation funny in itself. It is comic that a dramatist should propose to *do* the things he will later write about.

Notes

[1] *Random Records* (London, 1830) Vol. I, 142–3.
[2] *Letters and Journals,* ed. R.E. Prothero (London, 1898–1901) Vol. V, 461.
[3] The letter is quoted in full in J.F. Bagster-Collins, *George Colman the Younger* (New York, 1946) 146–8.
[4] *London Gazette,* 28 February 1824.
[5] First performed at the Haymarket on 17 July 1799.
[6] *Biographia Dramatica,* ed. Baker, Reed and Jones (London, 1812) Vol. II, 247.
[7] Bagster-Collins, 282.
[8] George Raymond, *The Life and Enterprises of Robert William Elliston* (London, 1857) 258.
[9] Quoted in R.B. Peake, *Memoirs of the Colman Family* (London, 1841) Vol. II, 20.
[10] R.B. Peake, Vol. II, 413.
[11] *Random Records,* Vol. II, 113.
[12] *Random Records,* Vol. II, 176–7.
[13] Hunt repeats this accusation often. See, for example, *Lord Byron and Some of His Contemporaries* (London, 1828) 407, where he pays Colman a back-handed compliment: 'At a farce he was admirable; and remains so, whether writing or licensing'.
[14] *Random Records,* Vol. II, 24.
[15] J. Adolphus, *Memoirs of John Bannister, Comedian* (London, 1839) Vol. II, 245.
[16] Mrs Mathews, *The Life and Correspondence of Charles Mathews the Elder, Comedian.* Abridged by Edmund Yates (London, 1860) 109.
[17] *Random Records,* Vol. II, 275.
[18] Bannister frequently played Young Philpot, who makes the reference to Inkle.
[19] Michael Booth, *English Melodrama* (London, 1965) 88.
[20] B. Walwyn, *An Essay on Comedy* (London, 1782) 18.
[21] According to Adolphus, it was Bannister who suggested to Colman that Inkle should change his mind and his heart. See Adolphus, Vol. I, 168.
[22] For a treatment of *Inkle and Yarico* as a document in the literature of the Noble Savage, see H.N. Fairchild, *The Noble Savage* (New York, 1928) 80–7.
[23] See, especially, Holcroft's Preface to the published text of *Duplicity* (London, 1781).
[24] Peake (Vol. II, 212) says that the number of acts was, initially, four, but this seems unlikely.
[25] James Boaden, *Memoirs of the Life of John Philip Kemble* (London, 1825) Vol. II, 146.
[26] Joseph Hatton, *Reminiscences of J.L. Toole* (London, 1889) 110.
[27] *English Melodrama,* 42.
[28] Quoted in Raymond, *The Life and Enterprises of Robert William Elliston,* 34.

[29] *Random Records,* Vol. II, 183–4.
[30] *Edinburgh Review* (July 1841) 414.
[31] Knight summarizes his case in *Lord Byron's Marriage. The Evidence of Asterisks* (London, 1957) 159–97, but he has more to say on Colman's authorship of 'Don Leon' in an article in *Twentieth Century,* June 1956. My quotations are from *Lord Byron's Marriage.*
[32] C.E. Pearce, *Madam Vestris and Her Times* (London, 1923) 25.
[33] *Random Records,* Vol. I, 322–3.

6 WILLIAM RUDDICK

Lord Byron's Historical Tragedies

Lord Byron was always interested in the theatre. He acted when a schoolboy at Harrow and frequented the London theatres whenever he was able. At the same time he relished the classical dramas of antiquity and in later life, when discussing the genesis of his poetic drama *Manfred,* he declared:

> Of the *Prometheus Vinctus* of Aeschylus I was passionately fond as a boy. The *Prometheus,* if not exactly in my plan, has always been so much in my head, that I can easily conceive its influence over all or anything that I have written. [1]

Classical and contemporary ideas were to achieve a new and individual integration in Byron's mature plays. But in his earliest dramatic writing it was the contemporary Gothic-historical influence that predominated. At the age of thirteen he read Harriet Lee's *Canterbury Tales* and attempted to dramatize one of its incidents in a play called *Ulric and Ilvina.* He destroyed the manuscript later, but the idea stayed in his mind and in 1815, when he was a member of the Drury Lane Committee (ploughing through what he afterwards claimed had amounted to nearly five hundred plays in search of one or two worth producing), he took up the Harriet Lee story once more and wrote the first act of *Werner.* The manuscript disappeared after he left England and it was not until 1821 that he rewrote and completed the play. It contrasts strangely with the three historical tragedies he had then just written in a much more restrained and classical manner and has done a certain amount to obscure the consistency of Byron's dramatic aims near the end of his life. *Werner* is essentially a much earlier and less deeply thought out play than *Marino Faliero, The Two Foscari,* or *Sardanapalus.* It is his most conventionally theatrical piece (and was, therefore, the most successful in the theatre in early Victorian days) and is unlike his other plays in the reliance it places on concealed identities, secret passages and other melodramatic stand-bys. But two points are worth making: first, it is unconventional in that it does not rely on a love story as a main source of interest (Byron tends to avoid love stories as leading to hackneyed situations and emotions: when love appears in his plays it is the mature love of an established relationship; stable, strong and generally linked with sentiments of patriotism and patriotic suffering): secondly, *Werner's* inspiration is historical, and history, as will be seen, holds an important place in Byron's mature thinking about the possibility of regenerating dramatic literature.

Byron's first mature dramatic work was the visionary, wild dramatic poem *Manfred,* into which he poured the turbulent emotions of the months following his departure from England in 1816. When he had written *Manfred* he turned away from dramatic themes for a time to complete *Childe Harold* and write the first cantos of *Don Juan.* But his interest stayed strong and when he was reunited with Shelley at Venice in 1818 their conversation soon turned to the drama. Shelley had encouraged Byron when he was composing *Manfred.* Now, as they discussed Shelley's ideas for a play about Tasso, Byron turned over the subjects of two of his later plays (*Cain* and *Sardanapalus*) and began to formulate theories for a new kind of drama. It was to be very far removed from either the Jacobean model that Shelley adopted in *The Cenci* or the popular historical-Gothic, sensational and rhetorical plays that Byron's experience with the Drury Lane Committee had shown him to be favoured by so many writers among his contemporaries.

Byron knew that contemporary drama was in an unhealthy condition. Like most creative dramatists of his day he felt that reforms were needed. Also, like most of these writers he looked for models on which to base a new kind of dramatic literature. He believed that the Shakespearean–Jacobean manner which most serious playwrights tended to adopt was quite exhausted. In 1821 he wrote to Shelley that 'I am not an admirer of our old dramatists *as models*' [2], and in a letter to John Murray of the same year he made the point again while indicating an alternative source of dramatic tradition which, he believed, held out more hope for the future:

> Your friend (William Gifford), like the public, is not aware, that my dramatic simplicity is *studiously* Greek, and must continue so: *no* reform ever succeeded at first. I admire the old English dramatists; but this is quite another field, and has nothing to do with theirs. I want to make a *regular* English drama, no matter whether for the Stage or not, which is not my object, – but a *mental* theatre. [3]
>
> (to John Murray, 23 August 1821)

This letter, like others Byron wrote at the time, shows that he had a very definite programme of reform for the drama in his mind. His own dramas were to be regular, and to understand his concept of regularity one need look no further than any standard Augustan discussion of Classical theatre (the passages on the Unities in Dryden's *Essay of Dramatic Poesy* for instance). Byron is orthodox in his interpretation of dramatic regularity. But there is real originality in the way he uses 'regular English drama's to create 'a mental theatre' of a psychologically and poetically novel sort.

In his mature historical tragedies Byron sought to create a controlled, powerful drama in which the excesses of stage melodrama would be avoided through the nature of his plots and rhetoric would be employed for its legitimate purpose: the expression and analysis of powerful feelings. His letters of 1821 frequently turn to these subjects. To Douglas Kinnaird, for example, he writes:

> With regard to... '*Simplicity*', I study to be so. It is an experiment whether the English *Closet* or *Mental* theatre will or will not bear a regular drama instead of the melo-drama. [4]
>
> (23 August 1821: the date of the letter to Murray quoted above)

On 20 September 1821 Byron explains to Murray that

> I am much mortified that Gifford don't take to my new dramas: to be sure, they are as opposite to the English drama as one thing can be to another; but I have a notion that, if understood, they will in time find favour (though *not* on the stage) with the reader. The Simplicity of plot is intentional, and the avoidance of *rant* also, as also the compression of the Speeches in the more severe situations. What I seek to show in *The Foscaris* is the *suppressed* passion, rather than the rant of the present day. [5]

At the end of the letter he adds that his dramatic method is 'more upon the Alfieri School than the English'.

Byron admired Alfieri's neo-Classical, French-influenced tragedies because they succeed in being passionate within the framework of the Unities. Alfieri represents a modern writer of genius working in the kind of tradition Byron wishes to see developing in his own contemporary theatre. In his own dramas, as in *English Bards and Scotch Reviewers* and *Don Juan,* he was trying to return to the classical standards of the previous age: the standards he had glanced at in his earlier satire when he urged Sheridan to

> Give, as thy last memorial to the age
> One Classic drama, and reform the stage.

In his own attempt to 'reform the stage', Byron wrote historical tragedies. He shared the view of many eighteenth-century thinkers that history was more valuable than fiction because of its truth, and also on account of the moral exemplars it contains. He wrote in his Journal that 'the moment I could read, my grand passion was history.' In a letter to John Murray from Venice, dated 2 April 1817, he showed the power history held over his imagination and the nature of its fascination:

> There is still, in the Doge's Palace, the black veil painted over Falieri's picture, and the staircase whereon he was first crowned Doge, and subsequently decapitated. This was the thing that most struck my imagination in Venice – more than the Rialto, which I visited for the sake of Shylock.

He mentions a novel about Venice he loved as a boy, then goes on:

> But I hate things *all fiction*; and therefore the *Merchant* and *Othello* have no great associations for me: but Pierre (in *Venice Preserved*) has. There should always be some foundation of fact for the most airy fabric, and pure invention is but the talent of a liar. [6]

Byron repeatedly stressed the trouble he went to in following his sources and dramatizing true history. After *Marino Faliero*'s publication he sent a letter to Murray containing new evidence which had just come to light: he exulted in the way it justified certain dramatic effects and speeches which he had been forced to invent and therefore demonstrated the truth to history of his imaginative recreation of Faliero's character. His tragedies were intended to be true to the recorded facts of human experience. Action and language were to represent a dramatically heightened version of the events of real life: the exaggerations of contemporary melodrama would be shown to be needless by practical justifications of the poetry and pathos implicit in historical events. In fact, Byron seems to have found in history the same attestations of emotional integrity that country life possessed for Wordsworth.

Early in 1821 an attempt was made to stage *Marino Faliero* in London. Byron was alarmed, since he felt sure the play would fail on the stage. His Journal shows the extent to which he knew he had moved away from the conventions of popular theatre and gives negative evidence of his dramatic aims:

> It is not intended for the stage. It is too regular – the time, twenty-four hours – the change of place not frequent – nothing *melo*-dramatic – no surprises, no starts, nor trap-doors, nor opportunities "for tossing their heads and kicking their heels" – and no *love* – the grand ingredient of a modern play. [7]

In place of love and trap-doors Byron placed historical events. History, he found, combined truth with imaginative stimulus. It had power to affect the reflecting mind, while the more romantic side of his imagination and his deep concern for political ideals led him to reflect on tragic situations in which insoluble paradoxes of situation led the mind to a strong awareness of pathos. For example, in his Journal entry of 28 January 1821 he records:

> Pondered the subjects of four tragedies to be written... and am not sure that I would not try Tiberius. I think that I could extract a something, of *my* tragic, at least, out of the gloomy sequestration and old age of the tyrant – and even out of his sojourn at Caprea – by softening the *details* and exhibiting the despair which must have led to those very vicious pleasures. For none but a powerful and gloomy mind overthrown would have had recourse to such solitary horrors – being also, at the same time, *old*, and the master of the world. [8]

Tiberius's story attracted Byron because of its emotionally-charged quality of paradox. The same is true of the tragedies he actually completed. Marino Faliero, for instance, is a Doge of Venice whose fear of the tyrannous power of its corrupt nobility leads him to join a revolt against the established authority of which he is the symbol. An essential starting point for these tragedies is a situation in which the hero is forced into a tragic awareness of the inadequacy of conventional attitudes to power and political morality. They are, in many respects, political plays, reflecting Byron's questioning of his own liberalism and the part he was playing in the contemporary cause of Italian independence. In *Sardanapalus* the whole ethics of involvement or non-involvement in major events are examined. The morality of these plays is a questioning one: they explore and illustrate the presence in historical events of political and moral issues that Byron felt to be in urgent need of definition as forces nascent in the intellectual movements of his age. It was to question the morality behind great events and analyse human reactions to the paradoxical situations they created that Byron developed the restricted plot action and simplified tragic style that he mentions in his letters.

Such general observations about the aims of Byron's historical tragedies require the support of concrete illustrations. Two of the plays are particularly worth scrutinizing: *Marino Faliero* for its demonstration of the power of historical paradoxes, and *Sardanapalus* for the development of the full capabilities of dramatic rhetoric in the service of Byron's new theatre of the mind.

Marino Faliero (1820) is the earliest of Byron's historical tragedies. It is worth looking at closely because it demonstrates particularly well the working out of his ideas for a new kind of drama.

'Simple and severe' *Faliero* certainly is. Its plot is rigorously simple and comes close to obeying all the rules. Its action is unified, but perhaps more significant is the extensive balancing of comparable incidents to be found in the two halves of the play (indeed in many respects its structure resembles that of a giant eighteenth-century balanced antithesis). The plot lends itself readily to such balances. It tells the story of Marino Faliero, a distinguished warrior who has spent his life in the service of the Venetian state and been called in old age to its supreme honour, the position of Doge. His wife is young, and the play opens just after Faliero has been insulted by the gross insinuations of Michael Steno, a patrician, whose fellows have met to pass judgment upon him. When the punishment is announced it is insultingly trivial and Faliero sees in the Forty's mocking support of one of its members yet another sign of both his own and the people's helplessness. He agrees to lead a revolutionary plot to depose the patricians and the second half of the play consists of its discovery, Faliero's trial and his eventual execution.

It is a simple story, but its situations build up an extensive network of paradoxes inside which the full pathos of the old Doge's situation and the nobility of his tragic revolt are revealed. Close examination of the plot reveals that Byron's method is to exploit the ironic and pathetic contrasts to be derived from the balancing of comparable (though finely distinguished) situations at similar points before and after the pivotal situation of the play – the lyrical scene at the beginning of Act Four in which the honest and imaginative nobleman Lioni muses on the beauty of Venice, creating an awareness of the timeless beauty of the city against which the complex web of political motivation in its government must be evaluated.

Marino Faliero is, as the balancing of its components suggests, a static play. This is intentional. The play is not a drama of events but of crucial situations, presented to us and then investigated in increasing depth through the sustained employment of lengthy monologues. Most critics do not seem to have realized this, mainly because of their natural tendency to read the play as a series of events. But in fact Byron's plays are transitional in form. Events there are, of course, but they are relatively few and their function, like that of the recitatives in opera seria, is to advance a tightly connected series of psychological and emotional tableaux, each one of which in turn is defined, expressed and analysed through the rhetoric of spacious set-speeches.

In his book called *Byron and the Spoiler's Art* [9], Paul West refers to the plays as 'pageants *à thèse*'. He claims that Byron is 'more interested in emotions than in ideas, in attitudes rather than motives, in flourish rather than steady observation, in similitudes rather than in analysis'. It might be truer to suggest that in these plays we find ideas expressed through emotions, motives through attitudes, steady observation behind the flourishes and analysis achieved through the similitudes.

Leigh Hunt said in 1816, when reviewing Byron's *Monody on the Death of Sheridan,* that Byron's talent 'does not lie so much in appealing to others, as in expressing himself. He does not make you so much a party as a witness'. In their formal speeches his characters create precisely this kind of effect, but it is an effect from which neither depth of motivation nor complex analysis are absent. Consider, for instance, the clarity and condensation of emotion that formal balance gives in a speech of Marino Faliero's to the conspirators:

> Mark with me
> The gloomy vices of this government.
> From the hour they made me Doge, the *Doge* THEY *made* me –
> Farewell the past! I died to all that had been,
> Or rather they to me: no friends, no kindness,
> No privacy of life – all were cut off:
> They came not near me, such approach gave umbrage;
> They could not love me, such was not the law;
> They thwarted me, 'twas the state's policy;
> They baffled me, 'twas the patrician's duty;
> They wronged me, for such was to right the state;
> They could not right me, that would give suspicion;
> So that I was a slave to my own subjects;
> So that I was a foe to my own friends;
> Begirt with spies for guards, with robes for power,
> With pomp for freedom, gaolers for a council,
> Inquisitors for friends, and hell for life!
>
> (Act 3, scene 2)

Opinions vary about the rhetorical style of these plays, but in the main Byron has surely had less than his due. As he said of *The Two Foscari,* 'I seek to show... the *suppressed* passion rather than the rant of the present day'. Suppressed passion is passion under the surface. Formal rhetoric of the kind illustrated above is too controlled to become rant: its antithetical balances and use of parallel phrases reveal feelings without releasing them. The motives present in a man's mind can be exposed without the possibility of their leading to immediate action, and through this a drama of psychological pressures is attained.

It is, too, a drama of psychological contrasts and paradoxes, for paradox is at the heart of Byronic drama. Faliero's own position is paradoxical: head of the state yet helpless, seeking to re-establish true authority by rebellion. Byron shows more skill than critics credit him with in the handling of such paradoxes. In the first half of *Marino Faliero,* for example, it is to Faliero's viewpoint and that of the conspirators that we are exposed. In the second half of the play the rebellion fails and it is the power (and attitude) of the patricians that dominates. Faliero is arraigned as a traitor to established authority: as the familiar words and accusations roll out the reader begins to doubt whether he may not have been over-impressed by the old Doge's reasoning in the earlier scenes. *Can* the power struggle have been as black and white as he made it seem? Were his motives wholly pure and untainted by the longing for absolute authority? But then, as the play ends, comes the final (and finest) structural balancing of related scenes. *Marino Faliero* began with a brief scene in which ordinary people meet and discuss Faliero's insult and the probable action of the patricians. At the end the people's voice is heard once more:

Third citizen Then they have murdered him who would have freed us.
Fourth citizen He was a kind man to the commons ever.
Fifth citizen Wisely they did to keep their portals barr'd.
Would we had known the work they were preparing
Ere we were summon'd here – we would have brought
Weapons, and forced them!

A final perspective is thus established. Faliero's assertions are attested by the people, his individual heroic tragedy integrated into the common desire for freedom.

Marino Faliero and the other tragedies give dramatic form to almost all the personal and political preoccupations that recur in Byron's poetry and prose writings. But the amount of personal bias he had brought into his rethinking of classical forms was not evident to more than a handful of his contemporaries. It was a lonely task. William Gifford, it is true, showed understanding and encouragement, but Shelley's response to *Faliero* was cool and he thought that its severity needed to be enriched by 'familiarity with the dramatic power of human nature'. Some such process of enrichment seemed to occur when Byron began writing his second historical tragedy, *Sardanapalus,* and it is in the rhetoric of this play that we find the full maturity of Byron's concept of 'mental theatre'.

Sardanapalus tells the story of a pacifist king, the last Assyrian descendent of Nimrod, the hunter, and Semiramis, the great conqueror. As both ruler and man he seems weak, but beneath he is strong: he is a character whose paradoxes of character, sexuality and political motivation embody most fully the tensions Byron was aware of within his own personality. The tight plotting of the story relies on careful contrasts of situation and character once again, but the interest is heightened by a strong love interest of a very complex kind. Sardanapalus's love tends to the soft and voluptuous, but Myrrha, the Greek slave who obeys and loves him, reveals a passion which is self-sacrificing and brave to the point of heroism.

The story of the two lovers may be seen as universalizing Byron's unease at his relationship with Teresa Guiccioli at a time when Italian nationalism called him towards active political engagement. But what is significant is that the play universalizes his often despondent moods in these months into a tragic story of almost Shakespearean richness of symbolism and poetry. In it, a great man who, somewhat in the manner of Hamlet, finds that his awareness of the moral complexities of action renders political firmness almost impossible, can only achieve the justification and fulfilment of his life in a tragic defeat and death. This, since it is the result not of cowardice but of his inability to push political ruthlessness to the necessary point of finality, is emotionally justified in a kind of final apotheosis. In the death-apotheosis in which the royal line of the hunter and the conqueror comes to its end, Sardanapalus's qualities of sensitivity and affection (the gentle opposites of the ruthless power-mania of his royal ancestors) are purged and spiritualized through the fire in which he chooses to perish at the moment of final defeat by his rebellious subjects. With poetic appropriateness his qualities find their culmination in fire and destruction, as did those of his ancestors, but the fire in which Sardanapalus and Myrrha die is not the symbol of a tyrant's conquest based on universal misery, but of universal sympathy and love.

The final scene of *Sardanapalus* imaginatively recreates one of the spectacular effects of cataclysmic destruction much admired on the contemporary stage in a way which is both brought about by the play's poetry and also constitutes its final summation. Sardanapalus and Myrrha ascend the pyre and she pauses for a moment:

Myrrha A single thought yet irks me.
Sardanapalus Say it.
Myrrha It is that no kind hand will gather
The dust of both into one urn.
Sardanapalus The better:
Rather let them be borne abroad upon
The winds of heaven, and scatter'd into air,
Than be polluted more by human hands
Of slaves and traitors. In this blazing palace,
And its enormous walls of reeking ruin,
We leave a nobler monument than Egypt

	Hath piled in her brick mountains, o'er dead kings...
Myrrha	Then farewell, thou earth!
	And loveliest spot of earth! farewell, Ionia!
	Be thou still free and beautiful, and far
	Aloof from desolation! My last prayer
	Was for thee, my last thoughts, save *one*, were of thee!
Sardanapalus	And that?
Myrrha	Is yours.

Act 5, scene 1

So, as the play ends, the purging fire brings together and immortalizes self-denying love, patriotism, and peace.

Sardanapalus, Byron's most personal play, is deeply fatalistic. From its very opening it moves inexorably on towards the tragedy of its conclusion, creating a complex web of ominously repeated portents and nature references. There is, for instance, the striking use of pathetic fallacy in the passages of nature description which open many of the scenes. The sun and sky appear to threaten mortal schemes, or else they remain aloof in a Turner-like blaze of pure but unsympathetic clarity and glory. Yet within the fatalistic confines of the plot there runs a contrasting movement towards the justification and appreciation of Sardanapalus's character and viewpoint.

At the opening of the play, his brother-in-law, the active and loyal warrior Salemenes, is musing on Sardanapalus's character:

> He must be roused. In his effeminate heart
> There is a careless courage which corruption
> Has not all quenched, and latent energies,
> Repress'd by circumstance, but not destroy'd –
> Steep'd, but not drown'd, in deep voluptuousness.

In a conversation which follows, the different viewpoints of the two men are established:

Salemenes	Semiramis – a woman only – led
	These our Assyrians to the solar shores
	Of Ganges.
Sardanapalus	'Tis most true. And *how* returned?
Salemenes	Why, like a *man* – a hero; baffled, but
	Not vanquished. With but twenty guards, she made
	Good her retreat to Bactria.
Sardanapalus	And how many
	Left she behind in India to the vultures?
Salemenes	Our annals say not.

(Act 1, scene 1)

The nature of Sardanapalus's courage – that of the man who understands too much and whose response to simple, heroic virtues is limited by his awareness of their limitations – must be made clear to Salemenes before the play's conclusion. So, likewise, must the validity of the king's love for his slave and the grandeur of the slave's devotion to her master. Salemenes is the central figure whose responses act for those of the average, straightforward member of Byron's ideal audience. And because Byron is now more fully aware of the poetic possibilities of his analytical mental theatre, the play addresses itself to the reader through a rich texture of metaphorical and symbolic devices. These have been discussed with admirable sensitivity and comprehensiveness in the essay *'The Two Eternities'* by G. Wilson Knight [10], who demonstrates the Shakespearean richness which Byron attains in this play. One might suggest that a great many of these poetic devices (especially the passages of cosmic nature description and the recurrent images associated with ancestral cruelty, jealousy and revengefulness), not only intensify the sense of inexorableness in Sardanapalus's self-justification through tragedy, but are also the result of Byron's increasing realization of the way in which a mental theatre could benefit from the enriching effects of poetry in increasing the reader's sense of setting and situation while creating an intensification of effect through rich poetry comparable to the intensifying power of visual spectacle and opulent splendour on the contemporary stage. In short, Byron exploits language to imitate and replace stage spectacle: his acceptance of the implications of 'closet drama' producing a backward movement or reversal of theatrical development; away from current visual elaboration, back once again to the poetic richness of Shakespeare (whose influence is so strongly present in this play) and the Elizabethan stage.

Yet, at the same time, a careful reading of Byron's historical tragedies reveals that he tended to choose stories which involved him in actions, situations, character-relationships and plot-sequences which were well within the experience of contemporary theatregoers. He shared, for example, the Italian taste for rich neo-classical exoticism which made grand operas such as Rossini's *Moses* and *Semiramide* a success at precisely this period. He was evidently responsive to movements in the contemporary theatre and this has, ironically, placed many difficulties in the way of a full understanding of his serious plays.

Byron's tragedies foreshadow the late nineteenth-century split into popular and intellectual theatre. The fundamental interest of his plays is intellectual, since he was working towards a new drama of situation in which the predicament of man as prisoner of his environment is deeply investigated: his main characters are trapped in hostile situations, their lives spent under pressure; Byron's attitude to their predicaments points the way forward to many developments in much more recent theatrical history. But his new approach is worked out through old-style material and since the element of historical spectacle is always present the plays were inevitably misunderstood by contemporary theatre managers. Charles Kean's 1853 production of *Sardanapalus* with scenery based on Layard's discoveries at Nineveh is perhaps the noblest but most misguided attempt at staging one of Byron's plays according to the old spectacular tradition.

Byron's historical tragedies are, in two senses, 'mental theatre'. They are plays about individual minds, and they are plays addressed to, and adapted for, the mind of the reader. Stage and scenic effects of an often recognizably early nineteenth-century kind are recreated through poetry and poetic description. To reproduce these in a stage production is to do again what Byron has already done through the descriptive rhetoric of his drama. They are plays addressed to the ear and to the inward eye. Perhaps our own age offers a new possibility for their successful performance through the verbal resources of radio drama.

Notes

[1] Quoted by John Buxton, *Byron and Shelley, the History of a Friendship* (London, 1968) 78.
[2] *Works of Lord Byron, Letters and Journals,* ed. R.E. Prothero, 6 vols., (London, 1898–1901) Vol. V, 268.
[3] *Letters and Journals,* Vol. V, 347.
[4] Peter Quennell, *Byron, a Self-Portrait* (London, 1950) Vol. II, 663.
[5] *Letters and Journals,* Vol. V, 372.
[6] *Letters and Journals,* Vol. IV, 93.
[7] Quennell, *op. cit.,* Vol. II, 562.
[8] Quennell, *op. cit.,* Vol. II, 576.
[9] Paul West, *Byron and the Spoiler's Art* (London, 1960) 127.
[10] In G. Wilson Knight, *The Burning Oracle* (London, 1939).

7 MICHAEL R. BOOTH

Early Victorian Farce: Dionysus Domesticated

When one surveys the mass theatrical market that existed in London alone, not to mention the provinces, in 1850, thirteen years after the accession of Queen Victoria and seven years after the passage of the Theatre Regulation Bill, even a brief treatment of one of the most popular contemporary dramatic forms, farce, seems impossible. A hundred years before, in 1750, the population of the metropolis was perhaps 750,000 and there were two theatres regularly open at which farces were performed as afterpieces. It is therefore possible to examine with some care the whole *corpus* of mid-eighteenth-century farce, since it is a significant but not overwhelming collection of material [1]. In 1850, however, London's population was about three million, and ten times the number of theatres were performing dramatic pieces. The writing of farces as afterpieces for all these theatres – scarcely a single night's playbill was without its farce – became a matter of mass production. For the purposes of this paper, then, I have selected from the period 1832–57 a fairly representative dozen for discussion; such a selection seems reasonable because it illustrates the principal characteristics and tendencies in the farce of the time.

Eighteenth-century farce is, generally speaking, a reduction to absurdity and an extension to extremes of satirical comedy, which attacked stereotyped 'humours' characters, occupations like medicine, the clergy, and the law, ruling passions, selfish and eccentric social behaviour. Towards the end of the century sentimentalism reached even farce, but by no means dominated it. The settings and characters of this farce are commonly middle, upper-middle and aristocratic in class, although the clever manservant and chambermaid are stock types. Eighteenth-century farce reflects the composition and interests of those classes that came to the Patent Theatres: the fashionable aristocracy and upper-middle class in the boxes, the middle class and the professions in the pit, the lower-middle class, servants, and journeymen in the galleries. In their selection of the farce repertory, eighteenth-century managers were careful to appeal to all their patrons.

By the 1830s and 1840s substantial changes had taken place in the audience. No longer was it socially as stable as the audience in a Patent Theatre of the last century. The concept of the same theatre for all classes of patron had disappeared. The working class, in addition to occupying the galleries of West End houses, as before, had their own neighbourhood theatres in the East End, on the South Bank, and on the fringes of the West End. (Before discussing the social implications of any Victorian play, therefore, it is useful to know the year of performance, the theatre of performance, the social status of that theatre and the nature of its audience.) No longer were there such sharp class divisions between boxes and pit. The fact that boxes were the worst attended section of West End theatres in the early part of Victoria's reign meant that managers and playwrights appealed more deliberately to the patrons of the cheaper seats; the prices of the more expensive seats were also dropped to attract a lower class of audience. Depending upon the theatre of performance, the middle and upper middle-class characteristics of the earlier farce survived to a greater or lesser extent or disappeared. The taste of the Victorian theatre patron, greatly changed from that of his eighteenth-century predecessor, largely determined the character of Victorian farce.

The mainstay of Victorian theatrical taste was undoubtedly melodrama in all its varieties, since these formed the substance of so many mainpieces as well as appearing on the bill as afterpieces. The one-act or short two-act farce, an afterpiece (and sometimes a curtain-raiser) until it was lengthened later in the century into a three-act play, ranked second in popularity. It is not then really surprising that one of the interesting aspects of early Victorian farce is its close link with melodrama. A notable feature of melodrama is the presence of comic man, comic woman, and scenes of low comedy juxtaposed with scenes of violence and pathos. In farce the reverse is not as common, but the emotional components of melodrama and much of its moral value system are not infrequently present.

J.B. Buckstone's *Married Life* (1834), an early three-act farce, contains four comic couples who fall out maritally for various reasons: Coddle complains of the cold and draughts; Mrs Coddle complains of the heat; the Younghusbands always contradict each other; Dismal is rude and surly to his wife; Dove, a former footman, irritates his middle-class wife by forgetting his elevated station and running to answer the door whenever he hears the bell; Mrs Dove annoys Dove by continually correcting his footman's vocabulary and pronunciation. Additional to this thoroughly farcical quartet is another couple, the Lynxes, who though part of the general plot and husband-wife quarrels and misunderstandings, are serious and very melodramatic characters. Mrs Lynx is obsessed with suspected infidelity on her husband's part, but not in a comic way, and gives vent to powerful and disordered speeches on the subject. Lynx, entirely faithful to his wife, is protecting the identity and honour of a mysterious young girl. The intensely emotional scenes between them come from melodrama, not farce, as does the husband's rescue of his wife from the assault of an off-stage villain. The comic effects of *Married Life* are obtained by common farcical techniques: the repetition and accumulation of eccentricities and misunderstandings, the successive introduction of 'humours' characters, the extremism of characterization, the open and sometimes lengthy confiding in the audience, the truncation of time so that comic events follow one another with ridiculous rapidity, the attention to physical stage business. These techniques are familiar from most farces of the period, but the undercurrent of melodramatic emotion is also essential to the play and not merely an aspect of sub-plot.

In another farce by Buckstone – an author equally at home in melodrama or farce – the melodramatic potential is obvious. The heroine of *A Rough Diamond* (1847) is a good, jolly, simple country girl, Margery. Her husband, Sir William, despairs of making her over into a refined society woman like the young wife of his uncle, Lord Plato. However, he revises his values when he sees the educated and elegant Lady Plato secretly renewing an affair with a former lover. There is something of Rousseau in this Victorian farce that is also present in melodrama: the moral superiority of the uncomplicated rural life over education and civilization. Sir William, the Platos, and Lady Plato's admirer, Captain Blenheim, are not comic characters at all; they exist merely to display the innate superiority of Margery and her country cousin, Joe. Their relationship, farcical though it is, is strongly suggestive of melodrama's moral dogma. This is most apparent at the splendid conclusion of a scene between them in which Margery is told what has happened since she left her home village:

Margery. And Harry Bacon, what's become of him?

Joe. Gone to sea, because Mary Brown took up with a tailor what opened a shop from London. And you recollect Tom Hammer, the blacksmith?

Margery. Yes.

Joe. Well, if he ain't gone and bought all Merryweather's pigs, I'm a Dutchman! And Merryweather's gone to America, and the eldest daughter's married Sam Holloway, the cutter, and folks say it ain't a good match, because he was a widow with three children all ready made, and she might have had Master Pollard, the schoolmaster, and he's gone and turned serious and won't let the boys play at no games, and so they're all going away to a new man that'll let 'em do just what they like; and Will Twig has been found out stealing chickens, and he's in prison; and Johnny Trotter, the postman, has opened a grocer's shop; and they've pulled down the old parsonage and are building a new 'un; and the doctor's got a large lamp over his door with big blue and red bull's eyes; and there's a new beadle, and the parish children have got the whooping cough, and Mrs. Jenkins' cow's dead. And that's all!

Margery. Oh, Joe, I can shut my eyes and see everything and everybody you've been talking about, oh, so plain! And to see you again does seem so like old times!

Joe. And didn't we have games? When you used to climb up the cherry-tree, and call out to me, "Joe, come and help me, or I shall tumble down and break something!"

Margery. Yes! And Joe, when my father used to take you and I to market, and we used to sit at the bottom of the cart and eat apples!

Joe. And when sometimes I used to try to give you a kiss, what knocks on my nose you used to give me!

Margery. Oh, didn't I?

Joe. And when I got savage, how I used to kick at you wi' my hob-nailed shoes! Oh, how friendly we was – wasn't we?

Margery. And how we did sing!

Joe. And dance!

Margery. And were so happy!

Joe. Oh, Margery!

Margery. Oh, Joe!

(*Joe catches her in his arms and kisses her.*)

In *A Rough Diamond* virtue and good-heartedness are enshrined in simple country folk and are contrasted with opposite qualities in the educated and fashionable. In W.B. Bernard's *The Middy Ashore* (1836), they reside in the midshipman-hero Harry Halcyon, his bosun Tom Cringle, and Lt. Morton of H.M.S. *Orion.* The sailor-hero and his comic partner are right out of nautical melodrama, and *The Middy Ashore,* like *A Rough Diamond,* assumes the moral attitudes of the melodramatic form. It also resembles Buckstone's play in plot. Halcyon's aunt, the fashionable and terribly snobbish Lady Starchington, despises what three years at sea have done to her nephew, and she tries, with the aid of the bored and equally snobbish Mr Tonnish, to give him social refinement and *savoir-faire.* By comic means the effort fails, and Halcyon and Tom Cringle also foil Lady Starchington's attempt to marry Halcyon's sister to Tonnish, rescuing her instead for the brave and honest Lt. Morton. *The Middy Ashore* establishes a clear moral pattern: the fashionable and elegant with a touch of villainy on the one hand, and opposed to them the simple and virtuous on the other, the sea serving the same moral purpose in this play as the country in *A Rough Diamond*.

Thus some part of the basic sub-structure and moral attitude of melodrama is carried over to farce, an interesting similarity in view of what might appear to be a total opposition between the two forms. Two of the best farces of the period deliberately set out to parody melodrama. Parodies of melodrama have been noted in burlesques from the beginning of the nineteenth century, but their presence in farce has gone without comment. The heroine of William Murray's *Diamond Cut Diamond* (1838), unable to decide between two suitors, Howard and Seymour, promises her hand to the one who prevails upon his rival to pass the boundaries of her estate and leave her. Each man, aided by a servant, resorts to every trick possible to force his rival from the estate; intrigues, mistakes, comic surprises, a quick succession of hurried entrances, exits, and ludicrous anti-climaxes – all contribute to the excellence of this farce. Additionally, each comic deception that one rival tries to practice on the other is a burlesque of a stock melodramatic situation. Howard's servant, after declaring, 'The virtuous man is never alone. Honour, conscience, morality, integrity, and sobriety are his constant associates' – the sort of moral platitude often on the lips of the melodramatic hero – immediately accepts a bribe to trick his master. Seymour's servant, equally bribed to trick *his* master, rushes in to Seymour with the news that his poor old mother lies on her deathbed anxiously asking for her son. Powerful filial sentiments are expressed with an appropriate sense of grief and duty before Seymour recalls that his mother died ten years ago. A fire bursts out in the distant village, and Seymour, crying to Howard, 'Follow me, and let us save the innocents, or perish in the attempt, rushes off. Howard, however, after announcing that 'it is so sweet to assist the afflicted...to save a child from the flames...to restore it to its raving mother', refuses to go, because this is a scheme of Seymour's. Two or three more such tricks, preceded by emotion-filled dialogue, follow, and finally Howard and Seymour fight a grimly serious duel. Seymour falls, and with his dying breath urges Howard to flee the wrath of the law. As soon as Howard is discerned galloping across the boundaries of the estate, the triumphant Seymour – for this was his winning trick, and the pistols were filled only with powder – rises and claims Charlotte.

Diamond Cut Diamond parodies melodramatic speeches, situations, and emotions, but John Maddison Morton's *Box and Cox* (1847) is a more extensive parody, involving plot machinery as well.

Box, the journeyman printer, and Cox, the journeyman hatter, find that not only do they live in the same room, but also that they are both engaged to be married to the dreadful Penelope Ann; finally, they discover that they are long-lost brothers [2]. The comic complications are considerable, and they depend largely on the surprises, mysteries, revelations, and coincidences of melodramatic plot machinery [3]. Furthermore, Box and Cox as characters are serious and emotional; the dialogue is sometimes melodramatically patterned. Box, for instance, ends his narration of his faked suicide with a mention of his suicide note containing 'these affecting farewell words, "This is thy work, oh Penelope Ann!"'

Cox. Penelope Ann! (***Starts up, takes Box by the arm, and leads him slowly to the front of stage.***) Penelope Ann?
Box. Penelope Ann!
Cox. Originally widow of William Wiggins?
Box. Widow of William Wiggins!
Cox. Proprietor of bathing machines?
Box. Proprietor of bathing machines!
Cox. At Margate?
Box. And Ramsgate!
Cox. It must be she! And you, sir – you are Box – the lamented, long-lost Box?
Box. I am!
Cox. And I was about to marry the interesting creature you so cruelly deceived.
Box. Oh! Then you are Cox?
Cox. I am!
Box. I heard of it. I congratulate you – I give you joy! And now I think I'll go and take a stroll.

Box's final line is comically anti-climactic only because of the previous melodramatic build-up. The climax of the play is constructed along familiar melodramatic lines:

Cox. What shall part us?
Box. What shall tear us asunder?
Cox. Box!
Box. (***About to embrace – Box stops, seizes Cox's hand, and looks eagerly in his face.***) You'll excuse the apparent insanity of the remark, but the more I gaze on your features, the more I'm convinced that you're my long-lost brother.
Cox. The very observation I was going to make to you!
Box. Ah – tell me – in mercy tell me – have you such a thing as a strawberry mark on your left arm?
Cox. No!
Box. Then it is he!
(***They rush into each other's arms.***)

Box and Cox is a parody of melodramatic sentiment as well as other aspects of melodrama, excess of sentiment being an important part of melodrama. Certainly sentimentalism and benevolism, though frequently casually and haphazardly expressed by the playwright, pervade early Victorian farce. The plot of Charles Dance's *Kill or Cure* (1832) concerns the attempts of the kindly Mildman to reconcile the perpetually quarrelling Browns. He finally does so, although not until the despairing Brown has been stomach-pumped for drinking milk that he thought was poison; the farce then passes immediately from this strongly physical comic incident to an ecstasy of ideal domestic sentiment:

Brown.	(*Taking her hand.*) Susan!
Mrs. Brown.	Peter!
Brown.	I'm afraid we look very ridiculous.
Mrs. Brown.	Never mind that; let us agree that it shall be for the last time.
Brown.	With all my heart – with all *my heart.* (*Rising and shaking hands with her.*)
Mrs. Brown.	What can we say to this kind gentleman?
Mildman.	Say nothing; but be happy – let me see you embrace one another, and I'm content. (*They embrace.*) John!
John.	Sir!
Mildman.	What did I tell you just now?
John.	What, when we were – ah – I know – Betty, lass, come. (*They embrace – Brown and Mrs. Brown, seeing these, embrace again – then all four embrace.*)
Mildman.	That's right – that's right – my favourite toast is, "Harmony all over the world."

The impossibly benevolent Mildman, a fairy godfather bringing domestic bliss, is strongly reminiscent of the virtuous, do-gooding spokesmen of temperance melodrama, such as Romaine in *Ten Nights in a Bar-Room.*

In a less overtly moralistic farce, Buckstone's *An Alarming Sacrifice* (1849), moral and sentimental assumptions are the basis of conduct. The thoughtless and extravagant Bob Ticket finds his uncle's will, which to his horror leaves the whole estate to the housekeeper, Susan Sweetapple. Bob's struggle with his conscience occurs as he looks in the mirror.

> Now, let my face tell me what I ought to do. I'll destroy the will; I'll burn it. Susan shall never know such a document ever existed. I will – I will – and enjoy my property, and – Oh, what a demon I do look! I'd no idea I could ever be so frightful. I'll try again. I'll be a man; I'll do the right thing; I'll tell the poor girl of her good fortune – put her in the possession of all. My heart will approve of my conduct, and I shall be one of the noblest works of creation, an honest man! Oh, what an angel sweetness beams in

> every feature; what a handsome fellow I am! Yes, and I'll behave as handsome. The struggle's over – an alarming sacrifice *shall* be made!

This struggle is comically portrayed, perhaps, but the moral decision arrived at is a serious one. After Susan gives Bob a place as a servant and forces him to run around waiting at table, she burns the will in a fit of conscience and good-heartedness; and the now thoughtful Bob offers to marry her, partly out of gratitude and partly out of respect for her virtue.

The hero of a much more genteel and upper middle-class farce, Blanchard Jerrold's *Cool as a Cucumber* (1851), is a charming and plausible impostor in the home of the well-to-do Barkins. Claiming to have met young Barkins in Europe, Plumper rearranges the furniture and pictures, orders wine, orders lunch, orders coffee to follow, makes love to the maid, makes love to Barkins' niece, keeps up an interminable lively chatter, and behaves throughout with supremely energetic insouciance. However, it is this devil-may-care fellow who gets old Barkins to agree to the marriage of his niece and young Barkins [4], and who arranges the final tableau. Plumper's intervention is comically contrived but thoroughly sentimental; indeed, the ingenious conclusion of *Cool as a Cucumber* is a mixture of farcical parody of melodrama and straightforward romantic sentiment. Old Barkins refuses to support the young couple if they marry; the wrathful Plumper orders the curtain down behind him, and berates Barkins to the audience for his attitude. Barkins cries out from behind the curtain that he relents; Plumper orders the curtain raised and calls for red fire and a tableau as the niece and son kneel conventionally beside Barkins.

Finally, the sentimentalism of early Victorian farce was tailor-made for the stage Irishman, a comic and sentimental type for generations. Two examples will suffice. In Bernard's *His Last Legs* (1839), O'Callaghan, down on his luck and his cash, impersonates a doctor in order to win a meal and a fee. At the end of a series of complications and misunderstandings he is responsible for reconciling the real doctor with his estranged wife and making possible the engagement of O'Callaghan's erstwhile patient and his loved one. O'Callaghan is a typical stage Irishman of the time: a clever, eccentric, credible, improvident, gold-hearted rogue, and the play combines the plot mechanisms of farce with the generous sentimentalism inherent both in contemporary farce and in the stage character of the Irishman. A coarser Irishman, the tinker Barney O'Toole in Samuel Lover's *Barney the Baron* (1857), wins a German castle in a lottery and arrives to take possession of his property. The comedy arises solely out of Barney's ignorance, his low eating and drinking habits, and the dressing up as a ghost by the castle porter to frighten Barney into selling the property to its rightful owner. This trick is revealed before the sale is concluded, but even a character like Barney can say with great moral dignity, 'Give me your fist. I have pledged my word and I won't break it if I can make two living couples happy.'

The basically sentimental outlook of Victorian farce, despite its necessary plot machinery of intrigue and calculated deception, is closely allied to the overwhelming domesticity of this and other kinds of Victorian drama. The best farce is the disciplined expression of moral and domestic anarchy, the plausible and logical presentation of a completely crazy world that all the characters take with the greatest seriousness, a world in which extraordinarily absurd and fantastic pressures on the ordinary individual drive him to the very extremity of his resources and his senses, a world in which he can survive only by pitting the ingenuity of his own insanity against the massive blows of hostile coincidence and a seemingly remorseless fate. Such a world is the world of the best French farce, the world of Labiche and Feydeau, whose undoubted domesticity is uncompromisingly ruthless, savage, and anti-familial, whose very chaos and controlled violence is a kind of inverse moral order of great rigidity. These are the characteristics of the best farce, and they are only occasionally evident in Victorian farce. Boucicault in *Forbidden Fruit* and Pinero in *The Schoolmistress, Dandy Dick,* and *The Magistrate* come nearest to expressing them later in the century. Labiche and Feydeau are not sentimental, nor do they write on that level of domesticity concerning the trivia of home, hearth, and daily living that cram the Victorian farce to bursting. One might say the domesticity of French farce is hard and sharp-edged, and the domesticity of Victorian farce soft and well-disposed. The difference occurs because the farce of Labiche and Feydeau is anti-idealistic and satirical in aim, whereas the purpose of the far less aggressive Victorian farce is to amuse in a jolly and properly moral way, to cast a friendly, avuncular light on the minor vicissitudes of home and family [5]. The ideals of love, marriage, and household that enervate so much serious Victorian drama also debilitate Victorian farce, yet simultaneously give it a sort of homey charm that the French farce eschews.

Another significant difference is that French farce was very much a middle and upper-middle class affair, whereas a significant proportion of the audience that enjoyed early Victorian farce was working and lower-middle class. Box and Cox, for example, are journeymen, one working for a printer, the other for a hatter. They live in *'decently furnished'* lodgings; Mrs Bouncer is of the respectable but enterprising landlady class. Cox is given a day off and contemplates an excursion to Gravesend for a shilling or to Greenwich for fourpence. The comedy of the first part of the play revolves around the mysterious disappearances and reappearances of Cox's breakfast and Box's breakfast: Cox's is a mutton chop, Box's a rasher of bacon and a penny roll. The fearful but prosperous Penelope Ann Wiggins, a cut above both of them in social standing, is a proprietor of bathing machines at Margate and Ramsgate. When she comes to deliver the news that she is marrying Knox, she arrives not in a cab but a twopenny omnibus.

The setting of J.S. Coyne's *How to Settle Accounts with Your Laundress* (1847) is a tailor's show-room in Jermyn Street. Whittington Widgetts, tailor to the fashionable, expects the ballet dancer Cheri Bounce to a little private dinner that he has ordered from the pub across the street. Enamoured of the elegant Miss Bounce and acutely conscious of his own rise in the tailoring business, Widgetts is forgetting his former love, the laundress Mary White, who enters wearing clogs, with a basket of laundry under her arm. She makes out Widgett's laundry list – four shirts, one false front, and a pair of white ducks – and to the tailor's embarrassment recalls their former courtship when, as Widgetts remembers, he was 'a journeyman tailor in a two-pair back, struggling to make love and trousers for the small remuneration of fifteen shillings a week.'

Mary. When you lived in Fuller's Rents, you used to walk out with me on a Sunday. You never walk with me at all now.
Widgetts. Walking's vulgar, my dear.
Mary. And you sometimes used to take me at half-price to the theatres.
Widgetts. Theatres is low, my dear.
Mary. And you remember how we used to go together to Greenwich, with a paper of ham sandwiches in my basket, and sit under the trees in the park, and talk, and laugh – law! how we used to talk of love and constancy and connubial felicitude in a little back parlour, and a heap of beautiful things.
Widgetts. (*Aside.*) A heap of rubbish.
Mary. And you know, Widgy dear, when we enter that happy state –
Widgetts. What state do you allude to, Miss White?
Mary. The marriage state, of course.
Widgetts. Oh, indeed – Ah!
Mary. You don't forget, I hope, that I have your promissory note on the back of twenty-nine unpaid washing bills to make me your lawful wife.

The denouement of the farce occurs when Mary White, resolving to break up the Cheri Bounce affair, leaves a suicide note, dumps a tailor's dummy dressed as herself upside down in a water butt, enters again disguised as a detective looking for Widgetts on a charge of murdering his laundress, and consumes the expensive dinner *tête-à-tête* with Cheri Bounce, while Widgetts fumes impotently, in hiding from the law disguised as a waiter at his own table. The deception is revealed at last; Widgetts leaves Miss Bounce to the tender attentions of her lover, a hairdresser at the opera, and promises to marry the laundress. The point of quoting and summarizing the plot of this play is to show that, as in *Box and Cox*, its subject matter and farcical complexities spring from the domestic detail and thoroughly domestic human relationships of that border area between working and lower-middle class life. The values and ideals of the play are also those of this area. *Box and Cox* was a Lyceum piece; *How to Settle Accounts with Your Laundress* was first performed at the Adelphi. Both theatres, and especially the latter, enjoyed substantial patronage from these classes [6].

The social level and matey domesticity of such settings and such comic business appear in many farces of the period. Bob Ticket, the hero of *An Alarming Sacrifice*, is by his own description 'principal duster at Gingham and Twill's, linen-drapers, Oxford Street.' The heroine, Susan Sweetapple, is a housekeeper. The climax of the play is precipitated by the resolution of a moral crisis in Susan's heart. The setting of the play is the *'Interior of a Neat Country House at Watford.' Kill or Cure* is set outside and then inside a country inn near Doncaster at the time of the races. In addition to the benevolent visitor, the principal characters are the landlord and landlady of the inn and the ostler and his sweetheart. The subject matter is the altruistic intervention of an outsider directed to the admirable domestic end of reconciling a bitterly quarrelling wife and husband. Interestingly enough, *Kill or Cure* was performed by Madame Vestris' company at the Olympic, a rather elegant little theatre that attracted fashionable audiences. There is nothing fashionable about the content or setting of *Kill or Cure*, yet it was performed fifty-eight times during the nine-year Vestris management [7]. Obviously the domestically homey appealed also to an audience of the kind that patronized the Olympic.

Even in the farces with more refined social settings – such as *A Rough Diamond, Married Life*, and *Cool as a Cucumber* – the appeal to the domestic ideal and domestic intimacy is strong. The first speech the audience hears from the country girl of *A Rough Diamond* goes as follows: 'How many pigs are there in the last litter? Oh, I know – eight! Well, you may send one to my cousin...two to my old dad, and one to Betsy Buncle, my old playfellow in Lancashire. The three black ones I shall want to have in the parlour to play with.' This seems satiric of quaint rustic gaucherie, since the audience has not met Margery before, but in the event she is the paragon of female virtue and the ideal of unspoiled domestic simplicity. The jealous wife of Thomas Bayly's *The Culprit* (1838), whose husband is a retired naval captain, admits to error when she discovers that his secret infatuation is with a Turkish pipe rather than another woman. She declares that 'when I married, I expected too much. I required my husband to give up an innocent indulgence which long habit had rendered essential to his comfort.' The exonerated husband triumphantly installs the hookah in his own home. The husband's marital superiority, an essential aspect of Victorian serious drama, is asserted or reasserted at the end of many a play during which the wife has too long had her own way. This superiority was held to be a necessary part of the ideal marriage, or at least the ideal stage marriage. That sort of marriage was taken very seriously, even in farce. It forms the subject of a harangue that Coddle delivers to the audience at the conclusion of *Married Life,* a farce-ending speech so solemn in content and so glowing with domestic idealism that it is worth quoting in its entirety. It is prefaced by a piece of comic though nonetheless idealistic stage business. Coddle addresses the assembled married couples:

Coddle. Whenever a disagreement breaks out among you in future, recall the memory of those inducements which first led you to think of each other, and you will find it to be a wonderful help to the restoration of peace. Do you all agree to this?

All. Yes, yes!

Coddle. Then follow my example, and ratify the agreement by a hearty conjugal embrace. I will give the word of command. Make ready! (*As Coddle puts his arm round his wife's waist, each of the husbands do the same to their wives.*) Present! (*Coddle takes his wife's chin between his fingers and thumb, and prepares to kiss her; all the husbands do the same.*) Fire! (*They all kiss and embrace at the same moment.*) There, this is the way that all matrimonial quarrels should end – and if *you* are of the same opinion (*to the audience*) then, indeed, will our conjugal joy be complete, and our light lesson not have been read in vain. You have seen the result of perpetual jealousy in the case of Mr. and Mrs. Lynx; of continual disputes and contradiction in that of Mr. and Mrs. Younghusband; of a want of cheerfulness in Mr. and Mrs. Dismal; of the impolicy of public correction in the instance of Mrs. Dove; and of the necessity of assimilating habits and tempers in the singular case of Mr. and Mrs. Coddle; and though these may not be one half the causes of quarrel between man and wife – yet even

> their exposure may serve as beacon lights to avoid the rocks of altercation when sailing on the sea of matrimony. So think of us, all ye anticipating and smiling single people; for you *must*, or *ought* all to be married, and the sooner the better – and remember us ye already paired; and let our example prove to you that to mutual forbearance, mutual confidence, mutual habits, mutual everything, must we owe mutual happiness. And where can the *best* of happiness be found, but in a loyal and affectionate married life!

It has already been suggested that the comic business and farcical entanglements of these plays arise from the domestic framework and the thematic material rather than pursuing their own separate mechanical course. A noteworthy aspect of this connection between domesticity and comic invention is the large number of farces with scenes in which physical comedy depends entirely upon eating and drinking [8]. In *Box and Cox* Box complains that although the last thing he cooked on his fire was a pork chop, his gridiron is now 'powerfully impregnated with the odour of red herrings.' He puts his rasher of bacon on to fry and retires for a nap. Cox enters, discovers the bacon, removes it indignantly, puts his mutton chop on the fire, and leaves the room to get his breakfast tray. Box discovers Cox's chop, hurls it out of the window in a melodramatic fury, and goes out to get his breakfast tray. Cox enters, is likewise infuriated by renewing his acquaintance with Box's bacon, and with equal rage hurls *it* out of the window. To their mutual amazement, Box and Cox then discover each other for the first time, each holding a loaded breakfast tray.

In *Barney the Baron* the audience is supposed to laugh at Barney because in his German castle he calls for 'plenty of tripe and onions, and liver and bacon, and cabbage, and a big bowl of praties.' However, *peeled* potatoes annoy Barney; he throws them at the servants and expresses great horror at the sight of a dish of sauerkraut. He carves clumsily, looks forward to breakfast on 'a few butter rolls and some boiled praties with the skins on them', and retires to bed clutching a bottle of wine. In *Cool as a Cucumber* Plumper's *sang-froid* is nowhere more admirable than when, as a complete stranger in the Barkins' house, he successively orders wine, lunch, and coffee and comments on their quality. The main comic scene in John Poole's *Deaf as a Post,* a slightly earlier farce of 1823, displays a crafty suitor who, pretending to deafness, takes his tightfisted rival's place at supper, eats his way through his rival's capon, orders bottles of port and madeira to be placed to his rival's account, and, calmly misunderstanding the fury of the now incoherent rival, kindly thanks him for paying for his meal.

The funniest moments of *An Alarming Sacrifice* and *How to Settle Accounts with Your Laundress* also occur at table. In the former, Bob Ticket, in his new capacity of unwilling servant to his uncle's housekeeper, suffers the indignity of waiting on three young ladies whom he had invited to dinner in his sadly vanished role of master of the house. The stage directions, dialogue, and business are explicitly alimentary:

	(Deborah appears at the R. with a tray on which are three dishes, one of hashed mutton, one of hot potatoes, and the third roast duck. Pugwash takes cover off the dish before him.)
Pugwash.	Here young man, take this cover.
	(Bob takes it.)
Miss Wadd.	Bob, some bread!
Skinner.	Bob, some ale!
Pugwash.	Bob, some pepper!
Susan.	Bob, some butter!
Miss Gimp.	Bob, some vinegar!
Miss Wadd.	Bob, some mustard!
Susan.	Hot plates, Bob!
	(Bob brings the articles as they are called for from a table at the back. Deborah enters with hot plates; Bob takes them, burns his fingers, and drops them.)

Widgetts in *How to Settle Accounts with Your Laundress* relishes the prospect of his specially ordered private dinner with Cheri Bounce, a dinner of lobster in the shell, kidneys, roast fowl and sausages, and champagne. However, this superb repast is eaten by Miss Bounce and the laundress disguised as a detective, with Widgetts, bullied unmercifully, waiting in a pair of false whiskers at his own table, in dread that at any moment he will be identified as a murderer. Widgetts' simultaneous terror of the law and fury at seeing his own dinner devoured, as well as his clumsy idiocy as a waiter – at one point he pops a kidney into his pocket in order to have something to eat – makes this the best scene in the play.

The linking of food and drink with physical business in a middle and especially a lower-middle or working-class setting places this kind of farce in a glorious fantasy world of lesser domesticity, a Grimaldi-like existence of endless fun where kidneys, mutton-chops, rashers of bacon, and potatoes without skins can, like strings of sausages and hot codlins, be elevated into a splendidly comic way of life.

What I have tried to demonstrate about the early Victorian farce – its closeness to melodrama, its moral and sentimental basis, its interest in lower-middle and working-class material, its domestic idealism and domestic naivety, its sense of fun rather than satire, the way in which physical business grows out of domestic settings and content – these are all, with the exception of the last point, aspects of theme and outlook. The topic cannot be left at that, however. The mention of comic business brings me to the actor; perhaps this is where I should have begun. During the first half of the nineteenth century the English stage was unusually blessed with low-comedy actors; all contemporary critics who reviewed them paid tribute to their ability to work creative miracles with farce and low-comedy material. The early years of the Victorian period saw many of these performers still on the stage, with fresh talent coming along to join them. The farces I have discussed here were acted by these same performers. It was Wright who played Widgetts, the tailor, in *How to Settle Accounts with Your Laundress*; Buckstone who played Box, Bob Ticket in *An Alarming Sacrifice,* Cousin Joe in *A Rough Diamond,* and Dove in *Married Life*; Liston who played the booby rival in *Deaf as a Post* and the quarrelsome publican in *Kill or Cure*; Charles Mathews who played the imposter Plumper in *Cool as a Cucumber*; Tyrone Power who played the rogue O'Callaghan in *His Last Legs.* This is only a partial list of the actors in these farces; I do not begin to enumerate the actresses. In respect for and admiration of such performers this paper ends; any headstone that we erect to the memory of the early Victorian farce should also bear their names.

Notes

[1] From 1747 to 1776 the total number of farces performed at Drury Lane and Covent Garden was only 46; of these a considerable proportion, including five of the nine most popular, date from before 1747. (Cf. *The London Stage, 1747–1776,* ed. George Winchester Stone, Jr., 1968, clxvi–clxvii.) Allardyce Nicoll lists 162 farces written during the 1747–76 period. (Cf. *A History of English Drama,* Vols. II and III, Cambridge, 1952–5.)

[2] The Martins in *The Bald Soprano* come to mind at once. Could Ionesco have known a French version of *Box and Cox,* or its French originals, *Une chambre à deux lits* and *Frisette?*

[3] *Box and Cox* is described on the title page as 'A Romance of Real Life', a direct parody of the subtitles of melodrama.

[4] The niece, like many young heroines in farces, is serious, romantic, and emotional, without a particle of comedy in her.

[5] The Lord Chamberlain, the local magistrate, and public opinion prevented Victorian farceurs from writing – even if they had wished to,

which is most doubtful – as witheringly about love and marriage and as openly about adultery as the French playwrights did.

[6] The fact that the humour of *Barney the Baron* is coarser than that of the other Irish farce, *His Last Legs,* may be explained in part by the former being an Adelphi play and the latter being from the Haymarket. The comedy of *How to Settle Accounts with Your Laundress* is grosser than that of *Box and Cox,* with its Lyceum pedigree.

[7] James H. Butler, 'An Examination of the Plays Produced by Madam Vestris During Her Management of the Olympic Theatre in London from January 3, 1831 to May 31, 1839', *Theatre Survey,* Vol. X (November, 1969) 139.

[8] The connection between low comedy and food and drink is, of course, a very old one on the stage. It is particularly strong in nineteenth-century pantomime. One also remembers the comic uses of food in the silent film.

8 JOHN HOPKIN

George Henry Lewes as Playwright: A Register of Pieces

George Henry Lewes's 'Receipt Book', housed in the Berg Collection in the New York Public Library and printed by Gordon Haight as an appendix to his edition of George Eliot's letters [1], records the payment Lewes received for his efforts as a playwright. The total sum comes to a little over £1,000, of which £800 were earned during the 1850s. Individual pieces such as *The Noble Heart* and *The Game of Speculation* brought in £100 and £50 respectively. Sums of £20 and of £50 are recorded for pieces 'on acct.' or 'in adv.'; £20 for an act written and £30 on 'completion of entry above'. The right of printing *The Lawyers* brought in £5, and that of three farces, £13. In 1852 Lewes recorded the sum of £80 earned from an agreement with Charles James Mathews 'on acct. of pieces done at his theatre' at £10 per week. Regular sums of £10 and £20 are subsequently recorded opposite the entry 'Chas. Mathews', but at monthly, not weekly intervals. From 1855 receipts from the Dramatic Authors' Society of sums ranging from £2.15s.4d. to £38.7s.6d., are recorded up until 1878, the year of Lewes's death.

Fascinating as the details of this 'Receipt Book' are, the items recorded do not provide a comprehensive checklist of Lewes's work as a playwright. It is the purpose of this paper to offer a register of pieces written by Lewes, to include those which were performed and printed and those which were rejected or unfinished.

Plays performed with year of performance

1. *The Noble Heart* – 1849
2. *The Game of Speculation* – 1851

3. *The Chain of Events* – 1852
4. *Taking by Storm* – 1852
5. *A Strange History* – 1852
6. *The Lawyers* – 1853
7. *Wanted a She-Wolf* – 1854
8. *Give a Dog a Bad Name* – 1854
9. *Sunshine Through the Clouds* – 1854
10. *A Cozy Couple* – 1855
11. *Buckstone's Adventures with a Polish Princess* – 1856
12. *Stay at Home* – 1856
13. *Thieves! Thieves!* – 1857
14. *Captain Bland* – 1864

1 The Noble Heart

First performed at the Theatre Royal Manchester on 17 April 1849 with Lewes playing the leading role of Don Gomez, possessor of the eponymous noble organ. The play was subsequently performed at the Theatre Royal Liverpool on 18 May 1849 before its presentation in London at the Olympic Theatre on 18 February 1850. For the London production Lewes relinquished the role of Don Gomez to Gustavus Brooke. Lewes later wrote of Brooke in the *Leader,* 10 September 1853, that there was a grace and power about him 'which must always carry by storm an audience not very critical as to intelligence and poetry'. The play ran for eight performances at the Olympic, the last being on March 1. It was billed to appear after Mrs Mowatt, who played the heroine Juanna, had recovered from her 'indisposition', but it was the bankruptcy of Mr Watts, the lessee, which closed both the play's run and the theatre. It was favourably reviewed both in the provinces and in London. Notices in the *Manchester Guardian, Manchester Examiner and Times* and the *Manchester Courier* all praised the author's efforts at dramatic construction and theatrical effectiveness, qualities also commended by the critic in the *Liverpool Mail.* When it opened at the Olympic it was reviewed in the leading London dailies and weeklies. The critic in the *Examiner* expressed the general reservations felt by the London critics on the play's dramatic power. He wrote in his notice of 23 February 1850:

> It is not Don Gomez, or Juanna, or Leon whom we seem to hear; but rather an intimate friend, or next-door neighbour, a philosophical critic of emotion, who is privy to all they are feeling and undergoing, understands it thoroughly, and is good enough to put it into very choice language for them and for us.

To the printed version of the play which appeared in 1850, Lewes added a Preface in which he expressed his dismay at what he called the prudery of theatrical aesthetics. He maintained that the character of the religious fanatic, who went under the name of Herman the Hermit, was a part new to the stage and strikingly dramatic. But Mr Ryder, who played the part of Herman in the London production, went in dread of being hissed for allusions to the Infinite and to Him, thus, Lewes maintained, rendering the part ineffective. On the naming of the Deity on the stage Lewes pointed out that an actor may be permitted to say '*Him* and point upwards, but he must not say *God'*. He had been obliged, he added, in a line which ran: 'The heart hath but one resting place – in God', to soften 'God' into 'Heaven'.

The Noble Heart was not revived on the London stage, but did find its way to America. It appeared on a joint bill with *The Creole Maiden, or the Cooper of Paris* at the Bowery Theatre New York on 5 February 1851, and was also put on by an amateur company of the Garrick Club of New York at the French Theatre on 15 April 1858. A playbill in the Harvard Theatre Collection of the Boston Museum records its performance at that theatre on 29 January 1855 with E.L. Davenport in the part of Don Gomez.

2 The Game of Speculation

First performed at the Lyceum Theatre on 2 October 1851. Adapted from a three-act version of a five-act play written by Balzac entitled *Le Faiseur.* The shortened version, by Adolphe D'Ennery was called *Mercadet* and first performed at the Théâtre Gymnase on 24 August 1851. Lewes's version, written under the pseudonym 'Slingsby Lawrence', was printed in Lacy's acting editions, volume five. Charles Mathews records ninety-four performances of the piece during its first season, 1851–2 [2]. The playbills show the play ran for ninety-two performances. The Lyceum closed on October 13 after the play's tenth performance and re-opened with this play on December 15. The last performance of the season took place on 27 March 1852.

The printed version carried the following advertisement signed 'S.L.':

> THE GAME OF SPECULATION is an adaptation of a posthumous work by the celebrated H. de Balzac. This version was written in less than thirteen hours and produced after only two rehearsals – a fact worth recording, when it is remembered how admirably it was played. CHARLES MATHEWS, whom I regard as the most accomplished living actor, played Mr Affable Hawk in a style which would have carried any Piece triumphantly.

It is also interesting to note that only six weeks elapsed between the appearance of the French play in Paris and the first performance of the English adaptation in London. John Hollingshead gave this account of the play's adaptation:

> When Balzac's *Mercadet* was produced in Paris, and there was a rush of the few London managers who were largely dependent on the French stage for comedy, Lewes was first in the field. He got the play on a Saturday morning from France. He went up to a room at the top of the theatre with half-a-dozen shorthand writers. He dictated *à la Masaniello,* to each and all in turn; the plan of the Parliamentary gallery of the House of Commons was adopted; the 'flimsy' was copied from shorthand into slips of English; the slips were sent down to the stage every half-hour to the actors, who were there, learning these fragments with one eye, while they were rehearsing, so to speak, with the other. This work went on through Saturday and Saturday night, a part of Sunday and Sunday night, and a greater part of Monday, and the result, the three-act comedy of the "Game of Speculation" was produced at the Lyceum Theatre on the same Monday night, spoken and acted to perfection. I was in the front row of the gallery – a place that suited my pocket. Was the dialogue slip-shod? No. Take 'what are creditors created for but to give credit' as a sample. Charles Mathews played the chief part, and no one, not even the French creator, could have played it better or so well. Was it badly adapted? No. Years afterwards, when I had the Gaiety Theatre, and Mr Alfred Wigan was my chief actor, the necessity of finding him a good play and part presented itself to my managerial mind. I turned to *Mercadet,* and Mr Alfred Wigan turned to 'Affable Hawk', the chief character. The next morning we shook our heads. It was no good. Mr George-Henry-Lewes-Slingsby-Lawrence had cut the ground from under us with his forty-eight hours' adaptation, his phonographic echo of Balzac.

It is unlikely that the piece was presented as quickly as Hollingshead recounts. The manuscript of the play (British Museum Add. MSS. 43,037) shows it was received for licensing on September 27, and the licence was sent on September 29 for performance on October 4. The play was actually performed on October 2, a Thursday, not a Monday evening. The play was, however, an unqualified success. There was some critical disagreement about its merits as compared with those of the original, but there was unanimous agreement about its effectiveness as a vehicle for the talents of Charles Mathews as the Affable Hawk. Edmund Yates considered the role as 'possibly the most suitable character ever written for Charles Mathews, and in the acting of which he absolutely revelled'. Mathews played the part twice in his American tour of 1857, on September 21 and November 19 at the Broadway Theatre, New York. He made his final appearance in the part at the Opéra Comique in Paris on 7 May 1877.

3 The Chain of Events

First performed at the Lyceum Theatre on 12 April 1852 and printed in *Lacy*, volume twenty-one. Adapted from *La Dame de la Halle* by Auguste Anicet-Bourgeois and Michel Masson, first performed at the Théâtre de l'Abmigu-Comique on 7 February 1852. The French original is printed in *Bibliothèque Dramatique* (Paris), tom. XL. According to Charles Mathews the English version ran for fifty-nine performances in the season 1851–2. The playbill of 29 June 1852 announced the play's sixty-first time of playing. The piece was primarily a vehicle for the scene painter, William Beverley. Henry Morley in his review of the performance in the *Examiner*, 17 April 1852, testified to Mr Beverley's skill:

> The scenery brought out the admirable talent of Mr Beverley in a new light, and showed him as happy in the treatment of real as of faery subjects. The moonlight scene of the Market of the Innocents was a masterpiece of picturesque design. One of the most striking effects we have ever witnessed on the stage was the shipwreck on the rocks of St Domingo; the reality was almost appalling.

Most reviewers praised the scenic effects, but some thought it moved too slowly. Edmund Yates was of the opinion that it proved something of a failure, turning out, as he observed Douglas Jerrold had said of the piece, to be a 'door-chain to keep people out of the house'. George Eliot saw it with Herbert Spencer and confided her impressions of the piece to Charles Bray:

> It is a very long chain and drags rather heavily. No sparkle, but a sort of Dickens-like sentimentality all through – in short, I think it might please you. As a series of tableaux I never saw anything to equal it, But to my mind it is execrable moral taste to have a storm and shipwreck with all its horrors on the stage. I could only scream and cover my eyes. It was revolting to hear the cheers and clapping of the audience. [3]

As Gordon Haight observed, George Eliot's severe criticism of the piece betrays no evidence of interest in Lewes at this time.

4 Taking by Storm

First performed at the Lyceum on 3 June 1852 and printed in *Lacy*, volume six. For this piece Lewes changed his pseudonym to that of 'Frank Churchill'. [4]

The piece was adapted from the French *Tambour Battant* by A. Decourcelle, T. Barrière and L. Morand, originally produced at the Théâtre de la Montansier on 30 October 1851 and printed in the *Bibliothèque Dramatique*, tom. XXXIX. Lewes's version ran for twenty-three nights in the first season and for the same number of nights in the following season. With characteristic verve 'Vivian' reviewed this piece by 'Frank Churchill' in the *Leader* on 5 June 1852:

> Taking by storm with a vengeance! "Was ever woman in this humour wooed – was ever woman in this humour won?" Never! Fancy a man come to your lodgings, dear madam, and taking *you* with them – taking you in spite of all resistance – taking you by sheer force of irresistible pertinacity and gay confidence! *That* does Charles Mathews; and your shouts of laughter prevent your discovering that the piece is outrageously improbable. I will not be wiser than my laughter, but will let this piece pass for an extravagance rendered amusing by good acting.

He reminded his readers of this criticism of the English version when he reviewed the French players in the original at the St James's Theatre on February 12 the following year. He declared that his praise of the acting in the English adaptation had made him an enemy of the author, but emphasized how large a contribution good acting made to the success of such pieces.

5 A Strange History

First performed at the Lyceum on 29 March 1853 and printed in *Lacy*, volume ten. This play was a joint adaptation by 'Slingsby Lawrence' and Charles Mathews of a French play, *Marianne,* by Auguste Anicet-Bourgeois and Michel Masson, first produced at the Théâtre de l'Ambigu-Comique on 29 September 1850 and printed in *Le Théâtre Contemporain Illustré* (Paris, 1853) 16e serie.

'Vivian' reviewed the piece in the columns of the *Leader* on April 2:

> There are materials in abundance, but there is not a good drama in *A Strange History*; and I seize this opportunity of giving Slingsby Lawrence a bit of my mind (he won't take it; authors never do; the "envy of critics!") as regards construction. (I say nothing of his *collaborateur* Charles Mathews; *que diable*! if I make him angry, he may print a broadside against me!) In dramatic art because it is dramatic and sets forth a story in action – there should be not only visible progress in the story, but that progress should *culminate* and, as quickly as possible....Now an audience never should get impatient. Arrive at your climax, or series of incidents leading to the climax, as quickly as you can, effectively. Now this, O Slingsby! – this, O angry Lawrence! – you have not done in *A Strange History*; and hence failure.

The critic in the *Times* of March 29 was less severe to the piece than the author, but the thing that took his eye was the scenic effects. During one scene the appearance of 'real water' so took the audience by surprise that they applauded loud and long. 'Mr. Beverley appeared', remarked the *Times* reviewer, 'and walked across the stage'. The notice in *The Critic* on April 1, while praising the skill of Mr Beverley, had this comment to make on the entertainment offered at the Lyceum:

> Its stage is degenerating into a picture-gallery, and its drama reminds one of a faded coquette, who paints her face with all the more consummate art, the sillier and more fantastical she becomes.

The piece survived only eleven performances, proving, as the critic in the *Spectator*, April 2, commented, to have been dull as well as strange.

6 The Lawyers

First presented at the Lyceum on 19 May 1853 and printed in *Lacy*, volume eleven. This proved to be as telling and lively as the previous piece had been strange and dull. It was adapted from the French play *Les Avocats* by P.F.P. Dumanoir and Clairville (L.F. Nicholiae), originally performed at the Théâtre du Gymnase on 9 August 1852 and printed in the *Bibliothèque Dramatique*, tom. XLIV. The critic in the *Times* praised the piece highly and had this to say about adaptations from the French in general and about *The Lawyers* in particular:

> In many adaptations the transfer from Paris to London is merely nominal, and M. Dubois, when he becomes Mr Wood, is as much a Frenchman in his habits and sentiments as when he originally figured on the Boulevard. But *The Lawyers* is a thoroughly English piece; the dialogue is written with English vigour, and the abuses of the Bar are satirized with a perfect feeling for the professional peculiarities of this country. Although the course of action borders on caricature, nothing can be more life-like than the deportment of the barristers as they lounge through the hall and utter frequent pleasantries on their engagements at the courts. And it is not the colouring alone that is original. The adapter has altered the plot of the Gymnase piece in several essential particulars, as will be seen at once by all who have witnessed the English version, when we state that the character who is so well acted by Mrs. Mathews, and is so important to the general effect, has no existence in the French original.

The reviewer in the *Spectator*, May 21, went so far as to say that such pieces as *The Lawyers* 'are doing more real service to the drama, and are presenting us with better pictures even of English life, than a host of "original" writers, who show their nationality by incoherence and absence of constructive art'.

7 Wanted a She-Wolf

First produced at the Lyceum 23 March 1854. The piece was not printed, but the manuscript is to be found among the plays from the Lord Chamberlain's Office (Vol. 190, play No. 17) now housed in the

British Museum. It was adapted from a piece by Alexandre Dumas entitled *Romulus* which was first produced at the Théâtre Français on 13 January 1854. The English version was not a success and was withdrawn after seven performances. 'Vivian' had this to say about the piece when he reviewed it in the columns of the *Leader*, March 25:

> *Wanted a She-Wolf* turned out to be one of the latest Parisian novelties – *Romulus*, a charming piece by Alexander Dumas and Regnier, out of a novel by Auguste Lafontaine, and done in English by some admirable Unknown omne ignotum pro mirifico! – so that you see four men with immortal souls have been employed on one act; parturiunt *mentes* nascitur ridicula scena! The piece so produced is, as I said, a charming piece – a little cabinet picture, representing two philosophers in the serenity of their studies, disturbed by the apparition of that phenomenon which may interest but must not disturb philosophers – a baby. To whom does this "specimen of mottled humanity in long clothes" belong? And "how gat it there?" Questions which perplex philosophy and agitate the piece. The child is adopted, and, because a foundling is christened *Romulus*. No sooner is that historical name bestowed on it, than Professor Placidus feels the historic necessity for a she-wolf to suckle it. Si nous avions une louve!

'Vivian' complained that the stupid British public did not see the joke. He praised the players, but commented with a not disinterested irony that the 'discerning public found very mediocre amusement in it'.

8 Give A Dog A Bad Name

First performed at the Lyceum on 18 April 1854 and printed in *Lacy*, volume twenty-four. It was adapted by 'Frank Churchill' from a French 'proverb in one act' entitled *Quand On Veut Tuer Son Chien* by T. Barrière and J. Lorin, originally performed at the Théâtre de Vaudeville on 30 April 1853 and printed in the *Bibliothèque Dramatique*, tom. LI. Charles Mathews records thirty performances during the season 1853–4, the playbills giving the piece a run of twenty-seven performances.

The critics gave the piece a mixed reception finding the situation of a bachelor mischievously prowling about a domestic hearth and exploiting the indifference of a husband to his faithful wife a bit too French for their tastes. It is interesting that the printed version ends with a fittingly moral sentiment from the errant bachelor which was not part of the manuscript version.

9 Sunshine Through The Clouds

First performed at the Lyceum on 15 June 1854 and printed in *Lacy*, volume fifteen. It was adapted from the French *La Joie Fait Peur* by Madame Émile de Girardin, originally performed at the Théâtre Français on 25 February 1854 and printed the same year. The English version was very successful. It played twenty times in its first season, but 'Slingsby Lawrence' did not appear on the playbill until the eleventh performance. Madame Vestris was highly praised for her portrayal of the part of Mrs Cleveland. George Eliot was moved by the performance which she described in a letter to Mrs Charles Bray dated 28 June 1854:

> I went to the Lyceum last night to see "Sunshine Through the Clouds" – a wonderfully original and beautiful piece by Madame de Girardin, which makes one cry rather too much for pleasure. Vestris acts finely the bereaved mother through all the gradations of doubt and hope to the actual recovery of her lost son. [5]

10 A Cozy Couple

First performed at the Lyceum on 15 March 1855 and printed in *Lacy*, volume twenty-four. The piece was adapted from *Le Village* by Octave Feuillet which did not appear at the Théâtre Français until 2 June 1856, but which had been published in 1854. The critics praised it as an original piece, the reviewer in the *Times* affirming that it 'is not, we believe, taken from the French'. The play painted the advantages of the domestic bliss of a cozy couple over the attractions of world-wide travel enjoyed by a bachelor friend. The charm of the piece lay in its portrayal with attention to detail and individual effects, of the couple and of the old friend. The critics were misled by its very un-French sentiments on the virtues of domestic life into assuming the piece original. But the play betrayed its French origins by its use of a relatively simple situation made theatrically effective by attention to naturalistic details in characterization.

11 Buckstone's Adventures with a Polish Princess

First performed at the Haymarket Theatre 29 June 1855 and printed in *Lacy*, volume twenty-two. It was simply a vehicle for Buckstone, the adventure being in effect a dream and the jokes broad. It was perhaps originally intended for another actor, as George Eliot mentions in her Journal on 7 December 1854 after having read a piece entitled *Robson's Adventures with a Russian Princess.*

12 Stay at Home

First performed at the Olympic Theatre on 11 February 1856.

It was not printed, but the manuscript is among the Lord Chamberlain's collection in the British Museum (Vol. 202, play No. 22) where it appears under the title *The Married Flirt or, a Conjugal Lesson.* The original was a French play called *Un Mari qui se Dérange* by Pierre Étienne Pistre and Eugène P. Basté, written under the pseudonyms Eugène Cormon and Eugène Grange, and originally performed at the Théâtre du Gymnase on 25 March 1846.

Two years before Lewes's version appeared, an adaptation by Palgrave Simpson and Charles Wray was performed at the Haymarket on 11 February 1854. 'Vivian' reviewed this adaptation, entitled *Ranelagh,* in the *Leader,* 18 February 1854. He was critical of the failure of the authors to exploit the possibilities of the original. He commented:

> The piece is amusing; but it might have been made more amusing, and more permanently so, had the grasp of realities been vigorous, and a picture of life been presented in lieu of this mere stage intrigue which we have all seen a hundred times.

Lewes attempted to inject vigorous realities into his version by a skilful transfer of the situation into contemporary London life. The critics were dubious about the propriety of a plot which involved a husband's boredom with home life and his intrigue with a lady writer, but the adaptor was praised for making the surface of verbal illusion thoroughly English.

13 Thieves! Thieves!

First produced at the Olympic Theatre on 12 March 1857. The piece was not printed, but the manuscript in the Lord Chamberlain's collection bears the name 'G.H. Lewes' on the title page. It is a one-act filler which received no comment from the critics and merited none.

14 Captain Bland

More interesting is this three-act play which Lewes started work on some time in September or October 1855. The details of Lewes's negotiations with Alfred Wigan to stage the play in London are to be found in his Journal, Number XI (1859–66), which is in the Yale University Library. Wigan actually paid Lewes £100, £50 in December 1860 and £50 in May 1861, but did not put the play on. Lewes complained of the bother the piece had caused him with its numerous revisions and rejections. The play was finally performed, not in London, but in New York. It received its premiere at Wallack's

Theatre on 30 May 1864. The play was not printed, but the manuscript is in the Theatre Collection of the New York Public Library. It ran for five performances only. Edgar W. Hirshberg gives a full account of the play and its New York reception in his article entitled '*Captain Bland* on the New York Stage', which appeared in the *Bulletin of the New York Public Library* for August 1953 [6].

Pieces Unacted and Unpublished

Among the rich collection of Lewes's papers at the Yale University Library, handsomely housed at the Beineke, are a number of dramatic pieces and rough drafts which were neither performed nor published. Among them is a three-act comedy entitled *Pretension, or The School for Parvenus.* This particular manuscript is a fair copy dated November 1843. However, among the Mathews Family papers at Princeton University Library [7], are four letters written by Lewes to Charles James Mathews trying to interest him in a 'new' comedy. On the evidence of the dramatis personae listed and plot-outline described in these letters, the comedy in question was this *Pretension.* One interesting fact arises from this correspondence. In a letter dated 16 October 1841 Lewes recounts his frustrations at being an unacted dramatist. He suggested to Mathews that they become collaborators – Mathews supplying the theatrical connections to expedite production of Lewes's pieces, profits to be shared equally. This suggestion eventually became a reality in 1850 after Charles Mathews and Madame Vestris had taken over the management of the Lyceum.

Other items among Lewes's papers include a 'Philosophical Farce' entitled *Drat That Dick,* and another one-act piece entitled *The Fox Who Got The Grapes.* This latter effort Lewes turned into a short story for *Blackwood's* called *'Mrs Beauchamp's Vengeance',* which appeared in the May issue, 1861. Lewes outlined other pieces, among them *Marguerite,* a five-act drama with a scene in a madhouse, *The Miser's Niece,* a comedy, and a play called *The Fool's Tragedy,* which was sent to Charles Dillon. He also sketched an outline of a five-act play entitled *Savollo* for George Eliot to complete. In his Journal for 8 February 1864 he recounted how he came to consider this scheme:

> In the evening we went to the Adelphi, having a private box sent to us, to see Miss Bateman in *Leah.* While wondering at the badness of the piece and the success it has with the playgoing public, I thought of writing one for Helen Faucit and amused myself with sketching a plot. The idea laid hold of me, and during a sleepless night, I made out the skeleton of the whole five acts. In the morning I suggested to Polly that *she* should do the piece. She rather

liked the suggestion, and when I had written out the barest possible outline of my plot, I read it to her. [8]

Nothing, however, came of the project. The outline up to the beginning of the third act is extant and has been published by Gordon Haight [9]. A few months before his death in 1878, Lewes also drew up a scenario and a list of characters for a stage version of *Daniel Deronda* [10].

As the purpose of this paper is to offer a checklist, with brief comments, of Lewes's work as a playwright, no attempt has been made to discuss and to evaluate these pieces. It seemed pointless to recount in detail the plots, situations, characterization and dialogue of plays which were written primarily to feed the appetite of the Victorian commercial theatre. I have compared the French originals with Lewes's adaptations and some interesting textual material can be found on the techniques of adaptation: the alteration in character and situation, the application of local colour with topical and topographical references, the changes in idiomatic speech, the British sense of humour and the British sense of morality. But for a more complete picture of how these adaptations were put together for performance this textual material must be supplemented by more information than is now readily available on the relevant theatrical conditions of the time.

Lewes had no illusions about his stature as a playwright. With characteristic flippancy masking his characteristic awareness, he confided to readers of the *Leader*, 29 May 1852, that he was thinking of adapting a play from the French. He exclaimed:

Ah! if I had but the talent requisite for the stage, what a piece I could write; unfortunately I only know what ought to be, and don't know how to do it. Que voulez-vous? One cannot make silk purses out of flannel waistcoats, and a dramatist must be *born* a dramatist. I resign myself.

Nevertheless, Lewes's flannel waistcoat provided material for some of the most successful adaptations presented on the mid-Victorian stage.

Notes

[1[*The George Eliot Letters*, ed. Gordon S. Haight (New Haven, 1954–5), Appendix to Vol. VII.

[2] *Life of Charles James Mathews*, ed. Charles Dickens (1879), contains an appendix to Vol. II which lists plays and performances with which Mathews was connected.

[3] *George Eliot Letters*, Vol. II, 18.

[4] Lewes discussed the novels of Jane Austen in an article called 'The

Lady Novelists' which appeared in the *Westminster Review*, July 1852.

[5] *George Eliot Letters*, Vol. II, 162.

[6] Professor Hirshberg wrote an unpublished Ph.D. thesis on Lewes's dramatic criticism, Yale 1953. I acknowledge my indebtedness to Professor Hirshberg, whose thesis provided some useful corroboration of my own researches.

[7] I wish to thank Princeton University Library for providing me with photostat copies of these letters.

[8] *George Eliot Letters*, Vol. IV, 132.

[9] *Ibid.*, Vol. IV, 132–3.

[10] *Ibid.*, Vol. VII, 13.

In addition to the pieces listed, Lewes recorded payment of £20 on 'account of the Comedy *A Certain Age*' in his Receipt Book for August 1851. The manuscript of a play with this title is among the plays from the Lord Chamberlain's Office now in the British Museum (Add. MSS 43035 ff. 132–74), but I have found no record of the play's performance.

9 JOSEPH W. DONOHUE, Jr.

The First Production of *The Importance of being Earnest:* A Proposal for a Reconstructive Study

On the evening of 14 February 1895 – Saint Valentine's Day, appropriately enough – a glittering and highly expectant audience assembled at George Alexander's fashionable St James's Theatre in King Street, having braved the snow and bitter cold of one of London's record frosts, to witness the first performance of Oscar Wilde's new play *The Importance of being Earnest,* subtitled, as their programmes informed them, 'A Trivial Comedy for Serious People'. It was, as the phrase goes, an auspicious beginning. Despite the misfortunes of the author, who within a few months was tried for immoral conduct and sentenced to two years in prison and who within five years died abroad in obscure exile, the play has become one of the most frequently performed pieces in the modern repertoire, internationally known and admired, difficult to do to perfection but almost as difficult to ruin. Alongside cordial reception by directors, players, and audiences, attention has been consistently paid by generations of critics, not only reviewers of first nights but writers, academic or otherwise, concerned with dramatic literature. On the stage and in the study (to adopt a familiar duality) *The Importance of being Earnest* has proved, in sum, a continuing success.

As such, it has intrigued still another class of appraiser, whose interests comprehend those just mentioned but whose approach, strongly retrospective, places him in a special category. He is, of course, the theatrical historian, and his profession is centuries old. But he has recently been attracting notice because of his conviction, astounding to some, that the theatrical performances of times gone by not only merit serious and sustained inspection but are in fact susceptible of it.

Sympathetic as he is to sentiments lamenting vanished greatness, such as Sheridan voiced in his celebrated *Verses To the Memory of Garrick* –

> Feeble Tradition is His Memory's Guard;
> By whose faint Breath his Merits must abide,
> Unvouch'd by Proof – to Substance unallied! –

the historian of the theatre is not to be put off by any suggestion that he is engaged in the pursuit of what has vanished into thin air. He is, surely, careful to distinguish his activities in manner and scope from those of certain predecessors who, he has been brought up to think, merely revel in nostalgia, like Dickensian ancients over a steaming bowl of punch. Yet he realizes too that the experience, subjective though it is, embodied in the writings of early memorialists and other writers whose historical methods he may regard with suspicion is something he must seek out, identify, and finally come to understand. The responses of his own contemporary audiences and readers may fall fairly easily within comprehension even as they are made, but his concern with the past requires the exercise of a special faculty, historical imagination, for which he is supposed to be known and on which he must stake his claim to attention.

The claim is undoubtedly a familiar one. But, let me suggest, opportunity exists to substantiate it more fully. I am presently involved in finding a way of extending the compass of historical imagination in dealing with theatrical events of the past – in finding a way of viewing within a wider context facts and records of the kind assembled by, say, Charles Shattuck in his presentation of Macready's *King John* or Alan Downer's of Kean's *Richard the Third* [1]. It is highly important, of course, to learn as nearly as possible just what took place, visually and aurally, on the stage itself. But it seems obvious that, unless we are able to understand the impact of image and sound on the audience – unless we are able to reconstruct not only performance itself but the cultural ambience in which it was received – we do not really comprehend what Macready or Kean and his compatriots were doing on that night and in that place.

My purpose here is to suggest the kind of study that can possibly be made, given a large archive of materials or even, as in the case of Wilde's play, almost an embarrassment of riches. I should like to set before you a proposal for a reconstructive study of *The Importance of being Earnest*, a work whose own wide appeal is enhanced by its appearance at a particularly interesting period of English cultural life, the nineties, and was in fact ineluctably a product of that 'decadent' age and its flourishing theatre: a great age of audiences and, so it has been maintained, an age of dramatic renaissance as well. In making this proposal it seems best to posit first of all a format, or framework, within which reconstruction can take place, and then to proceed by way of illustration and example. What follows is designed to do two things: to indicate something of the nature and variety of materials pertaining to the subject of Wilde's play, and to suggest (partly by implication) some general ideas about the possibilities of theatrical reconstruction itself.

The basic idea for the format is the familiar one of text preceded by introduction. The aim, however, is not simply to provide the performance text, important as that is, but to surround each page of text with as much recreative and illustrative documentation as can be retrieved and assembled. Without dwelling on the technical aspects of layout, the format can best be described as a facing-page presentation: on the recto, the text, below it textual notes and variant readings as in conventional scholarly editions of plays, and in the right margin schematic drawings, inferred from the stage directions, to indicate the positions and movements of the actors; on the facing verso page, in an arrangement suggesting variety but avoiding clutter, there will appear explanatory notes and, more frequently, verbal glosses, together with numerous photographs, many of them action shots of the first production itself, as well as drawings and sketches from contemporary periodicals. It will be obvious that the attempt is to give the reader materials enabling him to build in his own mind a unified impression of performance and at the same time to gauge the mentality of the audience that first witnessed it.

It will be obvious also that, as a result of this technique of presentation, much that might be thought of as material for the introduction will instead be placed piecemeal in the text. But there will still be much to impart to a reader about to undertake what will surely be demanding and concentrated study. Since the central exhibit, so to speak, is the text of performance, there will be need to explain its nature and the process by which it has been established, as well as the relevance of other texts and the composition of the play itself. Then should come a discussion of the production, including an illustrated description of the St James's Theatre, its manager George Alexander, and the reputation he built for certain kinds of plays and standards of performance, followed in turn by biographies of the cast, information about scenes and costumes, and perhaps other pertinent materials which do not adapt themselves well enough to the direct illumination of the text. Here it is hoped to include, with reference to one or two pages and their illustrative materials, a specimen of the sort of imaginative reconstruction that the reader is invited to make for himself throughout. Finally, a section of the introduction will deal with the reviews of the first night. Here, a discussion of specific critical points, including Wilde's unacknowledged but obvious debt to the plays of W.S. Gilbert, will serve to raise some larger and more general issues.

This, then, is the general proposal for a reconstructive presentation of the play in performance. It is appropriate now to proceed to some examples of this presentation. A simple instance is a reference that occurs fairly early in Act I. Algy has discovered that Ernest's real name is Jack, but he gleefully taxes him with the pretence by producing one of his friend's calling cards and reading it off: 'Mr. Ernest Worthing, B. 4, The Albany.' Albany, it is well known, is a London residence traditionally reserved for bachelors or at least for men living alone. Built by Henry Holland, the architect of Sheridan's Drury Lane, in 1802–3 as an addition to the renovated Melbourne House, fronting on Piccadilly next to Burlington House and the Royal Academy, the structure stretched north to Burlington Gardens, providing two ranges of chambers, lettered from A to L, on either side of a covered walk. There is a photograph that conveys the atmosphere of almost cloistral exclusiveness that reigned here and evidently attracted a number of famous or well-to-do men over the course of the nineteenth century, including Byron, 'Monk' Lewis, Bulwer, Gladstone, Macaulay, and Aubrey Tanqueray. But the question is, of course, why does this young man of duplicitous reputation, who is Ernest in town and Jack in the country, live in Albany? The answer fortunately may be inferred from several sources which, along with the photograph, can be presented by means of quotation and summary on the page facing the reference in the text.

From the beginning, the architectural plan of Albany provided a seclusion that, Macaulay thought, afforded 'a college life at the West End of London' [2]. There was also a feeling that, at least later in the century, Albany's location marked a class boundary, as an anecdote of Wilde suggests. Asked directions to Curzon Street, he replied, 'I am pleased...that I should be asked to direct you to so eminently desirable an address. Personally, I am unacquainted with any part of London east of Albany' [3] – an untruth, as would quickly appear in a discussion of the restaurants mentioned in texts of the play; but the point remains. Still, one wonders if this is the appropriate place for a character who, according to his staid, conservative elder brother, Cecily's 'Uncle Jack', is a reckless squanderer and loose liver who frequents such places of scarlet iniquity as Paris and who never pays his restaurant bills. There is no appropriateness, however. In giving Ernest a suite in Albany (the more proper reference drops the 'the', perhaps to avoid confusion with a public house) Wilde is exploiting what he knows he can count on: the St James's audience and its keen knowledge of reputations, personal and otherwise, current in late 1894 and early 1895. As the authors of the *Survey of London* explain, 'In the late nineteenth century Albany was in less favour as a place of residence than before or since, and the proprietors of chambers were having difficulty in disposing of them.... In about 1893 some fifteen sets were empty and were used as "luggage and lumber rooms". In June 1894 nine proprietors of chambers stated to the Trustees that they were "dissatisfied with the present condition of the property...." ' [4] In this same year John Lane, the publisher, bought the lease of G.1 and established there his publishing house The Bodley Head, then engaged in bringing out the early numbers of *The Yellow Book* [5].

What Wilde has done, then, is to evoke for a knowing audience an unmistakable suggestion of elegance gone to seed, and at the same time of an exclusiveness tinged with a shade of raciness missing from Algernon's more respectable address in Half-Moon Street. One can imagine what Lady Bracknell might have been given to say about *The Yellow Book* and its place of origin, had Wilde been so inclined. John Lane was a perfectly respectable publisher; all the same, when Wilde was arrested in April 1895 he had in his hand a book with a yellow cover. The conclusion leapt to was that it was *The Yellow Book,* clearly a case of guilt by association. The particular suite, B.4, on Ernest's card, has no significance so far as I can discover other than in the likelihood that it was empty at the time. The licensing copy reads 'E. 4', but these chambers became occupied apparently early enough in 1895 for a change in the interests of propriety while rehearsals were still going on. The rehearsal copy, now at Harvard, which postdates the licensing copy, leaves the letter blank, and 'B' has been inserted by hand, to appear as such consistently in the printed editions. This change, by the way, is a small bit of evidence useful in establishing the performance text, which will receive more attention in a moment.

But first, another example, this time of speeches and accompanying business. Knowledge of this point comes from the happy appearance of Max Beerbohm's note on the ending of Act I, written in his copy of the first edition. According to the licensing copy, submitted at the end of January, the act ends in this way, as Algy determines to use his customary disguise for a clandestine journey to the country:

Algy. To-morrow, my dear boy, I am going Bunburying.
Jack. What nonsense.
Algy. It isn't nonsense at all. I will certainly Bunbury to-morrow, if the weather is at all favourable.
Jack. I have never heard such nonsense in my life.
Algy. I love nonsense.

ACT DROP [6]

The first edition, which presents in general a notably different ending, concludes with a variant reading:

Jack. Oh, that's nonsense, Algy. You never talk anything but nonsense.
Algernon. Nobody ever does.
[*Jack looks indignantly at him, and leaves the room. Algernon lights a cigarette, reads his shirt-cuff, and smiles.*]

ACT DROP [7]

In his copy of this edition, after Algernon's final 'Nobody ever does', Max Beerbohm adds, 'And besides, I *love* nonsense!' Sure enough, the rehearsal text gives Algy this speech: 'Nobody ever does. Besides I love nonsense!' Then it continues with the words Algy reads off his shirt cuff, having surreptitiously copied onto it Jack's country address: 'The Manor House, Woolton, Hertfordshire.' This is added in manuscript, as is the stage direction *'Drinking as curtain falls'*. Once again Max bears out the authenticity of the rehearsal text, and at the same time indicates how several small but neatly climactic pieces of business have evolved from the vague ending of the licensing copy. Underneath the line 'And besides, I *love* nonsense!' added in his hand he continues: 'I have a good verbal and visual memory, and I can still hear Allen Aynesworth saying these words, and see him raising his glass of sherry as he said them and as the curtain fell. I don't see why Oscar cut them for the printed version; for they surely are just right.' [8]

Certainly they are 'just right'. But it may be that Wilde had no chance to decide on cutting the words in question. There is presently no way of knowing whether they were included in the copy of the play furnished by George Alexander to Wilde's publisher Leonard Smithers for the edition that Wilde saw through the press himself. In fact complex problems arise in attempting to establish the performance text of this play, problems which will require some pages of introduction to set out in full but which may be briefly discussed now.

This is not the occasion to advance in detail principles applying to the establishment of performance text. But there should be no doubt why such a text ought to be established. A comprehensive study of a production of a given play *must* determine the text of the play as spoken on the stage. It cannot rely merely on the first published edition, whether supervized by the author or not, nor on the author's original composition, whether in a fair or foul state, nor, surely, on whatever text happens to be nearest at hand. This is not to say, however, that no text except that of the promptbook or similar theatrical text such as a licensing copy is of relevance; quite the contrary. In the case of *The Importance of being Earnest,* not only is the prime piece of evidence, the promptbook, unlocated, but the text of a known and well authenticated rehearsal copy differs in some important respects from the licensing copy (which presumably was what the producer was legally bound to see performed) and is in fact understandable only with reference to earlier manuscripts, to the first edition published some four years after the first and only English production up to that date, to the Samuel French acting edition of around 1903, and perhaps even to a German translation published at this same time.

In view of the complexity of the situation it is necessary to state that I take the rehearsal copy to be an adequate reflection of the text actually spoken by the cast of the first performance, but it is also important to point out the differences in this text from the licensing copy, from earlier manuscripts, and from the first and later edition. Moreover, we must sooner or later take cognisance of the fact that strict adherence to the text of the rehearsal copy results in certain awkward variants from what must in fact have been performed, and that this strictness likewise rules out the inclusion (except as notes) of a few of Wilde's most choice speeches which only appeared later, in the first edition. Finally, we must address ourselves to the question of the purpose of establishing whatever text is ultimately decided on. This is a question not only of the words, or even of words and format, but also of the needs of more than one class of readers: general students and specialized scholars, to be sure, but potential directors and performers too. The reconstructive scholar must try to develop the best sense he can of how the past may serve the present – a task, I believe, as pertinent to the lightest and frothiest of farce comedies of the 1890s as it is to the most ponderous of tragedies by Webster, or Shakespeare, or Seneca.

One other explanation is due: this is that opportunity has been lacking to examine all the available textual materials. So far I have collated the texts of the licensing copy, now in the British Museum, the rehearsal copy used by George Alexander and bearing his signature and bookplate, now in the Harvard Theatre Collection, and the first edition, seen through the press by Wilde himself and published in London in February 1899 by Leonard Smithers. What is yet to be done is to examine the original manuscript and several early typescripts of the four-act version and then to assess the relevance of the German translation in four acts published in Leipzig in 1903; of the Samuel French acting edition negotiated for as early as 1900 and published no later than 1903; of texts of the first American production, by Charles Frohman, which took place in New York less than two months after the English production; and of a promptbook, now in the British Theatre Museum, bequeathed by Allan Aynesworth, the first Algernon Moncrieff, and mistakenly designated as the promptbook of the first production. (I began this study in the hope that it was just that; since then it has appeared clearly to be a book for a later production, perhaps the successful revival of the play in 1909, made on a copy of French's acting text. This book is of high interest, nevertheless, since a preliminary analysis shows its text and annotations to be very close to those of the Harvard rehearsal copy.)

Much work remains, then, but it is possible at this juncture to describe the three texts already collated and bearing most closely on the production itself. First, the licensing copy. Dated by the Lord Chamberlain's Office as 'January 30. 1895', it is a typescript of eighty-two pages, in three acts, stamped by 'Miss Dickens's Type Writing Office' on the inside front cover and elsewhere. The title page reads, 'Lady Lancing. A Serious Comedy for Trivial People. By Oscar Wilde.' Giving the play a false title was simply Wilde's habitual means of avoiding the premature publicizing of the real one. The Lord Chamberlain was, however, properly informed, since the label pasted on the typescript reads *'The Importance of being Earnest'*. But the label also reads, 'Comedy (4 acts)', a reflection perhaps of clerical carelessness but more likely of the very recent cutting of the play from four acts to three, a reduction borne out by this typescript. The work of at least four typists, perhaps five, some working in tandem and all of them apparently to a close deadline, it is nevertheless a neatly prepared script with stage directions underlined in red ink. Anyone who has tried to read the crabbed hands of manuscripts in the Lord Chamberlain's Collection will appreciate how vast an improvement a copy like this is. There are numerous textual variants from the first edition, which will come up for discussion shortly, but one of the crucial differences is in the names of two characters: the Lady Bracknell of the first and subsequent editions is here called Lady Brancaster, and Algernon Moncrieff's surname is given as Montford.

In another case of difference, the setting of Act III is indicated to be the same as that of Act II, the garden at the manor house, whereas subsequent texts remove the action of the third act indoors to a morning room. These differences, aside from questions of felicity or variety, are highly important because they afford proof presumptive that the Harvard rehearsal copy is of a later date and hence closer to the elusive ideal state I have been calling the performance text. This second text, also the product of Miss Dickens's efficient typing service, contains seventy-eight pages exclusive of preliminaries, a cast of characters including Lady Bracknell and Algernon Moncrieff, and an inserted indication of the setting for Act III as the morning room of the manor house. And it is an actual rehearsal text, with many diagrams indicating blocking and detailed directions for movement and business. A heavily marked copy, replete with changes in wording and directions, it has two distinct but closely complementary values: it provides extensive evidence of George Alexander's rehearsal habits and production methods, and it comes as close as is presently possible to what the audience actually saw and heard on the evening of 14 February 1895.

The third relevant text, that of the first edition, also a three-act text, was based on a copy provided by George Alexander. What apparently happened is that the publisher, Smithers, obtained a type-written transcript of Alexander's text which he sent to Wilde, then living in France; Wilde corrected it and sent it back to Smithers, who returned proof which Wilde duly read and corrected (the proof sheets are extant), providing the text Smithers published in February of 1899 [9]. The first edition is, then, based in all likelihood on what editors working in an earlier period would call the 'playhouse text'. One might conjecture that the transcript Alexander furnished to Smithers was made from the promptbook, which in turn very likely developed out of the Harvard rehearsal copy. But, however plausible, this is merely guesswork. All that can be said is that the transcript Alexander gave to Smithers may possibly have incorporated further textual changes from the rehearsal text and that Wilde himself may well have introduced still further changes. If this transcript were to turn up, we could fairly say that we have the performance text cornered if not caged.

Collation of these three texts raises some difficult textual questions, which I should like to illustrate. The proof presumptive afforded by the changes in character names and setting of Act III from the licensing copy to the rehearsal copy is corroborated by the many instances in which a reading in the rehearsal text agreeing with the licensing copy is changed (by an unknown hand) to agree with the first edition. Among these are some good examples of Wildean wit:

	licensing copy		*rehearsal copy*
Gwen.	Yes, but men often propose for practice. I know my brother Gerald does. He tells me so.	*Gwen.*	Yes, but men often propose for practice. I know my All my girl friends brother Gerald does. He tells me so.
Jack.	Miss Cardew is the grand-daughter of the late Mr. Thomas Cardew of 149, Belgrave Square, S.W. – Gervase Park, Dorking, Surrey; and the Glen, Fifeshire, N.B.	*Jack.*	Miss Cardew is the grand-daughter of the late Mr. Thomas Cardew of 149, Belgrave Square, S.W.; Gervase Park, Dorking, Sporran Surrey; and the Glen, Fifeshire, N.B.

Similar corroboration of the rehearsal text occurs in the many instances in which it already agrees with the first edition:

	licensing copy		*rehearsal copy / first edition*
Lady B.	Lady Bloxham? I don't know her. What number in Belgrave Square?	*Lady B.*	Lady Bloxham? I don't know her.
		Jack.	Oh, she goes about very little. She's a lady considerably advanced in years.
		Lady B.	Ah, now-a-days that is no guarantee of respectability of character. What number in Belgrave Square?

But, for all these instances suggestive of Wilde's salutary presence in rehearsal, there are other types of variants that perplex rather than clarify or amuse. Many instances occur in which the licensing and rehearsal copies agree, and in so doing differ from the first edition. Still more puzzling are cases in which the rehearsal copy differs from a reading held in common by the licensing copy and the first edition, or in which the rehearsal copy is changed, by the hand of the unknown annotator, from a reading agreeing with the first edition to one coinciding with the licensing copy. As if these were not enough to tax any editor's patience and understanding, there are quite a few instances where each text presents a reading at variance with the others. For example, when in Act III Jack decides that baptism will no longer be necessary, Canon Chasuble remarks:

licensing copy

I am grieved to hear such sentiments from you, Mr. Worthing. However, where adults are concerned, compulsory christening, except in the case of savage tribes, is distinctly uncanonical, so I shall return to the church at once.

rehearsal copy

I am grieved to hear such sentiments from you, Mr. Worthing. I shall return to the Church at once.

first edition

I am grieved to hear such sentiments from you, Mr. Worthing. They savour of the heretical views of the Anabaptists, views that I have completely refuted in four of my unpublished sermons. However, as your present mood seems to be one peculiarly secular, I will return to the church at once.

The problem, then, to recapitulate, is that, while the rehearsal text may be taken clearly as the closest we can presently come to performance, it has the disadvantage of varying in numerous important or not so important but still characteristic and interesting instances from the published version which quickly became and has remained the 'standard' text enjoyed by generations of playgoers and readers. But in fact both the rehearsal copy and the published text have the disadvantage of being a whole act shorter, and so at least quantitatively twenty-five per cent less amusing, than the original four-act version, which includes a very funny sequence in which Algernon, Bunburying as 'Ernest', is arrested for debt, having run up a bill at the Savoy Restaurant of £762.14s.2d. This version was published in transcription by the New York Public Library in 1956. But we know that Wilde himself revised it at least twice before George Alexander required him to reduce its length [10]. In 1957 the playwright's son, Vyvyan Holland, made an attempt to recapture this 'final' revised four-act version – the text of which is now missing – by reconstructing it from the German translation of four acts published in Leipzig in 1903 which could have been made only from a late four-act version. In doing so he consulted the original manuscript, the subsequent typescripts of the four-act version still fragmentarily available, and the three-act version of 1899, drawing on Wilde's own words wherever possible. The result is a very interesting but surely anomalous piece, a pastiche of virtually all the best ideas for dialogue for the play that Wilde ever put down on paper. It makes good reading, but it is as far from the concrete actuality of dramatic performance as one can presumably get. It calls for mention here simply to emphasize by contrast how important it is to establish this concreteness as solidly as possible. To do so, I am presently convinced, one must employ the Harvard rehearsal text, in the absence of the promptbook itself. But simply to print this text, as if with no regard either for what Wilde wrote earlier before circumstances required a truncated version or for what Wilde, having bowed to inevitability, himself saw through the press almost four years after the production – to print this text alone is to don theatrical blinders, proclaiming one's channel vision before an already assembled audience not only of directors and players but of students of dramatic art and general readers, all of whom have demonstrated their delight in this play over the course of three-quarters of a century and whose needs must by right be consulted. In view of this long and happy association, the scholar seeking to reconstruct performance will deserve nothing short of remaindering if he does not pay adequate attention to the implications of what he has set out to do.

Naturally one hopes that the format as already explained will indeed serve the interests not only of professional scholars, both theatrical and bibliographical, but of stage directors who may wish to emulate the approach or the production standards of a theatre of excellent repute or who simply need a source of good ideas for their own production of the play. Actors and actresses too may benefit from studying the particularities of gesture and business and overall style that it has fortunately been possible to recapture. But, aside from serving the needs of specialized persons, a reconstructive study can also appeal to the general student of plays and allied culture. With a view towards informing readers of this sort, I should like to attempt a partial description of the St James's theatre as a setting for the production of plays, a description that might appropriately find a place in the introduction to the proposed reconstruction.

It may seem that there is nothing new to be said about the St James's. Certainly, A.E.W. Mason's book *Sir George Alexander & The St. James' Theatre* (1935) is the best work on the subject and a fine example of its kind, dealing with the unusually successful career in theatrical management followed by Alexander for over a quarter of a century. Nevertheless it appears worthwhile to reopen discussion in order to explore the relationship of this theatre to its audience. As suggested earlier, one of the most important purposes of making a reconstructive study is to see the impact of performance on the audience that witnessed it. When we realize, for instance, that the line giving Thomas Cardew's third address as the Sporran, Fifeshire was delivered to a first-night audience that among many notables may well have included the Duke and Duchess of Fife [11], we must acknowledge that it is not enough simply to make convenient generalizations about an audience full of *Society*. To avoid mere vagueness we must go back to contemporary or near-contemporary accounts of what it was like to be a playgoer or an actor, or otherwise involved in theatrical enterprise, at the St James's in the 1890s.

One of the most informative accounts, of high interest because of its author's unique position, was written by George Alexander's wife Florence in a note appended to Mason's book:

> First nights at the St. James' Theatre were great events.... I sat in my box sick with anxiety, and between the acts I used to put on an apron and go behind the scenes to place all the little things on the stage myself until the men got used to it. I arranged the flowers; in those days we had so much detail, and I loved to make things look real. I ordered the gowns to suit the decorations of the scene so that nothing clashed or was ugly....
>
> Our first nights at the St. James' Theatre were like brilliant parties. Everybody knew everybody, everybody put on their best clothes, everybody wished us success. When I entered my box on a first night I always had a reception from the gallery. I do not know why, but I did. They were always so pleased and so kind to me. [12]

The account seems superficial, perhaps somewhat vague, and conveys sentiments only too familiar in reminiscences of the stage. But in fact there are several ideas, or assumptions, here to which we would do well to pay attention. The most obvious and important is the feeling of extensive rapport conveyed. Even the illusion of reality on the stage is one carefully arranged to suit a particular audience's sense of decorative unity and social propriety. This totality is achieved through the efforts of someone who, in the course of the evening, appears, prominent and influential, both before and behind the curtain. Social position and professional activity are felt to alternate naturally, and as easily as the donning of an apron. Florence Alexander's account is, in effect, a description of symbolic intercourse between an expectant audience and a troupe at work behind the footlights. Moreover, the ambience in which the performance occurs includes an assumption that those in control of the enterprise hold a position of social equality or, in some cases, superiority to those who have come to see it brought forward. It is important to understand that the sense in which the 'real' is achieved in the stage setting is inseparable from the audience's sense of being catered to by a group of persons whom they know professionally and socially, a group which in turn bases its claim to success on an intimate knowledge of what will please this audience. It may appear inaccurate to imply that such parts of the audience as pit and gallery know George and Florence Alexander and their compeers socially; but they do, by virtue of the fact that the auditorium of the theatre provides the ground where social intercourse of this sort can take place. The applause from the gallery accorded Florence Alexander when she entered her box on a first night epitomizes this relationship of players and production staff to audience. Only by developing the keenest sense we can of the totality of the enterprise, social as well as artistic, may we appreciate that relationship of performance to audience and so avoid the impoverished understanding of Wilde's play (or any other play) that is otherwise likely to remain.

An appreciation of this kind is what the reader of the proposed reconstructive study may achieve when, for example, he reaches the scene in Act II in which Jack, having decided that the time is ripe to kill off his fictitious younger brother Ernest, arrives in the garden of his country house dressed in the depths of mourning, complete to the last detail of a black-bordered handkerchief (black-tipped cigarettes having been rejected in rehearsal as too *outré*). The stage direction in the Harvard rehearsal copy reads: '(ENTER JACK from back of garden R. He goes C. He is dressed entirely in black.)' This is followed by a hand-written insertion: 'Dr. C. & Miss P. both turn come down stage then towards C. See Jack for first time.' The direction in the first edition adds some useful detail: '[*Enter Jack slowly from the back of the garden. He is dressed in the deepest mourning, with crape hat-band and black gloves.*]' Numerous reviews of opening night praise this entrance as the funniest and most well-realized moment of the performance, but one critic went to the trouble of describing how the effect took place. For this we have to thank William Archer, who wrote:

> Monsieur Sarcey himself (if Mr. Wilde will forgive my saying so) would "chortle in his joy" over John Worthing's entrance in deep mourning even down to his cane to announce the death of his brother Ernest, when we know that Ernest in the flesh – a false but undeniable Ernest – is at that moment in the house making love to Cecily. The audience does not instantly awaken to the meaning of his inky suit, but even as he marches solemnly down the stage, and before a word is spoken, you can feel the idea kindling from row to row, until a "sudden glory" of laughter fills the theatre. [13]

This gradual dawning of comic understanding (interestingly described by Archer in Hobbesean terms) says a good deal about the skill of the playwright, but we may also notice that Alexander, with similar skill, has blocked a double down-stage movement of Miss Prism and Canon Chasuble along with that of his own character, Jack Worthing, in such a way that the delayed reaction from the audience is enacted on the stage as well: an engaging example of the rapport evidently possible to achieve in this theatre.

There is in fact a rich communicativeness characteristic of Alexander's St James's that repays intensive study. Although habitual playgoers frequented many London theatres, not just the St James's, there was such a thing as a St James audience, whose special qualities were, understandably enough, most prominently displayed on first nights. That seasoned playgoer H.G. Hibbert remarked in his memoirs that 'the old hand could mostly identify the house if he glanced at the stalls through a hole in an unknown curtain.' [14] What he might see through a hole in the St James's, especially after the reception accorded *The Second Mrs Tanqueray* in 1893 had created a singular reputation for Alexander's prosperous theatre, was an audience of the sort that gathered for the first night of Henry Arthur Jones's comedy *The Masqueraders* in April 1894: '...the most brilliant audience of the season, the Princes and Princesses, the Chancellors and ex-Chancellors, the innumerable notables in every walk of life who crowded Mr. Alexander's fashionable playhouse.' [15] Among them would also number, of course, the dramatic critics, to the tune of from seventy to one hundred seats – an astonishing figure even when it is understood that many of these were so-called second seats, grudgingly if not irately issued to regular reviewers who, Hibbert explains, 'have a subsidiary job – a daily and perhaps also a weekly paper, an evening paper and perhaps also a provincial paper.' Who fills the second seat? 'The critic's wife, or his cousin, or his confidential secretary, or even an obliging tradesman', with the result that the theatre manager is placed in the position of having to entertain, as Hibbert puts it, 'a guest whom he did not select' (pp. 129–30). The phrase recalls Florence Alexander's description of a first night as a brilliant party, although ironically enough it was the more brilliant who were the paying guests, unless they had the good fortune of a complimentary seat from manager or author.

'Papering the house' is a practice as well known as it is ancient, but the situation governing a fashionable first night was not quite the same thing as the recruitment of an audience or the infiltration of a claque. In addition to critics, second-seaters, personal friends, and other special persons, there were the regulars who considered that they could count on a St James's play to be a 'St James's Play'. Despite the inevitable uncertainties of management, Alexander's reputation rose so high that, as his wife later boasted, 'he could always run a play for a month because he had a large clientele who never missed a play that he did, and that kept him going until his new play was ready.' [16] As likely as not, these were frequenters not only of stalls and dress circle but of pit and gallery. In her memoirs Julia Neilson recalled Fred Terry's regard for the pit as 'the backbone of the theatre' populated by a group of serious and knowledgeable persons whose innumerable half-crowns had brought them in return an unparalleled wisdom of judgment that could spell success, or its opposite. 'It is the people in the pit and gallery', she explained, 'who have paid their hard-earned money, and often waited for hours outside to see the performance, that really tell you the truth'. [17] These were the people who told a very unpleasant truth to Henry James on the evening of 5 January 1895, when Alexander brought out James's last attempt to write for the stage, *Guy Domville.* But, true to what Florence Alexander later remembered, Alexander did not withdraw this demonstrable failure until exactly one month later [18], only nine days before *The Importance of being Earnest* was to make its appearance.

Keeping in mind the legendary imperiousness of that part of the audience occupying less expensive seats, one senses a peculiar force in Florence Alexander's comment on the favourable reception regularly given her by the gallery. Nevertheless her relationship was to the audience as a whole, not only to its more vociferous elements, and clearly her self-imposed task was to set standards that the St James's audience could, depending on its social position, either admire from a distance or actively attempt to emulate. She stood, then, as a kind of emblem of a theatre that both led its audience and followed that audience's inclinations, an emblem exhibiting configurations of flairful taste, not to say zestful extravagance, often bordering on the limits of propriety but never exceeding them. Some men booked a seat at the St James's before adding to their wardrobe, so authoritative was George Alexander's command of tasteful new fashion; at the same time Florence Alexander 'was rather "extreme" with clothes on the stage', as she herself explained, 'for in those days people went to see the St. James' plays before ordering a new gown'. [19] On the opening night of *The Importance of being Earnest,* the fashion writer for *The Sketch* caught a glimpse of Mrs Alexander '(who sat well back in her box) in a plain but perfectly cut gown of dark-hued velvet, with diamonds in her hair by way of relief, and a bouquet of pink tulips and lilies of the valley'; she could afford to sit back, having assured herself that Rose Leclercq as Lady Bracknell and Irene Vanbrugh as her daughter Gwendolen Fairfax would appear, as this writer reported, 'the respective personifications of stately and piquant smartness'. [20] It was apparently no exaggeration for this admiring author to claim, in a subsequent article, that 'Mrs. Alexander's name stands very high in the list of the most perfectly dressed women in London, so her clothes are veritable treasure-troves to the seekers after smart things'. [21]

The St James's stood for a great deal more, however, than what was likely to monopolize the pages of a fashion column, however important (and I take it to be important) that aspect of the St James's Theatre is considered. The particular quality of this theatre is easy to over-simplify, as not a few writers have done in attempting to describe a 'St. James's Play'. In an early book, *Modern Men and Mummers,* Wilde's biographer Hesketh Pearson takes on the subject in a cynical, not to say vindictive, mood but nevertheless comes close to home. The passage merits quoting at some length:

> [George Alexander] was the best and most typical product of London Society for twenty-five years before August, 1914. He catered to the tastes and foibles of that Society in its theatre-going just as the manager of the Savoy Hotel catered to the tastes and foibles of that Society in its restaurant-going; and exactly in so far as such drama was more or less important than such tables d'hôte, was the manager of the St James's Theatre more or less important than the manager of the Savoy Hotel. He produced plays that were correctly risky, and they became the talk of a social world that was correctly risky. He seldom deviated one hair's breadth from the safe path of correct riskiness.
>
> For the most part, his theatre mirrored to absolute perfection the people who patronized its stalls. He knew, none better, that the stalls enjoyed the gilded pill of romance about themselves, and that the gallery loved to see the stalls swallow it. No real medicine was possible, for his audiences wouldn't pay to be choked or for the privilege of having a nasty taste in the mouth [*sic*]. The light parts had to be charmingly playful, the serious parts had to be pleasantly sentimental, and the plot had to savour of scandal without being in any way truthfully objectionable. Adultery was invariably touched on and inevitably touched up. Murder, suicide and dipsomania conformed to the limits of the respectable and were made unshockingly dramatic. The working classes were seldom, if ever, introduced. Significant social problems were carefully avoided. It was the drama of the genteel – the Apotheosis of the Butterfly. [22]

One's inclination may be to move to Alexander's defence after an assault of this kind, since it appears that the St James's is being made to stand as a scapegoat for the vices of the same self-satisfied and unreflective culture that Bernard Shaw described as ubiquitous in talking of pre-War Friday-to-Tuesday country manor society in his preface to *Heartbreak House.* But when one looks for examples of more adventurous, even daring plays to throw in the face of Pearson's accusations, the most 'avant-garde' (not really the word) to be found is probably *The Second Mrs Tanqueray,* a drama that admittedly caused a tremendous sensation when first produced but now appears to many readers – as it did then to Shaw, who pilloried it in the *Saturday Review* – an artful dodger of the problem it affects to raise.

Yet both Shaw's and Pearson's judgments, as well as those of uninvolved modern readers, are, however relevant, in a category separate and distinct from the response of audiences. It is all too obvious, but still necessary to reiterate, that plays are written and produced for those who will immediately go to see them. Whatever audiences from the playgoing or reading public subsequently accrue do so largely through happy (or unfortunate) accident. In the present instance, the first production of *The Importance of being Earnest,* written, as Wilde then remarked, 'by a butterfly, for butterflies', [23] Pearson's category of the 'correctly risky' is both appropriate and off the point: appropriate to Wilde's artistic experimentation, because of the high verbal extravagance and dandified attitude toward dramatic structure – deeply dependent on the old fashion of Gilbertian burlesque and at the same time playing games with it and with the fashionable society who recognized its technique; off the point, because Pearson paints in all too broad, black lines social and ethical qualities much more subtle, various, and rich. Important as it is for modern dramatic criticism to describe the nature and merits of the play itself, it is equally important for students of the drama and theatre to reconstruct, in whatever ways are most meaningful to themselves, Wilde's play, or any play, in the context of its original surroundings. Many avenues of interest converge in Wilde's amazingly substantial frivolous farce. One can scarcely hope to follow them all, even when supported by long draughts of a temperance beverage and by the largest and most commodious hand-bag that historical research affords. The proposal I have been making is an incomplete, roughly drawn map of the territory, an attempt to arrange in some kind of suggestive order such signposts of art and life as appear to have survived. It is unfinished, and even in published form will in a sense remain so, because for anything like fullness it requires the presence of an ambitious and imaginative reader willing to try – not to recapture shadows, but to imagine in a vivid and intelligible way what their substance and import may have been.

Notes

[1] Charles H. Shattuck, ed., *William Charles Macready's King John: A facsimile prompt-book* (Urbana, Ill., 1962); Alan S. Downer, ed., *Oxberry's 1822 Edition of King Richard III with the descriptive notes recording Edmund Kean's Performance* (London, 1959).

[2] E. Beresford Chancellor, *Wanderings in Piccadilly, Mayfair and Pall Mall* (London, 1908) 81.

[3] Harry Furniss, *Paradise in Piccadilly: The Story of Albany* (London, 1925) 128.

[4] *Survey of London,* Vol. XXXII: *The Parish of St James Westminster,* Part Two: *North of Piccadilly* (London, 1963) 377.

[5] *Survey of London,* XXXII 377, and Sheila Birkenhead, *Peace in Piccadilly: The Story of Albany* (London, 1958) 213.

[6] 'Lady Lancing. A Serious Comedy for Trivial People. By Oscar Wilde', British Museum Add. MS. 53567(17).

[7] *The Importance Of Being Earnest: A Trivial Comedy For Serious People By The Author Of Lady Windermere's Fan* (London, Leonard Smithers and Co., 1899).

[8] Copy in the possession of Sir Rupert Hart-Davis, quoted by kind permission of Sir Rupert Hart-Davis and Mrs Eva Reichmann.

[9] *The Letters of Oscar Wilde,* ed. Rupert Hart-Davis (New York, 1962) 734, 736, 738, 754, 758, 762–5, 770–1, 777, and 779–80.

[10] *The Importance of Being Earnest: A Trivial Comedy for Serious People In Four Acts as Originally Written by Oscar Wilde,* ed. Sarah Augusta Dickson, 2 vols. (New York, 1956). For information on the history of the revisions see Miss Dickson's Introduction, Vol. I, ix–xxi.

[11] A.E.W. Mason includes them in a list of habitual patrons – *Sir George Alexander & The St James' Theatre* (London, 1935) 133 – and they were in town during January and February of 1895 – *The Lady,* 17 January 1895, p. 63; 24 January 1895, p. 93, and 21 February 1895, p. 213, this last containing a report of the fancy skating costume worn by the Duchess, featuring a 'pouch' front imitative, one infers, of the traditional sporran.

[12] Mason, *Alexander & The St James',* 227–8.

[13] *The World,* 20 February 1895.

[14] H.G. Hibbert, *Fifty Years of a Londoner's Life* (London, 1916) 130.

[15] *The Theatre,* Vol. XXIII (1894) 326.

[16] Mason, *Alexander & The St James',* 231.

[17] *This For Remembrance* (London, 1940) 52.

[18] *The Era,* 9 February 1895, 10.

[19] Mason, *Alexander & The St James',* 233.

[20] *The Sketch,* 20 February 1895, 210.

[21] *The Sketch,* 27 March 1895, 489.

[22] Pearson, *Modern Men and Mummers* (London, 1921) 80–1.

[23] *Letters of Wilde,* ed. Hart-Davis, 382.

10 ARTHUR COLBY SPRAGUE

Dr Hennequin and the Well-Made Play

Alfred Hennequin was born in France in 1846, came to America in 1872 and was for many years an instructor in French at the University of Michigan. Later he had his own school of languages in Boston and died there in 1914. (This much seems clear, though there are discrepancies, some of them curious, in the biographical accounts.) He wrote a number of French–English text-books, which do not concern us, and *The Art of Playwriting: being a practical treatise on the elements of dramatic construction*, published in Boston by Houghton Mifflin in 1890, which does. This work is divided into two parts of about equal length, the first having to do with those parts of the theatre which concern a dramatist, the second with principles of construction and advice on how to write a play. The relationship between the parts is very close. The author of a well made play is expected to have a working knowledge of the stage of his own time and what he writes is conditioned at innumerable points by this knowledge.

The description given of the theatre, its artifices and complexities, has great interest. Dr Hennequin is no reformer. As a rule he accepts what he finds without criticism or humour. He is well informed. He has consulted people like Bronson Howard, 'that prince of gentlemen and first of American dramatists', and the actresses Madame Janauschek and Minnie Maddern Fiske. He defines terms and explains what goes on in 'the twilight region ... beyond the scenes'. His own writing deserves credit for its consistent intelligibility, and he seldom wastes or abuses words. If you are in doubt as to just what 'the tormentors' were, or to what extent they were to be used as exits and entrances, Hennequin will tell you clearly and well.

One reservation must, I suppose, be made. The theatre which he describes is in the first instance American. So far as England is concerned his book was somewhat out of date. Hennequin, one feels, would have been much more at home at the Princess's, Manchester, under Charles Calvert, than at Irving's Lyceum. The English plays most frequently referred to are *Richelieu* and *The Lady of Lyons, London Assurance,* Robertson's *Home* and, a little surprisingly, Gilbert's *Engaged* – and only the latest of these could be called at all recent in 1890. The theatre of which he writes was still 'a monstrous, unwieldy, mysterious instrument of interpretation, rusty with traditions, top-heavy with prejudices, stuffed to bursting with curious, antiquated machinery of which few know, or care to know, the meaning.'

At the beginning we are given a straightforward account in successive chapters of the theatre staff, the stage itself, scenery, stage directions and stage plans. As was only to be expected, there is no mention of the director, but the power ascribed to the stage manager is noteworthy ('A good stage manager has almost as much to do with the success of a play as the actors themselves.') There is the inclusion of that archaic figure The Gas-Man ('The term is still retained, in spite of the fact that electricity has, in many theatres, taken the place of gas as a means of illumination.')

Our interest mounts when we come to the three chapters on 'Different Kinds of Plays' which follow. Tragedy comes first, then 'the romantic *drame*' and soon after melodrama. In the romantic *drame*, theme is 'generally of little importance. The value of personal strength, courage, and manliness is most frequently touched upon .... Rapidity of movement through a series of quickly-culminating climaxes is the most striking characteristic of the plot.' Under style he notes that 'sentiments' are of frequent occurrence.

> A sentiment is a striking thought intended to appeal to the sensibilities of the audience (as the sense of justice, fair play, honor, patriotism, etc.) and carefully worded in language more or less poetical. 'Rags are royal rayment when worn for virtue's sake', is a well-known sentiment from Bartley Campbell's *White Slave.* In this country a good sentiment rarely fails to win a round of applause, but in the French theatres (excepting those of a 'popular' character) such bits of declamation frequently call out hisses.

After that, one waits with some eagerness for what Hennequin will say about melodrama. I shall quote the whole passage.

> (1) *Theme.* The theme borders nearly on that of the romantic *drame,* but it is treated in a strained and unbalanced fashion that robs it of its proper impressiveness for those who are not carried away by their emotions.

(2) *Characters.* The characters are taken from all ranks of life. The villain is here indispensable, and generally takes the form of a group of thoroughly vicious characters, who, after working great mischief, end by circumventing and destroying one another.

(3) *Plot.* The plots of melodrama are usually of a dark and gloomy character, full of startling incidents, bordering closely on the improbable. Intrigue and crime furnish the necessary complications.

(4) *Style.* By a sort of dramatic license, the writer of melodrama is allowed to indulge in 'gush' and 'rant' to an almost unlimited extent. Indeed, in most cases, this is the only kind of language which harmonizes with the extravagant characters and situations. In some of the older melodramas the style is bombastic and unnatural to such a degree that to the reader of the present day it sounds like burlesque. Many of the more recent melodramas, on the other hand, show an encouraging moderation both in plot and diction.

Nothing is said here about the spectacular side of melodrama although scenic sensation is so closely associated with the form as to belong, one might have supposed, to a definition of it. Hennequin goes on, however, in his next paragraph to notice 'spectacular drama', as such; a widely constituted group of plays which includes many melodramas and the 'English Christmas pantomimes'. *The Silver King* (ascribed to Wills) is of course a melodrama; Bronson Howard's *Shenandoah* (I still recall the noise and smoke of its battle scenes; it was my first play) is an incontestable example of spectacular drama.

Hennequin does better by a subject of at least equal interest: the classification of actors according to the parts which they habitually played. This classification as it existed in English provincial theatres of the nineteenth century has been thought to have some bearing on the original performance of Shakespeare's plays. Granville-Barker in a little known essay of his, 'The Casting of *Hamlet*', discussed the problem in the *London Mercury* for November 1936, turning for help on details to Sir Arthur Pinero. Professor T.W. Baldwin made too much of the relationship in his big book, *The Organization and Personnel of Shakespeare's Company.* Hennequin, in describing the distribution of parts as he found it, has in mind its immediate importance for the playwright. 'Although the conditions of dramatic production admit the possibility of an infinite variety of characters', he maintains that the history of the stage shows the prevalence of a small number of general types. 'These types occur over and over in the plays forming the *repertories* of modern theatrical companies', and actors are chosen with their representation in mind. What is more, 'plays are now usually written and arranged so as to require a certain number and proportion of male and female actors of the various classes'. The men were these:

(1) The Star
(2) The Leading Man
(3) The Heavy
(4) The First Old Man
(5) The Second Old Man
(6) The Comedian
(7) The Light Comedian
(8) The Low Comedian
(9) The Eccentric Comedian
(10) The Villain
(11) The Juvenile
(12) The Walking Gentleman
(13) The Utility Man
(14) The Super or 'Supe' (supernumerary).

The presence of both Star and Leading Man might suggest the occasional visits of players with great names, an arrangement not infrequently attended by mutual reproach, the touring stars (Macready especially) complaining of the poor quality of the local companies and they in turn grumbling over the ruinous terms exacted by their visitors. By the time Hennequin wrote, however, this was an outmoded system, and Hennequin himself goes on to refer to travelling companies. 'There are very few plays on the road that require more than ten characters', he remarks.

'Star plays' receive a paragraph. 'When star plays are written to order, the part of the star is usually emphasized at the expense of the rest of the characters.... Examples of star plays in which all the characters are given strongly marked individuality are rare outside the Shakespearean repertory'. The leading man has 'the male rôle next in importance to that of the star', and 'in stock companies' replaced the star when the play called for one. The idea of the leading man's stepping down to second place upon the visit of a star, as was once customary, goes unmentioned, as if the occasion for such descents no longer existed. Is there possibly a trace of humour in the comment, 'If a star is a lady, the leading man, in about ninety-nine cases out of a hundred, plays the part of her lover' – ? I am doubtful.

The Heavy and the First Old Man raise few questions. Hennequin's description of them is characteristic.

> *The Heavy.* An actor who habitually plays serious parts, devoid of comedy elements, and calling for considerable manifestation of strong feeling, is called a heavy. The parts of the King and of the Ghost in *Hamlet* would be taken by heavies. Actors of this type who are qualified to assume important rôles are spoken of as *leading heavies.*
>
> *First Old Man.* The *old men* are distinguished from the heavies by their gray hair. The most important old man character, in a play which calls for

> more than one, is called the *first old man.* The part is usually dignified, exhibiting the nobler and more pathetic qualities of old age, such as tenderness of feeling, magnanimity, etc. Less frequently the first old man portrays the vices of old age.
>
> *Second Old Man.* If the play calls for two characters representing old men, the less prominent of the two is called the *second old man.* The second old man is not infrequently a comic character.

Of the others I pause for *The Villain,* who appears a little incongruously here, as a concession to the vogue of melodrama.

> *The Villain.* The character in a play who represents the evil tendencies of human nature, and hence seeks to frustrate the purposes of the nobler characters, is called the *villain.* The villain may be either a heavy or a comedian. In the older plays, he was almost invariably the former, and when uncommonly wicked and blood-thirsty was known as the *heavy villain.* At the present day it is not unusual to give the villain a touch of comedy, generally of a satirical kind. There has been some discussion of late over the question whether the villain may not be dispensed with altogether, but until human nature undergoes a radical change it is not likely that this interesting character will be eliminated either from real life or from the drama.

As an afterthought, seemingly, for he is not mentioned in the list, Dr Hennequin adds 'The Character Actor': 'an actor who cultivates the power of representing with equal facility widely different characters.... If the characters represented embrace those commonly called for in the modern repertories, he is called an *all-round character actor'.*

If at this point we seem to be in danger of passing into a new age, the 'Classification of Female Rôles' is comfortably reassuring.

> (1) The Star
> (2) The Leading Lady
> (3) The Emotional Actress
> (4) The First Old Woman
> (5) The Second Old Woman
> (6) The Comedienne
> (7) The Soubrette
> (8) The Ingénue
> (9) The Adventuress
> (10) The Juvenile
> (11) The Walking Lady
> (12) The Utility Woman

Hennequin gives little space to them beyond a general statement:

> All that has been said with regard to male rôles applies equally well to the corresponding female rôles. The female rôles that have no correspondence whatever with male rôles are:-
>
> (1) The Soubrette
> (2) The Ingénue

> The *adventuress* answers in the main to the male villain, and the *emotional actress* to the male heavy.

Mention of one of Hennequin's actresses calls to mind a story told by the tragedian Frederick Warde in his book *Fifty Years of Make-Believe* (New York, 1920). Warde's apprenticeship in the profession began in Sunderland about 1870 with a company carefully arranged according to 'lines of business' (Warde was to play 'General Utility'). They were to open with *Macbeth,* to be followed by an adaptation of *Les Misérables,* about which much curiosity was expressed by the players. Several of them questioned Warde, who had read Hugo's novel. 'A mature lady in a poke bonnet and with much jewelry eagerly inquired: "Is there any first old woman in the book?" ' Warde, if we are to believe him, was puzzled by the question.

The Art of Playwriting was, as its title promised, a practical treatise. From it the aspiring dramatist was to learn what was required of a play if it was to succeed on the stage, and the demands were stringent. It was only sensible for him to consider the distribution of his characters among the specialists who were to enact them. He might be well advised to have a first old woman in his book. Then there was a great deal to learn about his opening scene. Matters of importance were not to be introduced too early. In every play, Dr Hennequin told him, certain passages were pretty sure to be unheard by most of the audience. Among these were the lines immediately after a laugh or 'a round of applause' – and Hennequin added wisely that the laugh is not always to be foreseen. There were, too, the first words spoken.

> The confusion in the audience during the first minute or so after the curtain rises renders it impossible for any except those in the front rows to hear what is said on the stage. Many dramatists make a practice of throwing in at the beginning a short lively scene of no relevance whatever to the rest of the play just to get the audience quiet.

He does not, of course, advocate such desperate expedients; nor does one think of the well-made play as opening with violent action of any sort. Scribe at his best is likely to proceed somewhat gingerly, though with an eye to the future.

The would-be dramatist had many things more to remember: the naming of characters, for instance, in preparation for their entrance. Again:

> It is a stage rule never to bring two important characters on the stage at the same moment. The attention of the audience is divided, and, worse than all else, the actors themselves have no means of knowing for whom the applause, if any, is intended.

(With us the question is raised, if it is raised at all, only after the fall of the curtain.) Attention must be paid also to the order of the scenes – a front scene being followed by a full one. Elaborate properties were not to be introduced into front scenes.

> When the flats are separated, the front of the stage becomes a part of the full scene, and, as a consequence, chairs, tables, etc., will either be left standing at the front, or must be carried out by the attendants amid the jeers of the galleries.... As the noise made in setting a scene is sometimes considerable, the front scene should be of a loud and stirring character. All attempts at subtle character-drawing or tender pathos are likely to be frustrated by the banging of hammers and the rumbling of stage machinery.

Not for nothing were such front scenes known as carpenters' scenes.

Hard as the tyro's task must have seemed, it was eased by means of a number of theatrical conventions; though some of these, as Hennequin's pages testify, were beginning to be regarded with suspicion. Convention, if one accepted it, made the whole matter of exposition beautifully simple, since two characters might 'relate to each other facts with which both are familiar'. (This was 'one of the most common' of conventions having to do with dialogue.) As illustration he quotes from a conversation between two stage characters, Mountraffe and Mrs Pinchbeck:

> *Mount.* Didn't you get married?
> *Mrs. P.* To a man old enough to be my father.
> *Mount.* What of that? I thought he had plenty of the ready.
> *Mrs. P.* He hadn't a penny.
> *Mount.* No, the old villain, so I found out when it was too late.

That came, I am sorry to say, from a play by Tom Robertson.

What, on the other hand, would Robertson have said of the statement that 'an "interior" is conventionally allowed to have as many entrances as the dramatist chooses to give it..... A room will frequently be represented, in violation of all probability, as having three entrances on each side.' It is only fair to add that Hennequin himself would have the number restricted, 'except in the lightest comedy'. 'Stage doors, in interiors,' he notes, 'are generally made to open outward.'

Time, for the playwright, might move too fast or too slow to suit his convenience. Yet Hennequin, having said as much, tries gravely to compute ratios and measure discrepancies.

> Generally the supposed duration of events upon the stage is about five or six times as long as the actual period occupied by the representation. That is, at the end of a dialogue of five minutes, it is allowable to make one of the characters say, 'Here we've been talking for a whole half-hour'.

A specific time is assigned, or at least suggested, for the writing of a stage letter: 'Letters or other documents written in the presence of the audience usually proceed at the rate employed in speaking very deliberately'. 'The actor', Hennequin adds, 'does not, of course, do any actual writing.'

To what extent, we may ask, was the author of *The Art of Playwriting* conscious of the great changes which were going on in the theatre; changes which were soon to make many of its traditions wholly obsolete. At moments, he seems, indeed, to lack his usual confidence. He is on the defensive as he begins his chapter on theatrical conventionalities.

> To the beginner, especially if his artistic sense is keen, many of the most binding traditions of the stage must at first seem thoroughly illogical and unnatural. Upon further acquaintance, it is true, they turn out to have a logic and a fitness of their own; but no mere exercise of reason or intuition would ever enable him to forecast them or to dispense with them altogether.

The manner in which asides and what he calls 'aparts' should be spoken, he explains, for once, only with some difficulty. The apart should be used sparingly. In a note he adds, significantly: 'On the whole actors have a great dislike for aparts and asides, and, if these are not very carefully worded, often find it difficult to do justice to their lines'. 'The stage whisper', he goes on, 'except as a broadly comic effect, is out of date.'

At one point I find myself very nearly on Hennequin's side. Having told us, what perhaps needed little telling at the time, that important actions should 'take place in the center of the stage, well forward', he lays down this rule: 'The actors should not be compelled by any action of the drama to turn their backs upon the audience, especially while speaking'. And there is an ominous footnote beginning: 'This rule must be insisted upon, although the customs of the modern stage are rapidly leaving it out of sight.' If only, I cannot help wishing, some vestige of these good principles had persisted!

In the last three chapters of all, the reader is given an exercise in imagination. Let him suppose himself commissioned to prepare 'a light comedy for a stock company with from eight to ten characters.' It is to have 'plenty of incidents and a little chance for the emotional on the part of the leading lady'. He has no further instructions. His first concern will be to find a plot. Among the stray ideas which he has set down in his scrapbook, or wherever he keeps them, he comes across something like this: 'A young woman and an elderly woman in love with the same man'. That he perceives at once is a good starting point, 'a good basis for a story'. It has as yet only three characters, however.

> A little reflection on the complications that are likely to arise will suggest that the conflict may be heightened by adding a male character who is in love with the elderly lady, and whom the elderly lady greatly respects, although she does not love him. There is a good reason for this in the necessity usually found in comedy, of pairing off the principal characters at the close.

He decides upon a French setting and characters. His plot, as it now stands, is as follows:

> Léonie (the young woman) and the Countess (the elderly lady), are in love with Henri. Gustave is in love with the Countess, who greatly respects him and might marry him were it not for Henri. In the end Léonie gets Henri, and the Countess accepts Gustave.

Next, the author asks himself questions. How, for instance, are the rival ladies to show their love for the young man?

> *Answer*: Suppose Henri to be in some serious danger. Then each can use her best efforts to extricate him. He will thus be under obligation to the one who saves his life. If this one is not the woman he loved, still further complications will ensue.

By the end of the first of these chapters, the general outline of the story is complete. What follows concerns the realizing of its possibilities as a play. Hennequin advises the writer on many matters: the exposition, for instance, which should be carefully planned with an eye to what might be and what might not be omitted; the division into acts and the effective ordering of scenes. The incidents must be so arranged as to achieve a climax, 'each situation becoming stronger than the preceding'; and after the climax they must serve to untie the knot without sacrificing all suspense until the very end. And there is the wise counsel, 'Do not make your characters say in words what they can say more forcibly in action'. Thus, 'when the Countess learns of Henri's love for Léonie, she should not be made to dissipate her emotion in words – a look will be vastly more impressive....'

Hennequin is willing to admit that the method he has described is not the only method by which plays may be composed. His may yet lead the aspiring writer to work in a systematic way. Then, in a final paragraph, with perhaps a touch of complaisance: 'The student will of course have recognised in the play just outlined the main points of Eugène Scribe's *Un Duel en Amour*, which Charles Reade Englished under the title of *The Ladies' Battle*....' a play, it is worth noting, produced originally in 1851.

I have emphasized, it may be over-emphasized, the old-fashioned side of *The Art of Playwriting.* The book cannot have seemed outmoded to those who continued to buy copies of it for many years to come. After the author's death the copyright was renewed in 1918 by Marie Hennequin. A friend at Houghton Mifflin's has given me figures on its annual sales at a still later time. Fourteen copies were sold in 1945. Is it conceivable that the purchaser of one of these set out in all seriousness to write a well-made play?

PART THREE

Shakespearean Production in the Nineteenth Century

11 JAN McDONALD

The Taming of the Shrew at the Haymarket Theatre, 1844 and 1847

It is to J.R. Planché that we must give credit for the idea of reviving *The Taming of the Shrew,* under Benjamin Webster's management, at the Haymarket Theatre in March 1844. He attributes his choice of this play to the return to the stage of Mrs Nisbett, then Lady Boothby, whom he thought would make an ideal Katharine, and he was encouraged in his desire to present the original text, including the Induction, by the presence in the Haymarket company of Strickland, whom he thought particularly suited to the part of Christopher Sly.

It is not surprising that the renowned antiquarian Planché was anxious to present the original text and eschew what he calls 'the miserable, mutilated form' [1] of Garrick's *Catharine and Petruchio,* but it is perhaps more difficult to understand why, thirty-seven years before William Poel's famous First Quarto *Hamlet,* the idea of presenting a play in what current opinion held to be an Elizabethan style should have occurred to him.

Perhaps the 'play within the play' structure of the *Shrew* is the main factor. This does present problems to any producer, and the solution of presenting it as originally done may come quickly to him. Possibly, too, Planché was influenced by the work of Tieck in Germany. Tieck, first as *dramaturg* of the Court Theatre in Dresden, and later at the Prussian Court, had presented Shakespeare's plays in a setting that imitated freely the Elizabethan stage as he conceived it. The ideas expressed in *Der junge Tischlermeister* (1836) anticipated the Munich *Bühnenreform* of 1889, and, by the time of his death in 1853, Tieck had presented *The Merchant of Venice* (1821),

Twelfth Night (1836), *A Midsummer Night's Dream* (1843) and *Macbeth* (1851) according to his principles. Planché would almost certainly have heard of his work, as Tieck was in fairly frequent correspondence with John Payne Collier, Crabb Robinson and Charles Kemble – the last had visited him in 1834 – and it is well known that his ideas were current in England. *The Times* review of the Haymarket *Shrew* does indeed refer to them.

The contemporary English views on Elizabethan staging are expressed by John Payne Collier [2] and Edmund Malone [3]. Collier, like Malone, disallows the use of any painted and movable scenery on the stage – Malone defines scenery as 'a painting in perspective on a cloth fastened to a wooden frame or roller' [4] – although both recognize the use of movable properties. Collier writes, 'Hangings on the stage made little pretension to be anything but coverings for the walls' [5]. Malone believes that for tragedy the curtains were black, and when they became worn they would be painted with pictures. Until the Restoration, these curtains ran upon a rod and opened in the centre. They were usually composed of arras and worsted. The back curtains in the Haymarket *Shrew* were made of tapestry, and did have a centre opening.

Two other nineteenth-century ideas on Elizabethan staging, particularly relevant to this production, should be mentioned here: first, the idea that the place of action was written on a placard or board. Collier cites as authorities the Induction to *Cynthia's Revels* by Ben Jonson [6], and Sir Philip Sidney's *Apologie for Poetrie*: 'What child is there, that coming to a play and seeing Thebes written in great letters upon an old door, doth believe it is Thebes' [7], and Collier adds a quotation from *A Fairy Pastoral, or the Forest Elves*, '...you may omitt the sayd properties, which be outward, and supplye their places with their nuncupations onely in text letters' [8]. In the Haymarket production, change of place was indicated by change of placards, attached to the tapestry curtain, the actors changing the notices as they left the stage in preparation for the next scene.

Secondly, Malone describes thus the method of presenting 'a play within a play'.

> The court or audience before whom the interlude was performed, sat in the balcony or upper stage, *for the nonce*, the performers entered between the curtain and the general audience, and on its being drawn, began their piece addressing themselves to the balcony, and regardless of the spectators in the theatre, to whom their backs must have been turned during the whole performance! [9]

Collier disagrees with this, citing the stage direction in *The Spanish Tragedy,* 'He knocks up the curtain', as an indication that the performers were discovered in, or acted in the alcove [10]. Wisely Planché did not attempt to copy Malone's idea. His 'stage audience' sat downstage right and downstage left, giving them a side view of the players, and the action took place facing the real audience.

There is no mention of a balcony or upper level in the Haymarket production. Perhaps it was felt that the play did not demand it.

Neither Malone nor Collier stresses the importance of the apron in the Elizabethan stage structure, and in 1843 Webster had greatly reduced the size of the Haymarket apron, 'a useless portion of the stage', as he described it [11], in order to accommodate more orchestra stalls. One could take it that what we regard as the great advantage of the Elizabethan stage, namely the intimacy between actor and audience, was not present in 1844, but *The Times* review does comment on the 'closeness of the action'. Perhaps the presence of the stage audience well downstage brought the actors more to the front.

The text used was probably the Folio text. Poel's antiquarian interests took him to the bad quarto of *Hamlet* for *his* revolutionary production, but Planché did not go back to the 1594 *Taming of a Shrew* for his script. Planché was of the opinion that the 'epilogue' was not lost, as Schlegel thought, but had never been written. In Planché's opinion no writer, not even Shakespeare, could finish the legendary Sly. At the last line of the Katharine and Petruchio story, the actors bowed, and the nobleman's servant lifted Sly out of his chair, and carried him offstage. Thus, wrote Planché, 'the termination which Schlegel claims to have been lost was indicated' [12]. Action supplied the lack of words. The *Morning Post* review of the first performance complains that at the end of the *fourth* act the stage audience went off stage and left the players to amuse themselves by finishing without any audience. At the end of the play the lord entered and paid the players. They exited, and Sly was borne across the stage asleep. No other reviewer mentions this, and, indeed, *Punch* describes a jerk of the leg given by Stuart, playing the Lord, during the banquet scene, which would indicate the presence of the stage audience during the last act. It is possible that the fourth act exit was changed, either during the first run in March, 1844, or for the 1847 production. Planché, in his *Recollections,* does confuse the two.

The play opened on a typical Victorian painted scene 'representing an inn' which Planché describes as 'a little alehouse on a heath, from which the drunken tinker is ejected by the hostess, and where he is found asleep in front of the door by the lord and his huntsmen'. Then occurs the only scene change to the Lord's bedroom, where the Katharine and Petruchio story is enacted by the strolling players, made up 'so as to give a sort of resemblance to Shakespeare, Ben Jonson, and Richard Tarleton', in an attempt to give added Elizabethan flavour.

This picture (Fig. 1) from *The Illustrated London News* gives an artist's impression of the second scene. The lord and his servant are downstage left, Sly and his party downstage right. They remain there throughout, their only contribution to the action being that Sly and the others were plied with drinks during the 'very short' intervals. The critic of *The Illustrated London News* complains that Sly could very profitably have contributed comments during the course of the action, as of course he did in the old *Taming of a Shrew* (1594), but clearly this was not done.

The set for 'the play within the play' presents some problems. *The Times* review states that 'two screens and a pair of curtains' were 'the whole dramatic apparatus'. The actors could make exits and entrances round the screens as well as through the centre gap in the curtain. It is difficult to ascertain from the drawing whether the screens referred to by *The Times* were the outer ones – modified Serlian wings very accurately decorated with Tudor ornamentation as one would expect under Planché's supervision – or the inner pilasters, which are only vaguely outlined.

The second problem is whether the side curtains between the pilasters and the wings were in fact practicable. Frank Marshall, in Volumes 3 and 4 of his edition of Shakespeare (1922), quotes Howe, who had played the part of Hortensio in this production, as saying these side curtains were maroon-coloured and were 'looped-up' – which would imply they were for decoration only – but a quotation from *The Times* review would lead one to believe that they were used. 'By mere substitution of one curtain for another, change of scene was indicated.' Without the prompt-book it is impossible to tell, but a scathing letter to *Oxberry's Weekly Budget* signed 'K', describes the set as 'two blankets suspended from a rod', and would add weight to the view that the second set of curtains was merely decorative.

The architectural feature at the top of the picture, which is somewhat distorted, is probably the artist's addition, but could be a border making part of the Lord's bedroom set.

In the picture, attached to the back curtain can be seen the placard indicating the place of action. The *Morning Post* criticizes the stage-management on the first performance, complaining that the place of action and the placards did not change simultaneously.

The last interesting feature of the setting was the drop-scene which preceded the drama, painted by Charles Marshall from Hollar's print of the Bankside, included to add to the Elizabethan flavour, but in a typically Victorian way. It was generally praised, except by the critic of *The Illustrated London News*, who considered it too 'clay-y', and the critic of the *Morning Post* who, although liking the scene, thought the painting of the water 'unfinished'.

The Elizabethan costumes in general were praised, and, considering Planché's interests, were no doubt reasonably accurate. They were thought 'very handsome and appropriate' by *The Times*, although a sarcastic critic in *Bentley's Miscellany* suggests that, since written notices were used to indicate scenes, costumes could have been shown in the same way, the actors wearing placards attached to the appropriate parts of their persons, reading 'a slashed doublet of fine green velvet' or 'a handsome pair of scarlet hose'. A more serious comment on the dressing of the Induction characters as real Elizabethans, comes from the *Athenaeum* critic. He felt that this led the audience to expect a type of acting very different from that which existed on the stage in his day, and writes, 'Webster's previous assumption of Shakespeare's semblance made his subsequent misconception and undignified personation of Petruchio more glaring'. Since so little was known of Elizabethan acting styles, and since the critic bases his ideas entirely on Hamlet's speech to the players, perhaps this is not a serious criticism, but clearly the disguises in the Induction were not uniformly approved.

The Shakespearean overture by Sir Henry Bishop is interesting. It is probably the same as that used in the gala performance given at Covent Garden in December 1847, in order to raise funds to restore Shakespeare's house. It consists of themes, previously written or chosen by him for earlier Shakespeare revivals, *Twelfth Night, The Tempest, A Midsummer Night's Dream, The Comedy of Errors* and *As You Like It,* the only new theme being one for *Macbeth,* together with pieces by Ford and Arne. Bishop's biographer, Northcott, does not include the 1844 Shakespearean Overture in his list of works, although the 1847 version is mentioned. The critic of *The Illustrated London News* did not approve – 'The Shakespearean overture is a sorry medley of tunes that have been huddled together most clumsily. It is said in the bills to be the composition (?) of Sir H.R. Bishop; if so we are sorry for it'. The interval music, to cover the plying of Sly with liquor, was under the direction of the Haymarket's regular conductor, Thomas German Reed, and was an arrangement of madrigals by Festa and Wilbye, and traditional English airs. Since the intervals were relatively short, the amount of music was minimal.

The cast (from a playbill for 27 March 1844) was as follows:–

Baptista – Mr. Gough
Vincentio – Mr. Tilbery
Lucentio – Mr. Holl
Hortensio – Mr. Howe
Gremio – Mr. James Bland
Petrucio – Mr. Webster
Grumio – Mr. Buckstone
Tranio – Mr. Bindal
Biondello – Mr. H. Widdicomb
Pedant – Mr. Sauter
Katharina – Mrs. Nisbett
Bianca – Miss Julia Bennett
Widow – Mrs. Stanley
Sly – Mr. Strickland
Lord – Mr. Stuart

With a few qualifications as to Webster's own performance, the acting was universally praised. This leads us to consider two points: firstly, while it is true that Webster had assembled around him at the Haymarket a very distinguished company, it is possible that, for the first time, the nineteenth-century critics were able to see acting untrammelled by complicating setting and costumes. As far as I can ascertain, there was no new style of playing approximating to Poel's 'tunes', that went with the new setting, but, and this leads me to the second point, the actors would have much less time between acts and scenes than they would have in a conventional production. They were not cumbered by complicated settings and innumerable properties, and this perhaps led to the speed and vivacity of playing that the critics comment on; and, since they were relying on themselves and each other more than on the props of spectacle, the style of setting could have led to the development of the accomplished 'ensemble' playing mentioned by the critic of *The Illustrated London News.*

Mrs Nisbett's performance excited ecstatic reviews, even from those who did not approve of the whole production. The *Morning Post* critic, who regarded the evening as a bore, attributes the volume of applause at the end to her delivery of her last speech, expounding the duties of a wife. This speech was described by the *Theatrical Journal* critic as 'an elaborate finish to an exquisite performance'. The quality she added to the part was that 'she did not suddenly sink into the abject slave of her husband's whim, but now and then broke out into the short ebullitions of hasty temper she was wont to indulge in' (*Theatrical Journal*), and that she always maintained her dignity so that 'through the veil of the termagant, the lady was still visible' (*Illustrated London News*). *The Dramatic Mirror,* referring to the 1847 revival, praises both her 'buoyancy and spirit' and 'her delicacy' and proclaims her 'the best Katharine on the stage', a view echoed by the critic in *Oxberry's Weekly Budget* – 'a most beautiful piece of acting'. The only murmur of dissent came from the critic of the *Athenaeum,* who made the point that, since Webster was so intent on being Elizabethan, the part of Katharine should have been played by a boy, and adds: '... Mrs. Nisbett's personal attractions procured immunity for a degree of vulgarity that would hardly have been tolerated by smooth-faced striplings who played women's parts in Shakespeare's time'.

Webster as Petruchio was not so highly praised. It was generally felt that he was uneasy in the part which was of 'too high a cast for him' (*Theatrical Journal*). Therefore he rushed the lines (*Times*). *The Illustrated London News* felt that there was more of the rude tyrant than the gentleman about him. Westland Marston, while acknowledging that Webster had 'few faults', wrote that his Petruchio 'seemed really violent and angry, and showed little enjoyment of the part he was masquerading' [13]. The *Morning Post* agrees about the coarseness, and complains about 'sing-song' delivery.

Nisbett shared the acting honours, not with Webster, but with Strickland as Sly, who was praised for his by-play, although, says the *Morning Post* critic, according to the original text he ought to have been in bed, not walking about in a dressing-gown and slippers. There is little indication as to what the by-play may have been. We only know it was 'humourously droll'. 'He was drunk all over, yet not dead drunk, or mad drunk, or half drunk; but in a twilight state, between part drunkenness and future sobriety' (*Dramatic Mirror*).

The other notable performance was Buckstone's Grumio. He played the part with his 'usual gusto' (*Athenaeum*) and was 'a relief to dreariness' for the *Morning Post* critic, who tells us that the piece of business when Grumio draws his sword and follows Petruchio from the stage, presumably after the abortive wedding banquet in Act III Sc. ii, earned three rounds of applause. He is criticized however by the same critic for 'a nasal twang' which was not felt to fit with the characterization.

The only other actor reviewed at length was Stuart who played the Lord, and he was the subject of an ironic review in *Punch*.

> Nothing can be finer than the acting of Mr. Stuart from first to last in the very arduous character assigned to him. There is something truly Shakespearian in his treatment of the wand which he holds in his hand, and which he twiddles about, from time to time between his fingers, with a nice appreciation of the highly dramatic situation into which he is thrown by the towering genius of the Swan of Avon. In the fourth act, Mr. Stuart rests his right arm on an adjacent chair but the point we admired most, was the truly Elizabethan jerk he gave to his left leg in the middle of the banquet scene.

The adjacent chair mentioned here is omitted in the *Illustrated London News* sketch.

The Times says the whole performance took three and a half hours. This seems extraordinarily long, especially as only one scene change is required and the act intervals were so short. Did they merely seem short to a Victorian audience? The Shakespearean overture would last about 12–15 minutes. One of the 1847 playbills announces the *Shrew* performance for 7 p.m., and second prices at 9, but, of course, the second-price audience could have seen the end of the *Shrew* for their money. Clearly the speed of delivery of Webster's company kept them a long way from observing the 'two-hours' traffic' of the stage.

One must now consider the general press and public opinions of the experiment. The newspapers were divided. Those *for* the Elizabethan setting included *Bentley's Miscellany, The Dramatic Mirror, John Bull, The Illustrated London News, Oxberry's Weekly Budget, The Theatrical Journal* and *The Times*.

Bentley's Miscellany praised the economy and simplicity of the production: 'Here at one blow by the substitution of a contrivance beautiful in its simplicity, the whole army of scene-painters, carpenters, and shifters are ingeniously swamped'. *The Illustrated London News* concurred, writing that the success of the *Shrew* showed that 'mere gew-gaw accessories of the stage are not necessary when there is the "Mens divinior poetae" present'. *The Times* explained that the setting gave 'closeness to the action, and, by constantly allowing a great deal of stage room, afforded a sort of freedom to all parties engaged'. An advantage of the setting noticed by *The Dramatic Mirror* reviewer was that the simple staging 'permitted the undivided attention of the audience to the business of the drama'. *John Bull* took the opportunity to point out that this production showed that if there was a decline in the drama, it was not due to a decline in public taste, for Webster's intelligent experiment had been 'attended with complete success'. To sum up those 'in favour': what they liked was the simplicity and economy of the setting, which they felt helped not only the actors, in giving them freedom of movement, but also the members of the audience, who were forced to use their imaginations, and could and did listen to the words of the play with more attention than was necessary or possible in a spectacular production.

Those 'against' range from the ironic reviewer of Stuart's performance in *Punch* to the furious 'K' whose letter was printed in *Oxberry's Weekly Budget. Punch* continues his irony in a later issue. On learning that the spectacular *Der Freischütz* is scheduled for the Haymarket, the writer suggests that the incantation scene be got up after the manner of *The Taming of the Shrew.* Moon, clouds, smoke, lightning, blue fire, lizards, toads, boas and bears, are to be represented by placards hung at appropriate points (Fig. 2).

Bentley's Miscellany, although favourably disposed in the main, ends on a warning note. If Webster's experiment was carried to its logical conclusion 'the imagination of the public (could be) at last educated to so high a point that they may be able to read a play at home, and fancy themselves at the theatre'.

More serious complaints were launched by the critics of the *Morning Post* and the *Athenaeum.* The *Morning Post* critic found the production a bore, first because of the restoration of the original text:

> [The managers] overlook the fact that the original text was not altered until it had been tried and found wanting in dramatic interest. We must plead guilty to the impeachment of preferring the pleasant abridgement of it in *Catherine and Petruchio* to the long, wearisome and yet unfinished comedy of five acts, with its preliminary induction without a conclusion.

The applause of the audience at the end is attributed to the snob appeal of the play. Told it was the *real* thing, the audience had to

like it, but there was little applause or laughter during the performance. The charge of being boring was also implicitly levelled against the production by Charles Kemble when, in a letter to *Punch*, he wrote 'Prince Albert will, in a short time, wholly renounce the idols of the Opera and as a most convincing proof of his belief in Shakespeare, sit out the *Petruchio* of Mr. Webster'.

The *Athenaeum* accuses the management of gimmickry and 'pedantic affectation of accuracy', but does perhaps make a valid point in objecting to the inconsistency of style in presenting the Induction with typical Victorian scenes, and 'the play within the play' in an imitation of the Elizabethan manner. It is in this point that the spirit of the Haymarket revival differs most from Poel's. Within a Victorian conception of a Tudor hall, the play was performed in what roughly approximated to an Elizabethan stage. The tone of the whole production was not Shakespearean or Elizabethan as Poel understood the words.

The most virulent attack, and that which most clearly shows the rage for spectacle that had such a strong hold on the nineteenth-century theatre, comes from the letter in *Oxberry's Weekly Budget.* The writer, 'K', agrees that the restoration of the text might well be justified, but the restoration of the 'primitive beauty' of the stage condition was 'a miserable failure'. Shakespeare, he claims, would have loved nineteenth-century methods of staging, and, like the critic of the *Athenaeum,* he levels the charge of 'pedantic affectation' against the production.

In general, however, the reception seems to have been favourable, and Webster revived the production for fourteen performances in October/November 1847. Howe claims this was not so much of a success, but *The Times* critic found it a very interesting performance, and 'the effect was given of the ancient method of dramatic representation in England, when the art of scene painting was unknown'. *The Illustrated London News* records that the house was well filled.

There were few major changes in cast. Webster and Nisbett continued as Petruchio and Katharine, but Vandenhoff took over from Holl as Lucentio, and Keeley from Buckstone as Grumio. Lambert played Sly. Webster, if we are to believe the critic of the *Dramatic Mirror,* had improved, and was less guilty of the 'coarseness' that was complained of in his earlier interpretation. He showed 'an hilarious freedom and boldness in his bearing that conveyed to us a perfect idea of a choleric man without the blustering vulgarity of the bully, or the rudeness of an illtempered brute'. Crabb Robinson, who did not see the first production, still complains of 'coarseness' [14]. From *The Illustrated London News* review, we learn that Webster continued 'with much effect on the audience' the traditional cracking of the whip in the character of Petruchio.

Keeley was praised for his 'rich and quiet drollery' and *The Times,* although not the *Dramatic Mirror,* preferred him to Buckstone. The performances of the minor characters were inferior to those of the original production. *The Times* felt greater attention should have been paid to metre, and criticized Vandenhoff's trick of pronouncing the Latin in the passages with Bianca, according to Italian, not English pronunciation. Vandenhoff replied almost in the terms of a Stanislavskian actor, citing Lucentio's birthplace Pisa, and upbringing in Florence, as authorities for his choice of pronunciation. Rightly, however, *The Times* reviewer points out that, on this level, the whole play should be in Italian, and the fact that Bianca repeated the Latin phrases in an English way led to a jarring inconsistency.

Lambert as Sly was not so highly praised as Strickland, but he did 'take great pains and showed some talent in the various expressions with which he listened to the play' (*Times*). What was missed was Strickland's 'unctuous drunkenness'. Rogers, as the Lord, in place of Stuart, apparently looked more like a suppressor than an encourager of drama.

Clearly Webster did not regard the revival as a failure, as he chose scenes from Acts I and IV to be his contribution to the Shakespeare Night at Covent Garden on 7 December 1847, 'in aid of the fund for the purchase and preservation of Shakespeare's House'. Other excerpts presented included scenes from *Henry IV*, parts I and II, *Henry VIII, Two Gentlemen of Verona, Romeo and Juliet, The Merry Wives of Windsor, The Tempest, The Winter's Tale,* and the programme involved almost all the leading actors in London. The setting of the extracts from the *Shrew* is described in the programme as 'A Gothic Hall'. It is possible that this was merely stock scenery from Covent Garden, but the specific nature of the other set descriptions, 'Juliet's bedroom', 'The island before the cell of Prospero', 'A street in Verona' would lead one to believe that the set of the *Shrew* was the set of the second scene of the Induction, i.e., the Lord's bedroom, and that it was performed in more or less the same way at Covent Garden, as it had been in the Haymarket.

Another money-making venture, the publication of a book called *Selections from Shakespeare's Plays as represented at the Royal Italian Opera, Covent Garden* (1847), leads to some confusion about the extracts actually performed. In the first place, the text quoted is not from Shakespeare's play, but from Garrick's alteration, revised by J.P. Kemble. It is impossible to believe that Webster's company, having restored the original text in 1844, and revived it only a month before this performance, would have gone back to *Katharine and Petruchio* for the gala. One must suppose that the compiler of the book was confused, and used the wrong text – no doubt an indication of the currency of the Garrick version at this time. Secondly, the extracts printed are very short – fifty-one lines in the first extract and only twelve in the second – hardly enough to give any idea of the play. And lastly, although the full cast, except for the Induction characters, is listed in the programme, in the printed text only three appear – Katharine, Petruchio and Grumio. In the printed extract Grumio has only three lines, yet *The Illustrated London News* records that Keeley was specially called for after the performance. The *Selections,* then, was probably thrown together, very hurriedly, and gives very little clue to what was actually performed.

Webster's contribution to the evening is not noticed particularly, most press attention being given to the prologue by Charles Knight, spoken by Samuel Phelps, and the inadequate acoustics of Covent Garden for Shakespeare.

The results of the production are disappointing. Webster did not try any other play on an Elizabethan stage, although public reaction had on the whole been favourable. *Katharine and Petruchio* was still performed, and although Phelps revived the original text at Sadler's Wells in 1856, he did not use Elizabethan staging. The only follow-up was in Edinburgh in February 1849, when the Garrick text plus the Induction was performed 'in the Baron's Hall, fitted up for a temporary theatre as in days of yore' [15].

A totally contrasting production of the full text was used by Augustin Daly to open his new theatre in 1893, but the settings were lavish. 'Mr. Daly, wisely considering that the omission of proper scenery was by no means essential, has mounted the play with liberality and good taste' [16].

The theatre had to wait for Poel before it gave widespread recognition to Planché's idea. Poel was apparently not influenced by the Haymarket productions, as he calls his *Hamlet* 'the first revival of the draped stage in this country or elsewhere' [17]. But we must beware of attributing too much foresight to Planché. As Stanley Wells points out [18], Planché was as much the forerunner of the Kean–Irving–Tree tradition, as of Poel's Elizabethan stage. He no doubt felt that *The Taming of the Shrew* was particularly suited to this treatment, and perhaps the accusation of some critics that he was only pursuing 'novelty' for its own sake could be justified. He was still presenting an Elizabethan stage within a Victorian setting. Let us not, however, ask too much of Planché and Webster. They were attempting to reconstruct an Elizabethan stage, without the benefit of a sixteenth-century education, or of the discoveries of the next hundred years, but with the possible disadvantage of their knowledge of all the conventions and trappings of a Victorian theatrical experience. Neither William Poel, nor Walter Hodges, nor any other restorer has had the advantage of this type of education, and their ideas are as much the product of their own time and experience as Planché's were of his. We must, therefore, give him credit for the idea, and for recognizing the interesting possibilities that arose from his experiment. He wrote in *Recollections and Reflections*: 'My restoration of this "gem" is one of the events in my theatrical career on which I look back with the greatest pride and gratification' [19].

[1] J.R. Planché, *Recollections and Reflections* (London, 1872) II, 83.
[2] John Payne Collier, *English Dramatic Poetry* (London, 1831) Vol. III.
[3] Edmond Malone and James Boswell, eds., *The Plays and Poems of William Shakespeare* (London, 1821) Vol. III.
[4] *Ibid.*, III, 86.
[5] Collier, *op. cit.*, III, 366.
[6] *Ibid.*, III, 369.
[7] *Ibid.*, III, 374.
[8] *Ibid.*, III, 358.
[9] Malone, *op. cit.*, III, 108.
[10] Collier, *op. cit.*, III, 364.
[11] Playbill for 28 April 1843.
[12] Planché, *op. cit.*, II, 85.
[13] Westland Marston, *Our Recent Actors* (London, 1888) 254.
[14] Eluned Brown, ed., *The London Theatre 1811–1866. Selections from the Diary of Henry Crabb Robinson* (London, 1966) 183.
[15] J.C. Dibdin, *Annals of the Edinburgh Stage* (Edinburgh, 1888) 407.
[16] Sir Henry Irving and Frank A. Marshall, eds., *The Works of William Shakespeare* (London, 1922) III, 146.
[17] Robert Speaight, *William Poel and the Elizabethan Revival* (London 1954) 51.
[18] Stanley Wells, 'Shakespeare in Planché's Extravaganzas', *Shakespeare Survey*, 16 (1963) 114.
[19] Planché, *op. cit.*, II, 86.

Reviews of the 1844 production cited in this paper are as follows: *The Morning Post*, 18 March 1844; *The Times*, 18 March 1844; *The Athenaeum*, 23 March 1844; *Illustrated London News*, 23 March 1844; *John Bull*, 23 March 1844; *The Theatrical Journal*, 23 March 1844; *Punch*, March 1844; *Bentley's Miscellany*, April 1844; *Oxberry's Weekly Budget*, April 1844.

Reviews of the 1847 production are as follows: *Illustrated London News*, 13 October 1847; *The Times*, 27 October 1847; *Dramatic Mirror*, 3 November 1847.

Review of the 1847 Shakespearean Gala at Covent Garden is from *The Illustrated London News*, 11 December 1847.

12 W. MOELWYN MERCHANT

On Looking at *The Merchant of Venice*

The title of this note isolates one aspect of a Shakespearean production, in order to focus one of the most teasing and controversial features of dramatic interpretation. No sensitive and attentive reader of the text fails to make his own imaginative 'production' of the play as he reads. It will be for him the ideal production, since it will correspond at all points with the temper, plot movement, characterization, sound and imagery of the play, and no actual production in the theatre can hope to give the reader so flexible and comprehensive a setting.

This is to state the simple core of the problem for the modern scholarly reader; the problem has another side: whether it was Shakespeare's intention to set the play within an elaborate visual framework which pieced out for the eye the poetic and dramatic dimension of the work. Though much work has now been completed on the early 'baroque' quality of the Jacobean theatre, much still remains to be done in relating this theatre research to dramatic criticism. One necessary approach is to explore the critical implications of the setting within a limited period and our present concern is with the décor of *The Merchant of Venice* in the nineteenth century.

Self-consciousness in the matter of 'accuracy' or 'propriety' in setting Shakespeare may be fairly precisely located: in 1824 J.R. Planché, an omni-competent craftsman, declared in his *Memoirs* the principles by which he had contrived the décor and costumes for *King John*: accuracy was the first consideration:

> It was not necessary to be an antiquary to see the absurdity of the soldiers before Angiers, at the beginning of the thirteenth century, being clothed precisely the same as those fighting at Bosworth at the end of the fifteenth.

The play-bill for 19 January 1824 makes the claim which sets the temper of nineteenth-century décor:

> This present Monday, January 19, 1824, will be revived Shakespeare's Tragedy of King John with an attention to Costume never equalled on the English Stage. Every Character will appear in the precise HABIT OF THE PERIOD, the whole of the Dresses and Decorations being executed from indisputable Authorities, such as Monumental Effigies, Seals, Illumined Mss., &c.

A year or two before this production of *King John* Richard Smirke (1778–1815) painted an elaborate 'Trial Scene from *The Merchant of Venice*' (now in the Memorial Theatre Gallery, Stratford-on-Avon); it is the first visual indication of the new temper in setting this play, for the costumes and setting are an amalgam of figures from mannerist Venetian painting, an accurate reference to Shakespeare's Italian contemporaries which would greatly have pleased Planché.

We can trace little advance on these principles until Charles Kean gave the whole matter of décor a new and controversial impetus in his productions at the Princess's Theatre. That these were notably elaborate and this elaboration was good theatrical business is undoubted; but Charles Kean was never unaware of his sober responsibilities as a Fellow of the Society of Antiquaries and his programme notes were burdened with intimidating scholarship; indeed it was frequently remarked, despite the popular esteem accorded the productions, that the text was frequently overborne by setting. G.H. Lewes wrote (25 June 1853) concerning the production of *Sardanapalus*:

> Got up with splendour and with care the piece undoubtedly is. All that archaeology could do has been done. Whether the result was worth the labour may be a question, even among those who think scenery and costume the 'be-all and the end-all' of the drama ... Is the Drama nothing more than a Magic Lantern on a large scale? Was Byron only a pretext for a panorama?... Why not give up the drama altogether, and make the Princess's Theatre a Gallery of Illustration?

Of Kean's *Macbeth* Lewes wrote:

> But there is a want perceptible through it all – the want of a poetical mind. Melodramatic effects he can reach – he falls short of poetry.

But Lewes was not the sole representative of informed or sensitive opinion in the middle of the century. *The Times* of 14 June 1854 carried a very full consideration of Charles Kean's production of *The Merchant of Venice*:

> In elaborate decoration the Merchant of Venice is surpassed by none of the famous 'revivals' at the Princess's Theatre, but it has this advantage, that the story is rather elucidated than entangled by the ornamental accessories that were so liberally introduced....
> In the first place, by employing every possible accessory of scenery and costume, Mr Kean has rendered the work thoroughly Venetian in its aspect....

> Bassanio and the others, when ... they make their appearance on the stage, invariably enter by means of gondolas, which regularly pass and re-pass under the bridge....

This is the key-note of all the nineteenth-century comment, that Kean 'has rendered the work thoroughly Venetian' and Henry Morley comments in 1853 in his *Journal of a London Playgoer*:

> Beyond question this is the best of Mr Kean's revivals.... The scenery is so contrived as to suggest the whole idea of Venice, and the play is only better understood when thus presented with the local colouring that was in Shakespeare's mind marked strongly by the scene-painter.

This then would appear to establish settled principles by which a distinguished production of *The Merchant of Venice* could come about and indeed the conjunction of a great visual intelligence, E.W. Godwin and a lively man of the theatre, Squire Bancroft, would appear to promise such a production. The documentation of E.W. Godwin's visual realization of Shakespeare is exceptionally rich; we have Godwin's own articles in *The Architect* in 1875 and the reprints of these articles with significant comment by his son Gordon Craig in *The Mask* in 1909–11. The finest of Godwin's articles is that on *The Merchant of Venice* and examination of its details shows both his debt to the prevailing critical temper of his age and the considerable gap between his highly sophisticated vision and the naiveties of his predecessors.

Godwin lays the ground-work for his architectural planning of the play by a close examination of Shakespeare's treatment of his sources and of the temper of the play; his aim is to determine the appropriate date for the setting and he deduced 'the year 1590 as the date best suited to the stage presentation'. Further examination of the plot structure is directed to the most economic setting of the production (a consideration which rarely concerned Kean). Godwin concludes that Venice and Belmont may be presented in no more than five scenes: A Street; Before Shylock's House; a Court of Justice; A Hall; a Garden. Further analysis reduces the architectural settings to three which he then proceeds to work out in precise detail.

The first ground plan conflates the first two scenes of the original analysis. In the diagram 'A is Shylock's house; B, the public place, with a fountain or well; D, a pent-house; E, narrow streets; F, Gothic and late Byzantine buildings; and M, N the proscenium'. The set is conceived not simply as a flexible setting for all the principal scenes in the first four acts in Venice but as a subtle comment on the Venice of 1590 and, by indirection, on Shakespeare's play:

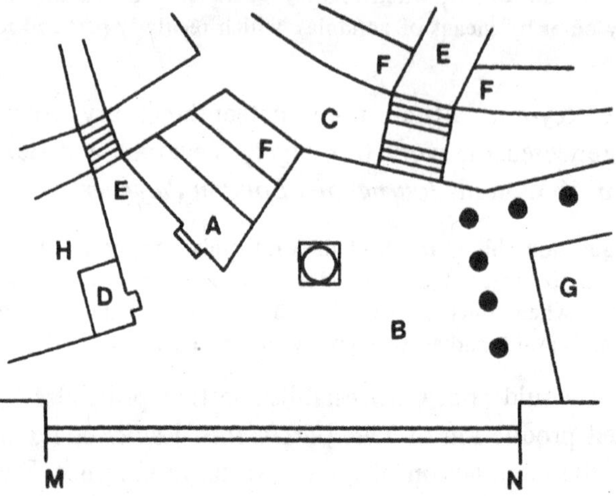

The three ground plans are taken from W. Moelwyn Merchant, *Shakespeare and the Artist,* published by Oxford University Press.

> It is essential first of all that the scene painter should bear in mind that in 1590 Venice was *neither a city of palaces nor a city of ruins,* and that along the canals and streets, two great styles of art, broadly speaking, prevailed and a third was gradually usurping the place of both; these three styles were the Byzantine, the Gothic; and the Renaissance.

But Godwin is not determining on an eclectic style in order to produce a complex theatre texture; on the contrary, this meeting-place of architectural styles is an indication of a decadence which pervades Shakespeare's play and determines its temper in the theatre:

> If we desire to realise the Venice of Shakespeare, we shall have to cover most of the brick with veneers of marble, either plain or in coloured diaper, or with stucco decorated with painted diapers....Venice was then in the full swing of the pride of life, and the very notion of decay or dilapidation must have been hateful to her, all the more hateful from an occasional gleam of consciousness that her power was already rapidly decaying.

No such delicacy of perception had hitherto related the Shakespearean text to the refinements of theatre setting; scholarship is here wholly subordinated to critical perception. At the same time the general principles by which the opulence and decay of Venice are determined are given the utmost precision; Godwin's first end is to define by particular examples the interplay of the three great styles he determined as the setting for Shakespeare's play – the Byzantine, the Gothic and the Renaissance.

> To the first belong the great church of St Mark, the churches of Murano and Torcello, sundry palaces...and a small house in the Rio de Ca' Foscari.

> To the second belong the church of the Frari...as well as a perfect crowd of palaces, of which those of the Doge, the Foscari...and the Ca'd'Oro are characteristic examples. To the third belong the Scuola of St Mark, that of St Rocco, the inner court of the Ducal Palace.

This stratification in Venice's architectural history he defines in accurate but general terms:

> Broadly speaking, this last mentioned style obtained from as early as 1485; the Gothic style prevailed during the thirteenth, fourteenth, and fifteenth centuries, overlapping the early Renaissance even to as late as the sixteenth century, and the Byzantine takes us back two hundred years more, through the twelfth-century palace, Fondaco de' Turchi, to the basilica of Torcello, built in 1,000, and the church of St Mark founded in 977.

On this secure foundation Godwin is now in a position to fill out the detail in his first diagram; this flexible and complex setting he has designed as a miniature conflation of the three styles he has analysed, a meeting-point of the grandeur and accelerating decadence of Shylock's Venice. He is therefore concerned to identify the main blocks of buildings (A, F, G, and H in his ground-plan), which could still be seen in his own day. They are fully listed:

> A. The Palazzo Badoer (painted stucco walls.)
> F. The Palazzo Giustiniani, the Fondaco de' Turchi, the Ca' d'Oro. (Showing three modes of surface ornamentation – stucco, white marble with low reliefs, and coloured marble diaper.)
> G. The Library of St Mark (new white stone) or the Prison.
> H. The semi-Byzantine house in the Corte del Remer (marble and brick veneered) or the work at Murano and Torcello.

This is admirably precise and there would be no difficulty whatever in recreating Godwin's setting from photographs and prints. He has in fact provided a sound working set and a full atmospheric context for the first three acts in Venice.

The fourth act raised a difficulty in historical terms. The large hall in which such a hearing as the trial scene would normally be held was for various reasons unsuitable. Godwin therefore determined on the smaller, more confined Sala dello Scrutinio, in the Ducal Palace. He described it as 'a fairly large room of the Sansovino series, decorated by paintings of Tintoretto, Marco Vecellio, and some others of a date later than our story.' His diagram is again admirably clear and practical.

> Considering all the circumstances of the case I again propose a diagonal set for this scene as shown in the diagram, where M N represents the proscenium, D the raised platform of the Doge, Magnificoes, &c., B the seat for Bassanio among the nobles, S and A positions of plaintiff and defendant, P Portia,

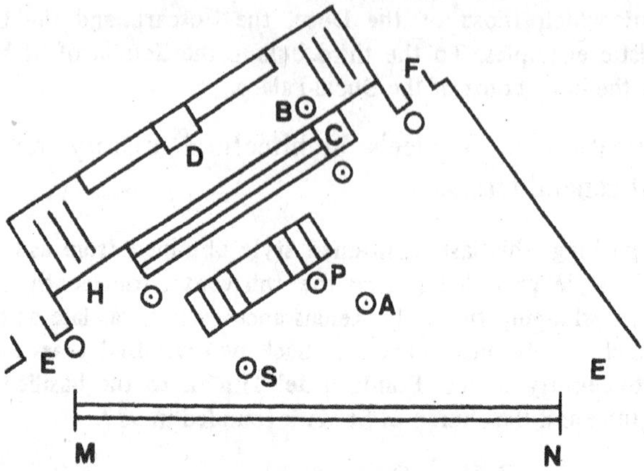

F official entrance, E E public entrances, C seat for the assessor-general, O O halberdiers, and H group of esquires of the Doge.

It is characteristic of Godwin's theatre sense, which is never subordinated by his search for historical and aesthetic accuracy, that the emotional stir of this scene is envisaged in terms of crowd grouping and that this is economically conceived:

> Now it is, I hope, manifest, that having placed the officials and dignitaries, an enormous concourse of the general public can easily be indicated by very small (if well organized) groups near the entrances E E, especially at that near N.

Belmont needed a wholly different mood and very subtly this is provided once more within the characteristic 'diagonal set'. The 'state room or hall' for the display of the caskets is so contrived as to suggest both intimacy and the extension of its space into a Palladian house with a vista of the garden with which the fifth act opens. This

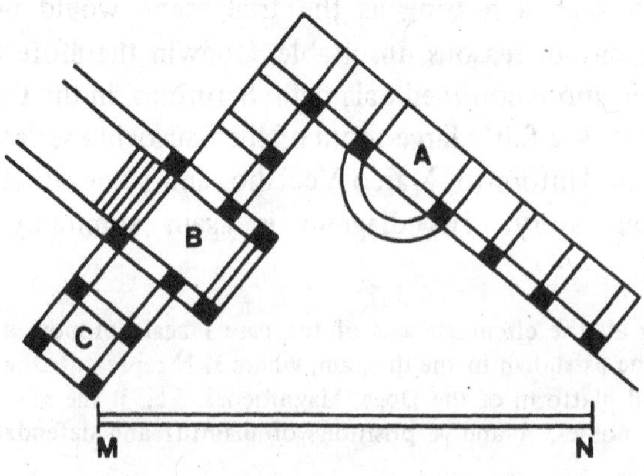

hall is described with something of the precision with which the opening Venetian scene is set:

> Assuming that Portia was descended from noble or rich ancestors, and that her house would naturally be one among the works of the first century of the revival, we may fairly take counsel with such artists as D. Ghirlandajo (1451–1495) and Bazzi (1480–1549), or such architects as Michelozzo (1402–1470) or Giulio Romano (1492–1546) in designing or arranging the room. On this basis I would suggest for this scene an architectural arrangement somewhat like that indicated in the diagram, where M N is the proscenium, A the platform for the caskets, B an ascending staircase, and C a corridor (open to the garden if required).

Godwin realizes here that texture is as important as space and his instruction to the designer is eminently practical:

> The arches of the arcade round the room may be hung with curtains, having large patterns in broad stripes, like those perceived in the Kensington Museum, and above the main arcade may be a smaller open arcade, as shown in one of Bazzi's paintings, published by the Arundel Society.

We are very fortunate that this critical exercise, conceived in the temper of Godwin's other Shakespearean essays, should have been immediately translated into production by Squire Bancroft at the Prince of Wales Theatre. The programme for the opening night (17 April 1895) contained a minimal acknowledgment to Godwin who was clearly the presiding mind in the visual side of the production:

> The text (for the arrangement of which Mr Bancroft is responsible) will be comprised in seven scenes, painted by Mr Gordon and Mr Harford, from drawings expressly made in Venice by Mr Gordon, who desires to acknowledge his obligation to Mr E.W. Godwin, F.S.A., for valuable aid in archaeological research.

The main departure from Godwin was in act four, where the trial scene was to dominate the whole conception of the play. Neither of the apartments between which Godwin had argued was now chosen: 'in the Doge's palace we saw plainly that the Sala della Bussola was the only one within our means to realise and this room we decided should be accurately reproduced for the trial.'

The Times for 19 April contains the most significant critical judgment on this setting and a measure of the change in temper between Kean's conception of realism and Godwin's:

> It is scarcely possible to convey in writing an appreciation of the manner in which...a picture of old Venice is presented. No attempt is made to emulate the gorgeous revival of Mr Charles Kean, but the most thorough feeling for propriety and finish prevails throughout.

This has been an account of a growing sense of responsibility towards the text in the course of the nineteenth century. It is true that sparer techniques were introduced under the combined impact of the visual genius of Gordon Craig and the historical researches into Elizabethan theatre practice by William Poel. But the history of décor has rarely found principles and theatre practice more harmoniously wedded by a sensitive appraisal of the text than in the work of E.W. Godwin.

13 KENNETH RICHARDS

Samuel Phelps's Production of *All's Well that Ends Well*

The production of *All's Well that Ends Well* is one of the least admired and least documented of the thirty-one Shakespeare plays Samuel Phelps mounted at Sadler's Wells during his management of the theatre from 1844–62. George Odell, in his *Shakespeare from Betterton to Irving* [1], notes that the play was performed but makes no other comment; John Coleman, in his biography of Phelps, explains that he did not see it [2]; and that confused, patch-work, but indispensable Phelps source-book, *The Life and Life-Work of Samuel Phelps* [3], only mentions the play in passing. The most detailed reports of the production in recent years have been supplied by Harold Child, in the stage history he contributed to the Cambridge edition, and by Professor Joseph Price, in his excellent study of the play, *The Unfortunate Comedy* [4]. It was not one of Phelps's striking productions: it did not attract great audiences, it was not presented with expensive scenic splendour, nor was it a revival that others quickly sought to emulate. Yet it commands interest as the only major production accorded the play on the Victorian professional stage; and further, of all Phelps's Shakespeare repertory this was, in its unspectacular way, perhaps the bravest and most adventurous production that he undertook. By the time that *All's Well* was produced in 1852, in Phelps's ninth season at Sadler's Wells, he had firmly established the policy that was to make his eighteen years at Islington a repertory achievement unique in the history of the British theatre. Following the example of his former manager Macready, Phelps had partially restored the Shakespeare Folio readings in a series of splendid and scholarly productions, most notable of which were *Macbeth* and *Richard III*, *King Lear* and *Antony and Cleopatra*. Going beyond the mere restoration of texts, he had brought back to the stage several of Shakespeare's plays which had long since fallen out of the repertory: the season before *All's Well* was produced, the Sadler's Wells company had given *Timon of Athens* its first presentation for more than two hundred years, and *All's Well* was quickly to be followed by a play equally unfamiliar to the playhouses, *Henry IV Part II.* Nor was the repertory of revivals solely Shakespearean, for the company had performed adaptations of, among others, *The City Madam, The Fatal Dowry, A King and No King, The Maid's Tragedy,* and *The Duchess of Malfi.*

The presentation of fine but rarely performed plays of the early stage was the conscious policy of the management at Sadler's Wells, a policy dictated by Phelps's earnest concern for a drama of quality and a theatre of social and educational purpose. The manifesto that Phelps and Mrs Warner issued when they entered into their management at the 'Wells' shows a profound sense of mission: to restore to the art of the theatre that dignity and seriousness that the erst-while Patent Houses had to all intents abandoned [5]. Yet while the policy of the company was admirably and unquestionably high-minded, it was also most expedient. Islington was not, as Phelps ruefully acknowledged to Coleman, the centre of the world: the district itself was unfashionable, and the little theatre, at the time Phelps took it over, was of low reputation [6]. Without an adventurous artistic policy it is doubtful if Phelps's management could have continued so successfully for so long, and his work at Sadler's Wells would today no doubt command little more attention than we give to the useful but modest achievement of, say, William Creswick at the Surrey. That Phelps should have sought both artistic distinction and economic stability for his company in the production of restored Shakespeare and the presentation of good but neglected masterpieces of the theatrical past is understandable enough. His seven years with Macready had given him living contact with a similar policy: one that his serious and scholarly disposition could approve, and that he could strive to emulate and surpass in his own theatre. But equally important, while working with Macready he had had a chance to see how insubstantial were the talents of contemporary writers for the theatre, and how little likely was a theatre to succeed, and particularly a small suburban theatre, if it relied on new drama of quality for its box-office successes. During his tenancy at Sadler's Wells Phelps received the manuscripts of more than two thousand new plays, but in his eighteen seasons there he produced only twelve of these, the majority in the early years of his management [7]. Some had a modest success; none made any distinctive contribution to the English drama. Nor could Phelps hope, at the suburban Sadler's Wells, to attract good new work by established contemporary dramatists: Bulwer Lytton's comment in a letter to Forster about his play *The Sea Captain,* which ostensibly he was reworking for Phelps, is suggestive of the kind of prejudice he could expect to encounter: 'I think it too good to throw away as an old play – on Sadlers Wells – ....better not speak to Phelps about The Sea Captain.' [8]

Given Phelps's taste for quality, for serious performance and for shaping the stage to social and intellectual ends, it was, then, both wise and necessary policy for him to seek variety and novelty at Sadler's Wells by resuscitating the actable drama of the past. At the same time, however, this was a strategy that had to be handled with caution. If pressed in too evangelical a spirit it could easily have proved disastrous, for there were many and powerful voices ready to decry the principle of mounting long neglected plays: as did the High Tory critics of *John Bull.* Further, many of the plays rejected by the nineteenth-century stage were inadmissible not because they were technically faulty, but because their manners and morals repelled the age. For all Phelps's adventurousness, he never attempted a Restoration comedy; and for all that he deplored Dr Bowdler, his own Shakespeare productions were all carefully pruned. Yet another problem was that the policy of bringing out seasonal novelties became the more difficult to sustain the longer Phelps's management survived, for inevitably 'the best were taken first, and the weakest plays left to the last, (*The Morning Advertiser*). More than one critic saw Phelps's later revivals, like *Pericles,* as manifestly scraping the barrel, and certainly his final seasons at Sadler's Wells put little that was new before the public. By the time he came to produce *All's Well* some of his most ardent admirers had come to think that the stock of plays worth rediscovering was as good as exhausted. It is in this context, of firm principle, re-enforced by expediency, but always hedged and threatened by the limitations imposed by a cautious and delicate public taste, that we must see this production of *All's Well that Ends Well.*

Phelps's decision to produce *All's Well* was, as we have said, a brave one, for the play has one of the thinnest production records in the Shakespeare canon. There is no report of its performance before the closure, and revivals of the play before this century have been comparatively few. Its fortunes were probably highest in the mid-eighteenth century, when Henry Giffard mounted it successfully at Goodman's Fields in 1741, and a year later it was given with similar approval at Drury Lane. Indeed, in the 1740s it was played some twenty-two times [9]. As far as we know, these performances were substantially of the Folio text, but in the next decade began the series of adaptations which governed the play's stage life until Benson produced it at Stratford in 1916. David Garrick was the first to revise it, reducing the romantic elements and bolstering the part of Parolles, to provide a comic vehicle for Woodward. It seems probable that this was the version that was most frequently acted in the theatres during Garrick's life-time, and the potentiality of the piece for comic treatment was further exploited in a farcical adaptation prepared for the Haymarket in 1785. In 1793 it was adapted yet again, this time by John Philip Kemble. Kemble's version, played the following year at Drury Lane, went a long way to restoring the original text, although in the process of doing so it reduced the importance of Parolles, heightened the pathetic-romantic element, and partially refined the text. This version of the play was substantially modified for Charles Kemble's production at Covent Garden in 1811, and the revised text was published in the same year [10]. Harold Child, in his stage history of *All's Well* in the Cambridge Shakespeare, remarks that Kemble's version restored the play 'pretty nearly to the original', and that Phelps's Sadler's Wells production was of the play 'as found in the Folio' [11]. Both observations are rather misleading. Kemble's 1811 version was much further from Shakespeare's text than was his adaptation of 1793, and it was not the Folio but an 1815 reprint of the Kemble 1811 edition that Phelps chose as the text for his production at Sadler's Wells [12].

Phelps might well have been daunted by the play's dismal stage history. After the successful revivals of the 1740s, it proved, even in Kemble's adaptation, a startlingly poor attraction. Kemble's own production at Drury Lane was no great success, for all that it had a brilliant cast, including the manager himself and the very popular Dorothy Jordan. Charles Kemble's Covent Garden revival was played only twice, on 24 May and 22 June 1811, and even an operatic version, put on in 1832, failed. Phelps, of course, had attempted, and was to attempt, even less frequently presented pieces, like *Timon of Athens* and *Pericles.* But these had certain saving graces. *Timon* contained little to disturb Victorian decorum, and its vanity of riches and ingratitude motives, though certainly stark, were not alien to the sterner morality of the period. *Pericles,* though it needed massive excision (especially in Act IV), was generally thought to make little claim as a play of logically developing plot, and at Sadler's Wells it was tricked up as a romantic spectacular melodrama of picturesque, but not always meaningful, scenes. *All's Well* was a very different case. It did not obviously lend itself to striking scenic treatment, nor, and much more important, for it was this that made the decision to produce it very ambitious, could it readily be adapted to Victorian taste. For even Kemble's carefully doctored text could not wholly conceal the implications of the bed-trick, and these Victorian morality refused to sanction. Condemnation of the plot of *All's Well* is general to the criticism of the period, and runs through all the reviews of Phelps's production. The strictures of *The Times* theatre critic, John Heraud, may be taken as standard:

> its infrequent production is not to be attributed to any unjust neglect, but lies in the nature of the play itself....the plot is indelicate, even beyond the limits usually conceded to Elizabethan dramatists, although these are allowed a pretty open field for the display of their eccentricities.

And the same critic assures us that if a young gentleman were asked by a young lady to outline the main incidents in this particular eccentricity, the best he could do would be to change the subject. Yet notwithstanding such a peril to maidenly modesty, when the curtain rose at seven in the evening on Wednesday, 1 September 1852, the little theatre at Islington was packed from pit to gallery with, we are assured, a most respectable auditory. At least some members of this audience it seems were ardent Shakespeare connoisseurs, for *The Daily News* describes spectators in 'the boxes text in hand – and all reverential and minutely attentive'. Attentive they might well have been, trying to relate their pocket Shakespeares to Kemble's version of the play.

Unfortunately, the production they saw cannot today be reconstructed in any detail. As the play was not a standard repertory piece we are unable to draw on a substantial number of reports and reviews written over a period of years, in order to piece together a reconstruction of the Sadler's Wells production. Nothing comparable to, let us say, Alan Downer's account of Macready's *Macbeth,* in *The Eminent Tragedian,* is possible for this *All's Well.* The press reviews are only marginally helpful, for they tend to be general rather than particular. Nor do any designs for the production appear to have survived. The play was decorated by Frederick and Charles Fenton, but the reviews, other than commenting favourably on the Florentine appropriateness of the costumes and settings, give us no details. As in most of Phelps's new productions, the décor was no doubt carefully and discreetly suited to mood and locale, but the production was not a spectacular one and the setting out certainly occasioned no particular comment. Nevertheless, we can, albeit in a slight and fragmentary way, get some impression of particular scenes and of the general principles that governed the production from the prompt-book preserved in the Finsbury Library.

Phelps seems to have acknowledged the essentially static quality of *All's Well* in Kemble's version, and to have exploited the comic Parolles scenes in order to punctuate with lively movement and broad humour a play that was in the main a highly formal debate. The elocutionary nature of the production was widely noted: 'The parts were rather spoken than acted', said the *Athenaeum*, 'and an air of polite reserve appeared to have been imposed on all the actors, save one. That one was the representative of *Parolles* – to which due prominence was given by Mr. Phelps'; and it was generally felt that Phelps's Parolles maintained 'an interest in an otherwise weak piece' (*Reynold's News*). Much of this weakness, it must be said, was inherent in Kemble's emasculated version of the play. The adaptation is, as one would expect, a very professional one, but for all that, in preparing his 1811 *All's Well* Kemble had disembowelled Shakespeare's text with the efficiency of a Samurai, pruning it of everything likely to offend the most delicate taste. By careful elimination, and by the redisposition of scenes, he shaped the play into a romantic and sentimental melodrama, with Helena its focus as the pathetic victim of scorned love who finally and triumphantly, but with the utmost of decorum, wins her man. References to her aggressive pursuit of Bertram, the aggression that so commended her to George Bernard Shaw, are drastically reduced as immodest, and what is brought to the fore is her selfless (one might almost say sexless) love for the wayward but basically decent young hero. The comic elements of the play are severely curtailed, diminishing the parts of Parolles and the Clown, and the roles of the Countess, the King, and Lafeu, are correspondingly cut to size to maintain dramatic balance. Words and phrases are substantially altered throughout, much of the figurative language of the play disappears, and references to the bed-trick and to Helena's conceiving of a child are eliminated. Phelps took over this text and presented it much as he found it. Phrases here and there are further softened in the name of decency: thus Bertram's 'wasting his manly marrow in her arms' is changed to 'wasting his manly strength within her arms', Parolles' description of Bertram as 'a whale to virginity' is cut, as is his 'for all that very ruttish', and so on. A few words and phrases are here and there reinstated from the Folio, mostly to give strong lines to Parolles. But otherwise Phelps stays very close to Kemble's version – that is, to a shortened, modified, and rather anaemic acting text, tailored to suit the most fastidious tastes of the age, and shorn of much of its verbal complexity. *The Times* observed with characteristic understatement 'we cannot help remarking that the sacrifices to delicacy weaken the real motives of the action' although at the same time it thoroughly approved of all the cuts; *The Daily News,* with equally characteristic bluntness, thought that the play as presented at Sadler's Wells bore as much relation to the original as did Garrick's *Macbeth.*

It may be surprising that Phelps, the celebrated 'restorer' of Shakespeare's texts, should have advanced such a version of *All's Well,* yet if he was to act the play at all it is difficult to see what else he could have done. Reversion to the complete Shakespeare text was clearly out of the question. Even when played in Kemble's version, the critics inveighed against the 'grossly indelicate plot' (*John Bull*), and even the sympathetic *Morning Advertiser* was moved to pronounce that 'No amount of cutting or transposition can eradicate this, the main idea, which crops up at every turn, and in every scene... namely, the distinction of the sexes'. Given such responses the mind boggles at the reception the Folio would have received. Nor would substantial cutting of the Folio have been a viable alternative, for to eliminate all that was likely to offend would have entailed a root and branch revision of precisely the kind that Kemble's text already provided. If Phelps was to produce the play at all, then, the Kemble adaptation was his most obvious and convenient choice.

And in fact, not only did Phelps stick closely to Kemble's text, but he drew heavily upon Kemble's acting directions, frequently adding to these, but rarely altering them, for in mounting the play he appears to have accepted that as it had been modified by the austere and classical Kemble, it called for a highly formal and stately orchestration, a presentation that was something of a compromise between a production proper and a recitation. Phelps we know, from the evidence of other prompt-copies, like the 1855 *King Lear,* was ready enough to break with traditional, markedly symmetrical stage groupings, in order to provide for a freer use of stage space and to develop strong dramatic tensions. But there is little sign of this kind of imaginative approach to staging in the prompt-copy of *All's Well.* Prompt-copies are, of course, notoriously deceptive, but as this is the basic evidence we have regarding the production it will be helpful to look briefly at the movements, groupings, and business it records.

The prompt-book shows much use of the customary paraphernalia of trumpet flourishes, martial manoeuvres, obeisances to royalty, formal blessings, and court processionals, but all are organized throughout in a very economic and traditional manner, while the patterns of stage movement are generally spare, conventional, and tied to symmetrical groupings. The danger of the production breaking its back, as productions of the play can so easily do, on what W.W. Lawrence called the two folk-tale episodes that comprise the plot [13] – 'the healing of the King' and 'the fulfilment of the tasks' – is reduced to a minimum in the Kemble adaptation, for his reshuffling of scenes and massive cutting of the exchanges between Helena and Parolles and the Countess and the Clown, noticeably increase the acting pace of the early scenes. Indeed, throughout the first two acts, the promptbook notations of Phelps's blocking suggest that he took full advantage of the contracted text to treat these acts as extended establishing scenes: movement is reduced to a minimum and is invariably movement on lines, exits and entrances are managed in the most economic way, and little provision is made for stage business. With the scenes so lightly orchestrated it is small, if obvious, gestures of hope and despair which operate to draw out the line of the play, as when Helena, responding to the Countess's

> Helen, you might be my daughter-in-law

has the instruction 'turns most hopefully to the Countess', but as the Countess continues

> Heaven shield you mean it not

'she turns away abashed'. Limited business of this kind serves to point attention to the submissive and sentimental heroine of Kemble's adaptation, for in the revised text it is Helena who dominates the first act of the play. Poor Fanny Cooper, who played Helena, at times gave the impression of not understanding her part, though in this she was not always helped by the text, which had been cut so ruthlessly that some speeches are bewilderingly enigmatic – as is Helena's soliloquy that closes Act I:

> Our remedies oft in ourselves do lie,
> Which we ascribe to chance. Whoever strove
> To show her merit, that did miss her love?
> The King's disease – my project may deceive me:
> But my intents are fixed, and will not leave me.

But it was generally agreed that Miss Cooper 'walked and sighed through Helena's wooings and wailings gracefully' (*The Daily News*). As Helena dominates the first act of the adaptation, so Bertram, by a redisposition of scenes, is made to dominate the opening of Act II, thus establishing a balance of romantic forces. Both the court scenes of Act II, the first from which Bertram departs to the Florentine wars, the second from which Helena leaves to seek the King's cure, were staged traditionally and with a minimum of movement, the focal point being inevitably the royal throne at stage centre. Again, one notices in the absence of business and the infrequency of moves, some confirmation of the reviewers' judgment that this was very much an elocutionary production.

More detailed orchestration begins in the third act. At the beginning of this act, which in Kemble opens with the scene of the recovered King inviting Helena to take her pick of the Court lords, the pace of the production slows perceptibly. The formal and catholic use of stage space that characterizes Acts I and II is here underscored by an elaborately organized 'order of entrance' in which '2 Chamberlains' precede the 'King leading Helena', followed by two pages and the young Lords walking in pairs. The subsequent disposition of the characters establishes a positional design based on the King at centre, which is virtually maintained throughout the scene, until Bertram, bending to the King's will and accepting Helena as his bride, crosses to Helena 'L.C.', and the Court recomposes an equally formal 'order of exit'. If the prompt-copy notations and the press reports are to be accepted, this entire scene of Helena's choice, Bertram's rejection of her love, and his over-ruling by the King, was staged as more of a debate than an action.

However, after the formal exit of the Court, Phelps takes the opportunity to substantially shift both pace and mood. The first two acts of the Kemble *All's Well* give little importance to Parolles, but after the betrothal the part comes into its own. Parolles and Lafeu are left on stage to comment on the marriage, and at Lafeu's

> Your lord and master did well to make his recantation

Phelps, as Parolles, indignantly snaps up the words:

> Recantation! My lord! My master!

taking them as his cue to launch into the swaggering, blustering characterization he assumed for the part. A brisk exchange at stage centre has Parolles 'vaporing', angrily pacing up and down, 'about to draw his sword' but stopping short, 'swaggering up to Lafeu', 'fuming and vaporing', and 'threatning a beating' to the old man, who remains ironically unimpressed by the antics. Phelps brings out the indignation by drawing an occasional word and phrase from the Folio to supplement Kemble, and his reading of Parolles as a booming *miles gloriosus*, nervous and insecure beneath his poltroon's arrogance, is said to have taken 'the audience by storm' (*The Literary Gazette*), though at least one critic, F.G. Tomlins of *The Morning Advertiser*, 'would have had less of the *Pistol* and more of the *Falstaff*'. The prompt-book notations suggest a broad and direct playing for audience response, but of Phelps's triumph in the part there was no doubt. He commanded 'incessant roars of laughter' said *The Times*, and one character trait particularly noted was 'the continual propelling of his arms', which was said to be 'as curious as it was artistic and provocative of mirth' (*The Illustrated London News*). The comic business with the arms was a palpable hit, and was a detail Phelps amplified for his superbly original Bottom when he produced *A Midsummer Night's Dream* the following season. Yet for all that he played for laughs, Phelps kept a tight hold on the part, and we are told that he was 'excessively amusing without buffoonery.... was light, comic, and whimsical, without burlesque' (*Lloyds Weekly*).

Phelps's acting at Sadler's Wells in the 1840s had consolidated his claim to be the first heir to Macready as the leading tragic actor of the day. In the early 1850s, however, the critics came increasingly to remark on his equally brilliant comic gifts: 'lately emerged as almost a new talent' (*Reynold's News*). The previous year he had revived Charles Macklin's neglected *The Man of The World*, and as the irascible Sir Pertinax MacSycophant gave one of his most celebrated comic performances. Four days before undertaking Parolles he had initiated the 1852–3 season with this play, and had then acted Falstaff in a repeat of *Henry IV*, *Part I*. Comedy was clearly in the ascendant, for his Parolles was quickly to be followed by a moving and delicately conceived Justice Shallow in *Henry IV, Part II*, and a year later he triumphantly acted Bottom in the first 'Wells' production of *A Midsummer Night's Dream*. With the exception of Garrick, Phelps was probably the most versatile of all English actors: equally accomplished in comedy and tragedy, in farce and melodrama. His Parolles was widely acknowledged by those who saw the Sadler's Wells *All's Well* as one of his most mature comic personations, and it was generally conceded that the chief interest in the production lay in his handling of this part. Yet there is no indication in the prompt-copy that Phelps sought to subordinate the romantic elements of the play to the comic. Comic business is subdued and appropriate throughout, and where it intrudes in the scenes of high romance it is introduced as light and momentary background to the larger purposes. Two instances will suffice to illustrate the way Phelps worked. In Act III, Helena, Diana, and the Widow watch the march of the Florentine army through the city gates: it is an occasion for martial pomp and ceremony, but Phelps introduces light comic business when Parolles 'kisses his hand to the peasants' as the army passes by. Again, at the end of the play, Lafeu, overcome by the reconciliation, weeps with joy, and Parolles comes downstage to offer him a 'ragged handkerchief'.

All the commentators were agreed that the drum scene and the unmasking of Parolles were the high points of the production, and the prompt-book shows that these scenes were worked up with great care. Particularly interesting in this fourth act is Phelps's sensitive use of lighting effects to sustain stage realism and to give a sense of continuity to the action. Preceding the drum sequence is a scene set in the Widow's house, where Helena and the Widow prepare the tricking of Bertram. Throughout the scene a lamp hangs 'suspended from the flies' stage centre and unlit. With the change to the French camp, this centre light is flown and we have directions for house lights to be put '¾ down', but at the next switch and a return to the Widow's house for a night scene, the house lights are put '½ up' and there is the instruction 'lamp from centre alight'. Finally, with the return to the camp, the house lights again go '½ down' for the gulling of Parolles, and are held until the blindfold is removed from his eyes, at which 'lights a little up'. Of course, such effects are modest indeed, particularly if we consider them in relation to the extended and sophisticated use of lighting suggested by the Phelps prompt-books of *Macbeth* and *A Midsummer Night's Dream,* but they do show a patient concern for detail, notably the last instance, which is a good example of the way Phelps thought out his lighting and could employ it at times in an imaginative and non-naturalistic way to achieve something approximating to audience involvement. However, as far as the grouping and organization of stage business is concerned in these scenes, although the prompt-book shows the usual careful preparation, the conventionality that we have noticed elsewhere is maintained: again Kemble's directions are followed closely, and such business as Phelps adds is what is most obviously suggested by the lines – as when Parolles says that Dumain is 'lousy' and 'Bertram and Lewis run away from Dumain affecting to avoid him. Soldiers laugh aside.' Equally traditional is the use of stage space: a sketch of positions for the gulling of Parolles shows Bertram, the Lords, and the Soldiers grouped in an arc about Parolles, who kneels stage centre in supplication. This is the first of five sketches of positions in the prompt-book (the other four all refer to the last scene of the play), and when we consider these together with the blocking notations they would seem to indicate that throughout the play the principle governing the composition of the stage-pictures was that of grouping in the shape of an arc.

But if it was the Parolles sequences that the critics, and no doubt the public, particularly admired, the prompt-book suggests that the most carefully and systematically worked scene was the last. Unlike Shakespeare's *All's Well,* the Kemble adaptation brings all the events that lead to the reconciliation together in the final act, building swiftly to a last scene climax by extensively cutting and contracting the functional scenes which serve to assemble the characters in the Countess of Rousillon's house. Here the blocking notations are considerably more detailed than elsewhere in the prompt-copy, and they are supplemented by rough positional sketches of key groupings at four stages in the action. It would be tedious to rehearse the arrangements of this last scene at length, but the general governing design can be indicated briefly. Again, as in the big Court scene in Act III, the action commences with a carefully drawn-up 'order of entrance', showing '2 attendants with wands preceding King and Countess', with the other characters following in pairs. Entrance is made through a back-stage centre-door which appears to have been something of a feature of the scene, and right centre of which stand an 'Oak Table and Large Chair'. The large chair serves as a throne for the King, and by contrasting with the regal throne shown in the Court scene of Act III discreetly indicates the shift in social position from the Court to the Countess of Rousillon's house. The characters are disposed symmetrically about the stage, with Lafeu, the King, and the Countess, grouped together down-stage centre for the discussion of Helena's supposed death, and for the return of Bertram. The preliminaries completed, Dumain exits 'L' to bring in Bertram, and as he does so the 'King goes up and sits in Chair brought forward by 2 attendants to centre'. Bertram enters 'L', kneels to the King, then moves 'R.C.' In other words, the opening 'stage-picture' is recomposed, with the addition of Bertram and with the King seated, for the ring sequence that follows: Bertram at R.C. shows the ring and passes it to Lafeu on his left, Lafeu inspects it and then passes it left to the King, who rises to receive it, and in turn shows it to the Countess standing on his left. It is good indication of how static was this production, that Phelps seems deliberately to have avoided the opportunity this passage of the ring provides for substantial stage movement. Indeed, the basic pattern of principal characters in essentially static poses dominating the fore-stage is maintained throughout the scene, modified only by the gradual accumulation of figures composing the arc form, first Diana and the Widow, and then Helena, as the play moves to its resolution. The final 'stage-picture' is thus one of a broad arc composed of all the principals, and out of this Helena steps, advancing down-stage centre to deliver the epilogue.

That this very formal and static production had a modest success says much for Phelps's directorial ability to keep a tight hold on an audience by careful attention to detail. As we have said, movement, business, and scenic effects, appear to have been minimal, and there is no evidence of that recourse to the more flamboyant display of stage machinery, like gauzes, diorama, and coloured lights, that we find in Phelps's productions of, say, *Macbeth,* or *Pericles,* or *A Midsummer Night's Dream.* Yet there is no suggestion in the reviews that the production flagged, or that its stately formality was tedious. The achievement, such as it was, seems to have lain in the fine precision of playing that by the 1850s Phelps had developed with his company. 'Phelps', said *The Daily News,* 'has got an excellent company together, working with wonderful smoothness into each other's hands', and the *Athenaeum* noted the care with which the production had been rehearsed, while *Lloyd's Weekly* considered that 'upon no similar occasion had greater attention been paid to the due preparation of a piece'. Of course, we must make allowance for journalistic exaggeration, for loose phrasing, and for different critical assumptions and standards. But the success of the production would seem to have been achieved by discreet, but precise, variation of tempo, by spare but meaningful stage movement, by the rigorous drilling of the company into a concern for cueing, pointing, intonation, and gesture – in short, by something approaching intelligent and disciplined ensemble playing. For Phelps's company at Sadler's Wells came close to being the first real ensemble group in the English theatre. Phelps had inherited from Macready just such a general concern for the details of staging, and what we know of his work at Sadler's Wells suggests that he strove to extend Macready's practice. Certainly he was dependent on group work in a way that Macready had not been, for where the 'Eminent Tragedian', in his major seasons, had been able to employ an impressive array of supporting players, Phelps's actors at Sadler's Wells were for the most part mediocre. Phelps spoke himself of the 'laborious rehearsals' and 'persistent drillings' that were the back-bone of his productions [14], and the importance he attached to frequent working-over and perfecting details of presentation was recalled by Tom Taylor, whose *The Fool's Revenge* was acted at Sadler's Wells in 1859:

> I never saw rehearsals more thorough, more careful, or more business-like. Phelps was as able as he was indefatigable in stage-management. He did the work of guidance and governance of his actors singly, and of the action as a whole .... rehearsal, as I saw it in the case of my own play at Sadler's Wells,

> was what rehearsal should be, continuous, well-considered, patient shaping of the play for public performance, in which not merely the groupings and movements of the personages were attended to, but the delivery of every speech watched – nay, the emphasis and pronunciation of every word noted. [15]

It is high praise, but the reviews of the period abound in similar praise of the quality of the stage-craft exhibited at Sadler's Wells. Of recent years we have become aware of the extent to which the reforms of the Meiningen company had been anticipated by a number of English companies in the middle years of the nineteenth century, and it is perhaps worth recalling that when Samuel Phelps took his Sadler's Wells company to Germany in 1859, one of the most enthusiastic members of his audience in Berlin was the young Duke of Saxe-Meiningen, who dated his own appreciation of the need for ensemble work and meticulous staging to his experience of Phelps's production of *King Lear,* a production that Phelps perfected in the 1850s [16]. It is productions like this *Lear,* or like his complexly, even sensationally, orchestrated *Macbeth,* or the delicately and beautifully staged *A Midsummer Night's Dream,* by which Phelps is most remembered, and clearly they are productions which link him to the central tradition of nineteenth-century staging innovations – to the development of increasingly subtle ensemble playing, which at its best operated within an aesthetic of historical accuracy and theatrical verisimilitude organized to match the temper of the text.

In this production of *All's Well,* however, although we may have had something like ensemble playing, we seem to be a far cry from the more familiar nineteenth-century scenic developments; closer in fact to that mode of staging which was soon to be castigated, in the words of *The Theatre,* as belonging to:

> those who cannot forget the habits prevalent in the 'good old times'. The moving from the centre of the stage and back again after every effective speech; the placing all the players at equal distances from one another, so that their out-stretched finger-tips would just meet; the restraint of all movement except 'crossings' etc. [17]

Phelps's *All's Well* was clearly not as dull and laborious in its staging as this, and perhaps the account itself is unduly disparaging of the unreformed stage, but it would seem clear, from the prompt-copy and the reports of the production, that the imaginative use of stage-area that we know Phelps to have been fully capable of, is noticeably wanting here. At the same time, we must acknowledge that what we tend to see as the progressively 'imaginative' use of stage-space in the work of Macready, Phelps, Kean and the Meiningen was, at least in part, simply a response to the increasing naturalistic impulse to upholster a play – for this upholstering included not only the provision of elaborate and historically accurate settings, but the massive accumulation of detail in characterization and stage-business. One is tempted to speculate that Phelps was essaying something rather different and very ambitious: that he was attempting in this production of *All's Well* to revitalize the older conventions of stage-craft, by an application of the increasing mid-nineteenth-century interest in detail, not to the peripheral *decoration* of a production, but by economy of movement, grouping and business, to emphasize in significant stage-action the central importance of the spoken word. There is sanction for such a view. Phelps was, in the words of an admirer, 'the last of the Romans'. He rejoiced in his elocutionary prowess, and at the 'Wells' he paid great attention to the quality and clarity of delivery of all his players. The tendency in his own verse-speaking in later years towards a slow and measured delivery, was said to have been a mannerism developed at Sadler's Wells, where slow and clear enunciation was an essential if the actors were to communicate sophisticated verse to a largely unlettered audience [18]. His productions (with the exception of *Pericles*) never exploited stage effects to the detriment of the spoken word. Henry Morley's comments on Phelps's production of *Timon of Athens* were echoed by many critics in the period when they assessed the stage-craft at Sadler's Wells:

> The scenery is always beautiful, but it is not allowed to draw attention from the poet, with whose whole conception it is made to blend in the most perfect harmony. The actors are content also to be subordinated to the play, learn doubtless at rehearsals how to subdue excesses of expression, that by giving undue force to one part would destroy the balance of the whole, and blend their work in such a way as to produce the right emphasis. [19]

Of course, we must not make too much of this. If the play was so conventionally organized, if it had about it that air of 'polite reserve' noted by the reviewers, and if the outlay on the production was, as it appears to have been, modest (and this at a time when Phelps was showing an increasing interest in scenic decoration – *Timon* the year before, *A Midsummer Night's Dream* the following year) then the reasons are not difficult to make out. Phelps could not help but be aware that in mounting the play he was taking on something of a risk – it did not quite have the novelty attraction of, say, *Timon* or *Pericles,* and the incident on which the plot turned was certain to qualify, in the minds of both reviewers and potential audience, enthusiasm for the project itself. Nor, in all likelihood, was it to be a production of which Phelps could be especially proud, and in terms of principle and policy deeply engaged, for it was not a major revival nor a 'restoration'. Having decided to risk the piece in Kemble's version, he staged it with conservative caution, financial economy, and with a judiciously polite restraint. Nevertheless, a study of this production of *All's Well* is a useful corrective to our tendency to see Phelps's important work in the more spectacular productions which set him in the main-stream of nineteenth-century staging development. It serves to remind us that there was another tradition, less celebrated, less exciting perhaps, and certainly less easy to recall, that was, as it were, the *arrière garde* in the long march from Inigo Jones to Beerbohm Tree, in the shift from a stage dominated by the spoken word, to one where the spoken word was accompanied by, and often submerged beneath, all the accessories that painters, costumiers, machinists and lighting-men could devise. It is the tradition suggested in those phrases that still crop up in mid-nineteenth-century theatrical criticism – phrases which compliment an actor on the quality of his elocution and characterize roles as elocutionary parts. Of this tradition Phelps was the last great exemplar. It was surely his recognition of this that made Johnston Forbes-Robertson name Phelps, rather than Irving, the finest actor he had ever seen.

But whatever Phelps's intentions with this *All's Well*, it was not so much the quality and characteristics of the production that engaged the attention of the critics, as what they felt to be the basic indecorum of the play itself. The fiercest attack came from the Tory *John Bull*: scenting something questionable, it savaged the 'grossly indelicate plot', sank its teeth into the misguided policy of revivals, and dismissed the whole 'Wells' undertaking as 'utterly hopeless'. No other reviewer was so hostile, yet in nearly every case the most enthusiastic praise was qualified by hesitation over the plot and doubts about the play's stage-worthiness. The general impression was that Phelps had done a good job with rather poor and decidedly dubious material. *The Illustrated London News* thought it 'a perilous venture', and *The Daily News* was confident that it 'could not be produced out of Sadler's Wells'. But perhaps the truest comment was that made by *Lloyd's Weekly*: the play, it said, is not calculated 'to overflow the coffers of the Sadler's Wells treasury'. It did not. More successful than his predecessors with the play, Phelps managed to get eleven performances out of it, but he never chose to revive it in later seasons. He several times contemplated, but never effected, a production of *Troilus and Cressida.* Even more than *All's Well*, the plot of that play would have offended the age. Perhaps the guarded and qualified reception accorded his production of *All's Well that Ends Well* finally decided Phelps to err on the side of caution and not to risk giving that offence.

Notes

[1] G.C.D. Odell, *Shakespeare from Betterton to Irving*, 2 Vols., (New York, 1920).

[2] John Coleman, *Memoirs of Samuel Phelps* (London, 1886).

[3] W. May Phelps and John Forbes-Robertson, *The Life and Life-Work of Samuel Phelps* (London, 1886).

[4] Joseph G. Price, *The Unfortunate Comedy: A study of All's Well that Ends Well and its critics* (Liverpool, 1968).

[5] See W. May Phelps, *op. cit.*, 64–5; and John Coleman, *op. cit.*, 196–205.

[6] See Charles Dickens's account of the theatre and its audience in *Household Words.*

[7] W. May Phelps, *op. cit.*, 7.

[8] Charles H. Shattuck, ed., *Bulwer and Macready, A Chronicle of the Early Victorian Theatre* (Urbana, 1958) 237.

[9] C.B. Hogan, *Shakespeare in the Theatre: 1701–1800*, Vols. I–III (Oxford, 1952–7).

[10] For an examination of the Garrick and Kemble adaptations see a fine article by Joseph G. Price, 'From Farce to Romance. *All's Well that Ends Well 1756–1811'*, *Shakespeare Jahrbuch*, Band 99 (1963) 57–71. See also *The Unfortunate Comedy*, *op. cit.*

[11] Cambridge *All's Well that Ends Well*, 188–9.

[12] Prompt-copy in Finsbury Library. I am grateful to the staff of Finsbury Library for putting this and other items in their Sadler's Wells Collection at my disposal.

[13] W.W. Lawrence, *Shakespeare's Problem Comedies* (New York, 1931).

[14] Godfrey Turner, 'Scenery, Dresses, and Decoration', *The Theatre*, N.S. Vol. III, (1884) 126–37.

[15] *The Theatre*, N.S. Vol. I (1878) 338–44.

[16] E.L. Stahl, *Shakespeare und das Deutsche Theater* (Stuttgart, 1947) 486.

[17] *The Theatre*, N.S. Vol. II (1879) 272.

[18] Westland Marston, *Our Recent Actors*, 2 vols. (London, 1888) Vol. 2, 21

[19] Henry Morley, *Journal of a London Playgoer* (London, 1866) 154.

Dates of reviews in newspapers and journals have not been given as they all appeared within three or four days of the first production on Wednesday, 1 September 1852.

